TARIKH-I-AKBARI

تاریخ اکبری

تالیف

محمد عارف قندهاری

TARIKH-I-AKBARI

Muhammad Arif Qandhari

An Annotated Translation
with Introduction by
TASNEEM AHMAD

Foreword by
IRFAN HABIB

PRAGATI PUBLICATIONS

PRAGATI PUBLICATIONS
9926, Library Road, Azad Market
Delhi 110 006

First Published 1993

ISBN: 81-7307-013-X

Published by Pramod Kapoor for Pragati Publications,
9926, Library Road, Azad Market, Delhi 110 006

Printed in India
at H.B. Printing Works, Delhi 110 006

To the memory of

my revered *Ustad*

PROFESSOR S. NURUL HASAN

FOREWORD

Akbar's reign saw a remarkable efflorescence of historiography. Abu'l Fazl's *Akbar Nama,* of which the celebrated *Ain-i-Akbari* is a part, presents a remarkable reconstruction of history through the use of archival materials, statistics, memoirs and even "oral history". Abu'l Fazl's vision of history is no longer that of a mere court chronicle. Yet by its very eminence the *Akbar Nama* tends to overshadow the other historical works of Akbar's reign. One of these works, whose rediscovery is relatively recent, is Muhammad Arif Qandhari's *Tarikh-i-Akbari.*

A comparison of Muhammad Arif Qandhari's text with other historical works shows that none of the later historians of Akbar's time had access to his work. It was only in Jahangir's reign, as Dr Tasneem Ahmad points out in his introduction, that this text came to be known to historians like Fireshta and Nihawandi. This invests the *Tarikh-i-Akbari* with the additional value of being a highly independent source with which we can check the statements of Abu'l Fazl and subsequent historians. That the corroboration it offers is quite considerable, enhances our confidence in the factual accuracy of the histories compiled later in Akbar's reign. At the same time Muhammad Arif Qandhari does add considerably to our knowledge:

For example, he gives the text of a rescript of Akbar to Bairam Khan not otherwise known; and he gives much information about the building of Fatehpur Sikri, and about the early paintings patronised by Akbar. Moreover, he gives the picture of Akbar drawn before his maturer religious views had been fully articulated, and his account is, therefore, a corrective to the view already advanced by the Jesuits in early 1580s that Muslims generally tended to regard Akbar as heterodox.

The *Tarikh-i-Akbari* has been excellently edited and annotated by Muinuddin Nadvi, Azhar Ali Dehlawi and Imtiaz Ali Arshi. What it now needed was a full-scale English translation. This has been provided by Dr Tasneem Ahmad in a very competent manner, aiming at faithful accuracy and at a critical assessment of the information here received by comparing it with that offered by other sources.

The publication of Dr Tasneem Ahmad's translation is a notable contribution to the National celebration of the 450th Anniversary of Akbar's birth. I feel confident that it would reinforce the interest in Akbar's age widespread among those who have a care for the long process of the creation of a composite culture and a unity that together constitute what is India.

7 July 1993

IRFAN HABIB

ACKNOWLEDGEMENTS

I sincerely acknowledge my debt to those without whose encouragement, guidance and assistance this work could not have been undertaken. Though the list is long, I may however, be excused not to mention all names.

The first and foremost, I express my profound sense of gratitude, very personal regards and respects to Professor Irfan Habib, who encouraged and guided me at every stage of the work. In spite of his very pressing engagements and pre-occupation, he ungrudgingly spared his valuable time to examine with care every intricate problem, arising out during the course of work. My debt to my revered teacher, Professor Satish Chandra is incalculable. He took great pains in reading and correcting the work and his considered suggestions have paid me rich dividend. I owe a debt of gratitude to my revered *Ustad*, Professor S. Nurul Hasan, who gave me the idea of this work. During the course of work, his suggestions to modify my choice of a particular word in favour of more suitable one or to alter the construction of a passage in order to make it nearer to Arif's own conception has paid me rich dividend. Grateful thanks are also due to Professor J.S. Grewal for his benevolent guidance and help. I am also thankful to Dr Basudev Chatterjee who helped me in the preparation of Introduction and Shri S.P. Das for the preparation of Index. Very personal and warm thanks are due to my dear teacher, Professor M.A. Ansari and friends Professor Jaweed Ashraf, Dr Momin Mohiuddin, Dr S.H. Qasmi, Dr S. Hasàn Mahmud and Mrs Shama Mitra Chenoy for their help. I will remain indebted without mentioning the encouragement and cooperation, extended by Professor Rajendra Joshi and his family.

I record with pleasure the facilities offered to me by the authorities of various libraries in Delhi, Aligarh, Rampur, and Allahabad. I am also thankful to my colleagues in the Council who helped me during the course of work.

I cannot restrain myself from mentioning the patient cooperation, extended by my wife, Nahid Tasneem and daughters Zareen and Farheen (Anu) during the course of work which resulted in completion.

I am deeply obliged to Shri Buddhadev Bhattacharyya for his valuable guidance in regard to design and production of the book and Vinod Kapoor of Pragati Publications, Delhi, who took very personal interest in getting the work published. However, I stand responsible for the shortcomings and faults, if any.

TASNEEM AHMAD

CONTENTS

INTRODUCTION

Tarikh-i-Akbari, also known as *Tarikh-i-Qandhari*, or *Muzaffar Nama*[1] is an exceptionally important work on the life and times of Emperor Akbar, and deserves closer attention than it has received from modern scholars whose major preoccupation has been with Abul Fazl's *Akbar Nama*[2] or Badauni's *Muntakhab-ut-Tawarikh*.[3] It is the first chronicle of Emperor Akbar's reign and is a vital source of information particularly on the early year's of his career. While it is certain that Abul Fazl did not use it, Farishta in his *Gulshan-i-Ibrahimi*[4] and Nihawandi in his *Maasir-i-Rahimi*[5] explicitly acknowledge their indebtedness to *Tarikh-i-Akbari*.

There is scant information about the author of *Tarikh-i-Akbari*, Muhammad Arif Qandhari.[6] From the available evidence it appears that he was brought up in an orthodox family and was a scholar of repute, conversant with a number of Islamic sciences and an erudite Persian writer. Arif joined the service of Bairam Khan[7] when he was the *hakim* of Qandhar and became the Khan's *Mir-i-Saman*.[8] We learn from his account that after Bairam Khan was assassinated by an 'irreligious Afghan' while on a pilgrimage to Mecca, Arif escaped along with the Khan's young son, Mirza Muhammad Rahim,[9] and some other relatives. He accompanied Mirza Rahim to Ahmadabad, and then fulfilled his cherished desire to perform *Haj*.[10] Upon his return he joined the service of Muzaffar Khan[11] with whom he had been closely associated from the days when the latter was the *diwan-i-buyutat* in the household of Bairam Khan. When Muzaffar Khan became the Wazir of the empire for the second time, Arif came to Agra in 1577 A.D., but he was dismissed from the service by the Khan, and then re-employed. He also went to Delhi and had an audience with the emperor. He was assigned the *mansab* of the *diwan* of Sarkar of Punjab on the recommendation of Shaikh-ul-Islam, Maulana Abdullah but he did not accept it since he was more inclined to lead the life of a *darwesh* and a *faqir* (renouncer).[12]

According to Arif's testimony, it was Muzaffar Khan who entrusted the compilation of *Tarikh-i-Akbari* to him, possibly in acknowledgement of his scholarship as well as his rich personal experience. He was either an eye-witness to the happenings, or had access to information about them from Bairam Khan, Muzaffar Khan and others who were close to the court.

Arif does not mention the date of the completion of his *Tarikh,* nor do other contemporary sources. The date can, however, be conjectured on the basis of events described in its last chapter. The narrative describes events until the end of Safar, A.H. 988/March, 1580 A.D. It does not mention the events leading to Muzaffar Khan's discomfiture at the hand of the Afghans in the east and his subsequent death there. So it seems plausible that Arif presented *Tarikh-i-Akbari* to Muzaffar Khan before his departure to Bengal in March, 1580 A.D. who bestowed a *Khilat* (robe) upon him and he lived thereafter without adding anything further.[13] Second, he followed his master and he too perished with him.

The *Tarikh-i-Akbari* consists of forty-four chapters. The events of Humayun's reign, including his relationship with his brothers, are described briefly. The account becomes a detailed one from the accession of Akbar onwards. As far as the literary features of the *Tarikh* are concerned, the most notable is that it opens with the *maqta* or the conclusion, followed by the *dibacha* (preface). Arif states that he consciously sought to avoid the styles of *Muzaffar Nama,*[14] which was so abstruse as to be of use only to the learned and the specialist, and of the *Taj-ul-Maasir,*[15] which was an exercise in linguistic embellishment and verbosity, inappropriate for its subject matter. His own style, however, remains highly ornamental and verbose, and not as straightforward and economical as claimed.

Arif was a traditional loyalist who believed in the metaphysic of the divinity of royalty.[16] Emperor Akbar is in the seventh generation from Amir Timur. Mystery is enshrined in "seven" by God; the blue dome (*asman,* the sky) contains seven edifices, while planets, seas, metals, days of week, organs of human body are all seven in numbers. Even the Holy Quran has been sent down in seven parts (*lughats*). Rebellions or sedition against an emperor such as Akbar, therefore, were the result of evil disposition and wicked thoughts arising from bad company and wrong counsel. Arif depicts Akbar's conquests as measures to bestow the blessings of a sound, humane and tolerant administration, not as acts of aggrandisement. Akbar's action against rebels, according to Arif, were not only politically but also morally necessary, and complemented his policy of peace with all.[17]

Despite some chronological inaccuracies (e.g. the construction of the Fatehpur Sikri preceding that of Agra fort, and looseness in the use of administrative terms (e.g. use of the terms *Sarkar* and *Vilayat* interchangeably), there is a mine of information on the diverse aspects of the life and times of Akbar.

This annotated translation of the *Tarikh-i-Akbari*, by making this valuable source of information accessible to a wider range of readers, will, it is hoped, encourage further interest in a crucial period of Indian history.

Notes

1. I am behodent to Professor Irfan Habib for enlightening me that the *Tarikh-i-Akbari* of Arif Qandhari is the first chronicle of Emperor Akbar's reign which presents the emperor changing India, while its compiler happens to be a privileged witness.
2. *Akbar Nama*, a detailed history of Akbar's reign with an account of his predecessors, commonly said to be divided into three daftars, of which the first completed in Shaban A.H. 1004/March 1596 A.D., the 41st regnal year, is sub-divided into two parts: (1) Akbar's birth, genealogy of the Timurids, reign of Babur and Humayun, (2) Akbar's reign from the first to the middle of the 17th year (i.e., to the birth of Daniyal (9 Jamadi II, A.H. 980/17 September, 1572 A.D.), the second continues the narrative from the middle of the 17th year to the end of 46th while the third, known by the independent title *Ain-i-Akbari*, deals with the administration and statistics of the empire.

   The celebrated author, Abul Fazl was the second son of the scholar and Sufi, Shaikh Mubarak Naguri. He was assassinated at the instigation of Prince Salim by Bundela Chief, Bir Singh Deo, who sent his head to Salim at Allahabad. His body was taken to Antri near Gwalior and buried there. For details see C.S. Storey, *Persian Literature*, Vol. I;

Part I., pp. 541-51. S.A.A. Rizvi, *Religious and Intellectual History of the Muslims in Akbar's Reign with Special Reference to Abul Fazl*, New Delhi, Munshiram Manoharlal, 1975.

3. *Muntakhab-ut-Tawarikh* often called *Tarikh-i-Badauni*, comprises the history of India from the time of Subuktigin A.H. 367/997-98 A.D. to A.H. 1004/1595-96 A.D., i.e., fortieth year of Akbar's reign. It may be said lux in details, both petty squabbles and heroic conflicts, and almost seeming to glorify the traditional alama. Badauni was born on 17th Rabi II, A.H. 947/21st August, 1540 A.D. at Todah (now in Jaipur) and he died in A.H. 1004/1595-96 A.D. For details see English translation, 3 Vols., Delhi, *Idarah-i-Adabiyat-i-Dilli*, 1973 (reprint). See also Harbans, Mukhia, *Historians and Historiography During the Reign of Akbar*, Delhi, Vikas, 1977.

4. *Gulshan-i-Ibrahimi* or *Tarikh-i-Farishta* of Muhammad Qasim Hindu Shah is a general history of India, beginning with an account of the beliefs of the Hindus and their early rajas. The narrative then turns to the coming of Islam in India and proceeds upto the sixteenth century. It was written in A.H. 1015/1606-7 A.D. For details see J.S. Briggs, *History of the Rise of Mohammadan Power in India*, 4 Vols., Bib. Ind., Calcutta, 1940.

5. *Maasir-i-Rahimi* of Abdul Baqi Nihawandi is primarily a biography of Mirza Abdul Rahim Khan-i-Khana, though it contains an account of the Muslim rulers of India from the Ghaznavids to Jahangir. For details see Text edited by M. Hidayat Husain, 3 Vols., Bib. Ind., Calcutta, 1940.

6. According to Bayazid, "Haji Arif". *Tarikh-i-Humayun Wa Akbar*, 186. Farishta, who mentions his name at a few places, has named him Haji Muhammad Qandhari. *Gulshan-i-Ibrahimi*, I, 4, 27, 132, 300, 307 and II, 301 and 311. While Baqi Nihawandi has mentioned his name at four places in his work. He mentiones his name Arif Muhammad and Muhammad Arif Qandhari at two places respectively. *Maasir-i-Rahimi*, I, 38 and 62; II, 1 and 8.

7. Bairam Khan belonged to the Baharul Turkman tribe. His lineage is traced to Mirza Jahan Shah. In the time of Humayun, he rose to the office of Vakil and Amir-ul-Umara and held the mansab of 5000. He achieved distinction in the service of Prince Akbar and he was his tutor also. He held Qandhar in Afif and consolidated the Mughal Empire in Hindustan. *ZK, 11 and 12*, For details see *AN, NM, MR, HI, TA, MT*, and M. Athar Ali, *The Apparatus of Empire, Awards of the Ranks, Offices and Titles to the Mughal Nobility (1574-1658)*, Delhi, Oxford University Press, 1985 (hereafter Athar Ali).

8. *Maasir-i-Rahimi*, Vol. I, 62 and Vol. II, 109.

9. Abdur Rahim, son of Bairam Khan was in his tenth year when his father attained martyrdom. He was brought to the imperial court and

the emperor entrusted the charge of his education to Mir (Hakim) Abul Fath and Raja Man Singh. Later, he was married to Mirza Aziz Koka's sister. He rendered valuable services and won great victories also. As a scholar he did not only earn name and fame, but he patronised scholars and learned men also. It may be said that he was par excellence among the great nobles. He died in Delhi in A.H. 1036/1627-28 A.D. While marching against Mahabat Khan. His mausoleum stands nearby Humayun's. *ZK*, pp. 31-64. For details see *AN, TA, TM, LJ, TJ, Farishta, S.S.* and *MU* and Athar Ali.

10. *Tarikh-i-Akbari*, p. 64.
11. Muzaffar Khan/Muzaffar Nishan was a clerk from Turbat. He was a retainer of Bairam Khan and he worked as *diwan-i-buyutat* in the latter's household. Bairam Khan sent the Khan as his envoy to seek help from Muhammad Khan Uzbeg Darvesh who arrested him and he was imprisoned in Gwalior fort. In spite of the insistence of some of the nobles, Akbar did not take his life. He was released and given the charge of diwan of Punjab. In 1563, he was appointed the full-fledged revenue and finance minister of the empire. Later, on 18th November 1573 he was made Wazir (prime minister) but he lost the post within a few months. He, however, was re-assigned the post of Wazir in October 1577 A.D. and remained till one year and a half. On March 14, 1579 A.D., he was appointed the subedar of Bengal and he was slain by the rebels on April, 19, 1580 A.D. *Z.K. fol. 343-A.* For details see also *AN*, Vol. II, pp. 178-79, 197-98 and Vol. III, 67-68, 85, 215, 16, 265 and 304, *Tarikh-i-Humayun Wa Akbar*, pp. 237-39, *MU*, III, p. 221 and Athar Ali.
12. *Tarikh-i-Akbari*, p. 234.
13. There seems to be two manuscripts of Arif's work. The manuscript which was in the possession of Nawab Rampur was later edited by Haji Moinuddin Nadvi, Saiyed Azhar Ali Dehlvi and Imtiaz Ali Arshi. It does not contain that Arif presented his work to Muzaffar Khan, who bestowed a *Khilat* (robe) on him while Cambridge University manuscript contains these informations. The text published from Rampur acknowledges this fact.

    Tarikh-i-Akbari of Muhammad Arif Qandhari was first introduced by Sri Ram Sharma who wrote an article entitled *Tarikh-i-Muhammad Arif Qandhari*, on the basis of manuscript, provided to Sir Jadu Nath Sarkar by Nawab Rampur. See *JRAS*, 1933, pp. 807-11 and Storey, p. 541.
14. This is a history of Muzaffar (dynasty). They were the rulers of Kirman and Shiraz. For details see Rieu, *Catalogue of Persian MSS in the British Museum*, No. 28.
15. The *Taj-ul-Maasir*, written by Sadr-ud-din Muhammad, son of Hasan Nizami, is a verbose, rhetorical and uninformative account, in prose and verse, of the Indian wars of Muiz-ud-din, Qutbuddin (who

reigned during A.H. 602/1206-7 A.D. - A.H. 606/1210 A.D. to whom the work is chiefly devoted) and Iltutmish. For details see Storey, pp. 493-95.

16. This doctrine is fully supported by Baruni, vide his *Fatawa-i-Jahandari*, text edited by Mrs A.S. Khan, Lahore, 1972, English translation by M. Habib and Mrs A.S. Khan, under *The Political Theory of the Delhi Sultanate*, Allahabad, Kitab Mahal, 1961.
17. See also K.A. Nizami, *Akbar and Religion*, Delhi, Idarah-i-Adbiyat-i-Dilli, 1989.

OCCURRENCE 1

Maqta[1] Comprises the Deeds of Abu-al-Muzaffar Jalal-ud-Din Muhammad Akbar and the Description of Happenings of the Reign of the Great Conqueror (May God Preserve His Kingdom for Ever!), Followed with *Muqaddama, Maqsad* and *Khatama*

In the name of Allah, the Compassionate, the Merciful. (p. 2)

Muqaddama[2]

In the *muqaddama* are narrated events and deeds of the reign of the good-natured Emperor Akbar.

O! that personality, whose seat is the imperial throne, who is sheltered under the imperial crown, by your world organising will, the garden of the realm and the nation has become well-ordered.

It is clearly reflected like a picture in the mirror of the heart and mind of the enlightened and learned persons as well as the historians that when the *matla* (preface) of this book, which constitutes the beginning (of this book), with all its contents decorated with the ornament of grace of the ever-lasting reign, reached the stage of completion, came the turn of *maqta* which comprises the account of the reign of Emperor Akbar which forms the conclusion of this well-arranged work as well and it has been compiled in the same manner. The reason is in accordance with the injunction of the *Quran* (may God preserve his good name among the future generations!), poets as well as prose-writers, who have ornamented their writings with the narration of the active life of the emperor (Akbar) as also of the other kings of your. And they have, in their introductions, given beautiful descriptions of kings and rulers. In this way they have thrown round the neck and ears of every age (or generation) the precious ornaments of the grandeur of the reign of the emperors, and filled the skirt (sheet) of the years with the pride of the goodness of the enlightened emperor. And he has established (pitched) the banners of reasoning of his secret favours, conferred upon the enlightened persons of the age whose knowledge and abilities were lying enclosed in a ring as it were. (p. 3) Also by means of new and strange methods he has brought under his administration (subjugated) the various sultans of the day by possessing great prowess and armies from beginning to end. (And he also collected the whole of the accounts of the happenings of the good and noble wazirs and then he also completed the notices of other Khalifahs of yester years and also stories worth of pride of the ancient rulers which have been fully recorded after the example, set by Abu-al-Qasim Firdausi[3] who was the pioneer of the poets and a most marvellous master of poetry and who had in his great work, the *Shah Nama,* a treasury of the most precious pearls of literature, mentioned the names of the famous men of the world). He has first referred to Alexander,[4] the Great and then turned his pen of praises towards Yaminuddaula Subuktigin.[5] Seeing all this, the flames of shame burst forth in the heart of the writer of these pages for if a poet could give such a wonderful expression in praise of the son of Subuktigin, then why art thou silent in belauding the Sultan, son of Sultan (i.e. who belongs to the pedigree of Kings), the ruler of the world, administrating the law and justice of Jamshed,[6] upholding the faith like Faridun,[7] expounder of the laws like the Solomon[8] (Hazrat Sulaiman) and whose face is turned towards paradise like Minu-chihr.[9]

Masnavi (rhyme)

The chief of chiefs, a king who is the slasher of necks, rival of Faridun, nay, successor of Sikandar (Alexander), the Great, star of skies and moonfaced, before whose dazzling light even fires pale into insignificance.[10]

The Sultan s/o Sultan s/o Sultan, the Khaqan s/o Khaqan s/o Khaqan, Sahib-qiran (the victorious king) who has adorned the throne of the realm, Jalal-ud-Din Muhammad Akbar Padshah Ghazi, before whose majesty two hundred Subuktigins bend their back in submission (p4) and in the row of his slaves a hundred Mahmud stand in awe like Ayaz[11] (his own slave).

Bait[12] *(verse)*

A thousand beggars of his camp (palace) are like Mahmud and a thousand of his slaves are like Ayaz.

Consequently it became inevitable that I set my fingers in motion to jot down the many great qualities of this stable and enduring kingdom, and raise high the crown of pride, because it would be necessary to write down the description of the reign of the emperor, *Jam Jah,* in such a manner that he might appear to be equal to Sikandar Zulqarnain. Sultan Mahmud Subuktigin had conquered Khurasan and Ghazni with the assistance of the rulers of the Samani dynasty. He had also subjugated some portions of Ghazni and Hindustan, but the fame of his rule did not go beyond these regions. However, the account of the reign of Emperor Akbar is such that in describing its great merits, the power of the pen should be used in full force because his reign has lasted through many generations and he is the monarch of the earth and his times.

Masnavi[13] *(rhyme)*

Thou art a successor of kings, generation after generation, who have conquered the world in no time. Their kingdom is comparable to a fruit-bearing tree and thy sword is like the sun which has taken possession of the land and waters.

Your grand ancestors had for ages ruled distant countries, Rume to Hind, Khurasan to Sindh, China to Iran and Persia to Turan.

Bait (verse)

All the (*sic.*) directions are resting on his shoulders and the rings of nine skies are hanging in his ears. (By the grace and kindness of Allah, the king (Akbar) has laid the foundations of his empire and consequent wars, in the country of Hindustan, praise be on him that he has defeated all the other kings and by his wise policy he has promoted the good of his subjects. (p. 5) If Alexander the Great had earned fame by inventing his administrative regulations, in the emperor's enlightened mind (a spotless mirror of faith in which) the secret of his (Alexander's) benign administration are fully adhered. And in his enlightened mind the mirror of all those tactics are reflected in which are clearly seen the secret methods of conquering and taking into possession various countries. The wisemen have said:

Masnavi (*rhyme*)

Oh! that person who is famous like Khizr and Sikandar and whose command and justice shine like light in the realm. Sikandar forged a mirror out of iron and Hazrat Khizr went round in search of the water of eternal life, but your chest (heart) is itself a lighted mirror and the water of life is itself present in your bowl.

If Sikandar raised a solid wall of iron to protect his empire against the attacks of the powerful race of Yajuj-Majuj,[15] you have by your good luck removed and suppressed by your forceful justice the trouble-makers and oppressors of the society and in this way you have put to an end all evils and vices.

In consequence of the peace and security established by his effective administrative system, the country is enjoying a peaceful life, free from fear and anxiety, that the young one of kid is being nursed on the milk of a lion(ness). The protection of the king is even available to the weakest person. If any watchman or even a Kotwal happens to pass by the house of a widow, he feels frightened lest his shadow might not fall on the walls of that woman because his (king's) protection and help is readily available to every helpless and poor person.

Qita[16] (*distich*)

When the moon established its banner in the air of the country it sees nowhere the smoke of tyranny or oppression nor does it see the dust of disturbances anywhere due to the King's justice and watchfulness. In the same way, the fortresses of the bodies of men have been enriched by the watchfulness of the Kotwali or alertness of the body.

(If any shiqdar[17] happens to pass through his pargana or dominion, he keeps shivering with fear lest his visit might not be a cause of throwing the slightest dust on the face of the farmer). (p6)

Masnavi (*rhyme*)

He performs many worthy acts by his faith and wisdom and spreads the hand of his justice even up to the bazars, removes or suppresses tyranny and injustice, protects those who have been oppressed and even kills the tyrants and oppressors.

If Alexander covered the whole world by means of his prowess, the emperor (Akbar) has filled the world with fragrance by means of the incense of numerous brilliant qualities. From East to West, ambassadors of all countries of the world have been adorned with royal robes. All men point towards him as the repository of unlimited praiseworthy attributes, of perfect humility, combined with dignity and wisdom as well as cleverness and finesse.

Bait (*verse*)

If in my admiration for you I were to call you the second Sikandar, it would be just and fair because you have given better protection to your kingdom and subjects than that even provided by Sikandar.

Duaa (*prayer*)

May God perpetuate for all time the bright sun of the reign of the King of the world! May He preserve the shadow (protection) of his just Wazir, Muzaffar Nishan over the world forever, and may his prowess and empire grow day and night, by the blessings of the Prophet who was the best of men!

(After these introductory remarks it would have become clear and bright as the sun, to the wise and farsighted persons that Allah, the Giver of things unasked has, among mankind made Kings and Prophets, worth of respect and reverence. He has raised to a high rank the Prophets who bring men towards their creator and allotted them a seat in the heavens, and the Kings who destroy or put an end to the tyranny of tyrants, He has raised to such a lofty pedestal that their drums (fish-standards) fly on the highest coast of skies).[18]

Masnavi (*rhyme*)

It is only by His grace that men attain high rank and dignity in life; some become messengers (of God) while some become Kings. (p. 7) It is due to His unique wisdom that kingdom and faith are twin children and these two cannot be separated from each other.

On the basis of the reasons set forth in this *muqaddama,* this poor, indigent and humble pilgrim of Holy Mecca, Haji Muhammad Arif Qandhari[19] (may Allah preserve him!) has resolved to reduce to writing, in the *maqta* of this *Tarikh,* the events of the reign of the emperor (Akbar), conqueror of the countries (regions), and praying for the progress of his reign day and night, bring it to a conclusion!

Bait (*verse*)

I have brought this account (beginning) from *matla* up to *maqta* for the reason that no other title of this can be more suitable than *maqta.*[20]

Hence my mind became occupied naturally in arranging and systematising the events of his reign. Then my pen, filled with the scent of ambergris in order to attain the above-mentioned purpose, began to spread the fragrance of ideas in such a way that the real story might not be hidden under the debris of inundation, (magical language or similies and metaphors). But may be that the sweet-singing Tuti of my tongue might begin to fly in the wind of the art of writing, and the nightingale of my sentiments might begin to relate the stories and might make the repetition of prayer for the emperor at the end of each story!

Masnavi (*rhyme*)

Beware! O, skilful narrator ot the incidents, thy heart holdsth the mysteries and thy mind is like a treasury; therefore thou ought to go on offering a prayer after every story and incident. But the idea arises in the heart of the worker that he should regard this fruit alone as enough in the garden of his objective.

In the course of describing the events whenever it may be necessary to write your famous and great name and (your) titles, although your famous name has the qualities of mushk (musk) and amber (whose fragrance itself spreads far and wide), as it has been said, the famous name is like musk, so the more it is repeated, it givesth off more and more fragrance but if I were to have the honour of recounting the title every time, then it would certainly prolong the narration unnecessarily. Hence it seems proper that I should speak of the emperor of the seven-regions as Khaqan Akbar,[21] and the preserver of the wise, the receiver of God's pardon, Nasiruddin Muhammad Humayun Badshah,[22] I may name him as 'Jannat Ashiani'[23] and the guardian of right and truth, conversant with the laws of government, Zahiruddin Muhammad Babur Badshah,[24] (p. 8) I may call him 'Firdaus Makani' so that the curtain of doubt may be removed from the eyes of the readers by means of these distinctions.

(It is a fact that for the right of enjoying or possessing a kingdom, high and noble descent and greatness of the ancestors has much importance and it is well-known that the emperor's pedigree comes down from Sahib-qiran). Moreover, Khaqan Akbar enjoys the honour of having descended through his mother from Shaikh-ul-Islam Zinda Pil, Ahmad-al-Jami[25] (may God enlighten his mind!).

Misraa (*a hemistich*)

My pen is helpless in giving a detailed account thereof. The reason simply is that the emperor's ancestors right from his father up to Hazrat Adam[26] himself have all been either Kings or symbol of kings.

Masnavi (*rhyme*)

Monarchy has come down from generation to generation in your family. Among the kings who else has been able to maintain the continuation of this dynasty (but yourself).

Excepting yourself who else can achieve such high dignity that may fit him to adorn the imperial throne. The son dominates his officers on account of wearing crown, and his father is his progenitor due to his great personal qualities. You may go on counting from here up to Sahib-qiran, and then you will realise the true pedigree of the royal house.

Nukta (*a quaint conceit*)

If we take into account his genealogy, we will know that Emperor Akbar is in the 7th generation from Amir Timur. In this is enshrined a mystery of God who is all wise and possessor of perfect knowledge. The wonderful mystery is this: God, the Almighty (whose kindnesses are many) has made this blue dome, which is called *asman* (sky) in seven layers; and in the same way He has created seven planets, so also the earth together with the seven-seas is divided into seven regions, called *Haft Iqlim* (climates); metals obtained from the earth are also seven, on the basis of which the edifice of the kingdom rests (p. 9); and then the number of days is also seven and the organs of human body are also divided seven, which have been brought from nonexistence into the valley of existence, and the holy Quran has been sent into seven *lughats* (parts), which are: (1) Qureish, (2) Hamadan, (3) Ti, (4) Hamir, (5) Hazil, (6) Haluh (7) Hawazin-i-Yamen. Further the *Qiraats* are also seven, and the *Sura-i-Fatiha*, without which *namaz* cannot be complete, contains seven *Ayats* (verses); and the Hajis, that is, pilgrims to Mecca have to run seven times between hillocks, called Safa and Marwah (near

Mecca), and they also circumambulate the Kaaba seven times. Similarly the dream of Walid-i-Riyan and its divination by Prophet Yusuf in prison, is also mentioned in the *Quran* in the *Ayat* which means; seven fat cows are being devoured by seven lean and lank cows and there are seven green and flourishing bunches while other seven are dry. So all wondrous and strange things should be attributed to God. By all this my object is to convey that the personality of Khaqan Akbar is endowed with infinite superiority.

In short, the purpose of describing all these things is that those who study this history may observe that this time of day is the spring time for the enjoyment of youth of the emperor, and it is a time of the distinction of victory and success. For this reason his fortune of blessed nature has adorned him with respectable attributes of sobriety and wisdom, found in elderly men. He is also equipped with the courage of those valorous men who have experienced many vicissitudes of life. On the nugget of his royal faith is inscribed the impress of purity and rectitude. The flags of the emperor's justice are so high that the name Kaisar seems pale before it.

Masnavi (*rhyme*)

As the Almighty has raised him to the throne of the ruler after the fashion of Sikandar-like dignity and grandeur, then what wonder if this king of Sikandar's greatness and magnificence, should also conquer and annex countries as Sikandar had done. Indeed he would surpass Sikandar himself in conquering countries, and that the extent of his dominions will cover the seven-climes. "You are always a conqueror of countries like Sikandar, and are endowed with the same attributes of nature. May your life be as long as that of Hazrat Nuh!"[27]

Men of the world know very well that so long as the world lasts, any adventurous king or famous emperor or farsighted minister who may have brought into brilliant light the rites and rituals of the Faith and have rung the organ of art into the ear of the tyrannous sky; none of them have ever invented any such proverbs. Nor does any such picture appear on the tablet of mental reflection. (p. 10) The sky sans feet or head would take years to circle round this polestar, the centre or axle (of the universe). But it so happened that all these necessary things were gathered together, and a star rose from its source. Therefore it is but proper and graceful that the corpus of the realm may be enlivened by good news just as the flower is refreshed by the morning breeze. All that has happened, is due to the benevolence of the king whose benevolence is like the morning dew in a forest. There can be no doubt that the collection of such memorable affairs and putting together matters worth of pride would add a thousand years to the age of the reign, so that it will become a source of wonder and envy for future generations, and they would naturally feel ashamed.

Bait (*verse*)

May the kings learn the ways of charity and mercy and thereafter the wazirs might learn the art of government and administration!

Eminent men of knowledge or masters of eloquence, who know how to distinguish the heavy from the light (small), fine from coarse, bad from good, pure from impure, acceptable from rejected one, are not unaware that those authors and compilers who move their pen to record the past monuments and history and reduce to black and white the glorious attributes and memorials of great rulers, do so with the object of exhibiting the beauty and high ornamentation of their language. Among these the charming language of the author of *Taj-ul-Maasir*,[28] for instance, makes the men of learning dance with joy and the drops of whose pen refresh the gardens of greatness. Similarly the author of the *Tarikh-i-al-Muzaffar*,[29] has jotted down the galaxy of the founder (or this dynasty) and filled his sentences with subtle bons mots. May Allah preserve the purity of (their narratives!).

This humble being (the author) had noted well on the tablet of his mind the idea that he should follow in the footsteps of these respectable persons. In the fine art of penmanship, this book would have been written in the manner of those authors. But I desisted and gave up the attempt of following these authors because the *Taj-ul-Maasir* is a garden, full of blossoming flowers of many kinds, all of which have been ornamented by means of similes and metaphors and everywhere in that garden plants of ideas are bestrewn, which are themselves decorated with subtle remarks. (p. 11) Hence when those who are in search of stories and parables (i.e. past events) open that work to study it, they are lost in amusement by the play of the art of fine writing and thus their real purpose is missed and the author of *Tarikh-i-al-Muzaffar,* in order to exhibit his great learning and ability, has made his language so tortuous and involved that except for some very learned and intellectual persons no one can grasp the sense, nor can any one enjoy his writing. Another reason of my shunning to copy these fellows is that I am aware of the poverty of my knowledge and further I wish that the sense of my text and manner of writing be so clear that all those who are familiar with the style and method of writing of this author, might easily be benefited by the meaning of this book and enjoy it thoroughly. He (Allah) alone can make everything easy because He is all powerful. Hence it seemed proper that first of all description must be given of the realm of the perfect man, Khaqan Akbar, and then should be narrated his victories, other events and happenings which are current, in great detail and are heard from the mouth of all men — all these should be related in accordance with the demand of the time, clearly and fully.

Bait (*verse*)

I have written down in detail and systematical order whatever I heard and all that is currently known.

Nukta (*a mystic note*)

To those who appreciate good writing and who are writers themselves, I pray and expect that they may peruse this history and the above-mentioned gentlemen, nobles and attendants of the court, may kindly compare these true facts and should not refrain from bearing witness to them.

The readers of the *Muzaffar Nama*, particularly commander of the army of Hindustan, councillor of the King of the World, Saifuddin Muzaffar Khan, in obedience to whose gracious desire this history was composed has bestowed on me a robe by way of reward. And in general any Khusrau of the assembly of Isfandiyar, might compare these true words which I have collected together and test their accuracy and they should not hesitate to give them due praise.

Qita (*distich*)

If the cloudy sky had not obliged the morning breeze, it would have remained a mere wind. How then the rose would have been plucked and separated from the thorn? (p. 12) If the sun and moon had not taken pains to train them how then the drops would have become pearls and how a drop of blood would have assumed the form of musk? Discourse can only be attained by means of training and education; for it is training alone which makes a man out of clay (converts clay into man. But Allah alone knows all).

Hazrat Maulana Sharfuddin Ali Yazdi[30] has written a few verses in praise (of the king) which it seems apt to reproduce here.

Abiyat (*verses*)

The extraordinary qualities of the king are greater than anything we can imagine. When I found the dress woven with my praises too small for his lofty stature, then I resolved to prepare a dignified robe for His Majesty out of the warp and woof of stories of kings. I shall start by relating the story of the birth of the King, that is to say, how the sun of the empire rose.[31]

Duaa (*prayer*) *for His Majesty*

May the Lord, whose name is high and esteemed above all, be endowed with everlasting youth and the wealth of both the worlds, and with all manner of pure qualities, for years! The king who resembles the Sun in his countenance, Jupiter in his books, possesses the capabilities of Solomon on the throne, is lucky like Faridun, like Alexander in his realm, just like the Kaisar, and in his largesse and liberty has the attributes of Sanjar. May the Lord preserve his empire and keep happy the hearts of his subjects!

Duaa (*prayer*) *for the Reign and Long Life of the Princes*

The highest or best gift of God and perfect greatness, (as has been said), "Wealth and progeny are the ornament of life in the world"). The king too has been endowed with that ornament, the fortunate princes, descendants of Humayun, each of them shines like the moon of the 14th (full of brightness), nay like the sun himself, the illuminer of the world; they are shedding their light over one quarter of the globe. (p. 13)

Qita (*distich*)

All the princes are the stars of the sky of good luck and in their midst the king is like the moon. Their praiseworthy civility and good manners are the shining mirrors of their nobleness and their dignified personality is the wealth of respect and honour they enjoy.

Because the account of each of the princes is to come in its proper place, it seems better to finish it with a prayer. Therefore I pray that *Allah Tala* may preserve by the grace of the Prophet and his honourable progeny protect these pearls of the royal family in peace, from the lot of ruin till the end of the age. And these princes under the care of the emperor of the world may continue to be benefited with the fruits of good life, and he may entrust each one of them with the government of a separate dominion!

Bait (*verse*)

While one of them may conquer the world like Sikandar, the other may obtain everlasting life like (Hazrat) Khizr.

Duaa (prayer)

The advisers of government and ministers of state, who are the creators of justice, are the framers of rules and regulations of good government, as the following couplet says:

To establish good administration and organisation is higher than the ability to perform one's religious duties.

Bait (verse)

May God give us ability! May Allah carry to unlimited heights, under the auspices of His great and fortunate Majesty the administration of the country! May the officers who are as lofty as the Saturn and dignified and dominant as the Mars and the kings who have the face of a lion and frightfulness of Rustam,[32] and the amirs having the countenance of Minu-Chihr and the standard-bearers of the social pleasures of Khusrau,[33] and learned persons possessing the brilliance and sharpness . . . of Mercury! May they be protected from evil eye![34] (p. 14)

Notes

1. In ordinary sense the word *maqta* (conclusion or last part) implies the last verse of a poem.
2. Arif seems to have used the word *maqta* to signify the concluding part of the book which, as he says, he has finished the *matla*. It is in the nature of a *dibacha* (preface) of the *maqta* which he seems to begin. It is strange that he has not spelt out the contents of his given *matla*. However, it will be hazardous to presume that the *matla* which is in the nature of only a preface, comprises anything related to pre-Akbari period.
3. The famous Persian poet who composed the great epic poem *Shah Nama* which is a poetical and most romantic history of the ancient Persian monarchs. Firdausi is justly considered as the Homer of the East.
4. Two Princes of this name are much celebrated in the east, both distinguished by the title of Zulqarnain, having two horns (of the world), implying that they conquered the globe from east to west; the first supposed to be the most ancient kings; the other, Alexander of Macedon.
5. He was the founder of the Ghaznavid dynasty, which flourished in

the beginning of the eleventh century. For details see M. Habib, *Sultan Mahmud of Ghazni*, Delhi, S. Chand & Co., 1967.

6. Name of a Persian king.
7. Name of an ancient and celebrated King of Persia. The commencement of whose reign is placed about seven hundred and fifty years before the Christian era.
8. Belonging to the time of Prophet Sulaiman.
9. Name of the son of Iraj, who was the seventh king of Pashdadian dynasty.
10. This is a gist of the verses.
11. Name of a favourite (slave) of Sultan Mahmud of Ghazni.
12. It implies verse, couplet and a distich.
13. Poetry composed of a distich, corresponding to measure, each consisting of a prayer of rhymes.
14. East, West, South and North.
15. Gog and Magog, belonging to the race of Eastern Scythia, beyond Imaus.
16. A kind of verse in which the meaning of the first verse of each stanza is completed in the last.
17. An officer appointed to collect the revenue from a certain portion of land. For details see Minhaj Siraj, *Tabaqat-i-Nasiri* and Zia-ud-din Baruni, *Tarikh-i-Firozeshahi.*
18. This doctrine is fully supported by Baruni, vide *The Political Theory of the Delhi Sultanate,* translation of *Fatawa-i-Jahandari,* Afsar Khan, introduction by M. Habib, para III, p. 138.
19. The few references by Farishta in his *Gulshan-i-Ibrahimi/Tarikh-i-Farishta* (hereafter *Farishta*) to a certain Haji Muhammad Qandhari (though he has omitted his proper name, Arif) does not seem to provide sufficient ground to identify him as the same person as is generally believed by modern historians.
20. Arif seems to have brought his preface to a close here.
21. The title 'Khaqan' has been used for the emperors of China or Chinese Tatary. Here it implies to an emperor or a king.
22. Humayun was born on Tuesday, March 6, 1508 AD. He ascended the throne after the death of his father, Babur. The date of Babur's death is variously given by Gulbadan Begum, Abul Fazl, Nizamuddin and Farishta which follows likewise:- Monday, 5th Jamadi I, A.H. 937; Tuesday, 6th Jamad, I, A.H. 937; Monday, 5th Jamadi I, A.H. 937. So the 5th Jamadi I., corresponds to Sunday, December 25, 1530 A.D., but the week is clearly mentioned by the royal authoress. She seems more likely to remember the day. So it can safely be said that Humayun wore the crown on 9th (Thursday) and it is supported by Khwandamir

also who was present there but the day is given Friday by him. On the basis of Gulbadan Begum's recording, the date of his accession will be Thursday 9th Jamadi I, A.H. 937/29th December, 1530 AD. Humayun after his defeat at Chausa, escaped to Persia. He recaptured Hindustan in 1555 A.D. and died in 1556 A.D. For details see *Tuzuk-i-Baburi, Tazkirat-ul-Waqiat, Humayun Nama, Tarikh-i-Humayun Wa Akbar, Tarikh-i-Rashidi, Qanun-i-Humayuni, Akbar Nama, Tabaqat-i-Akbari* and *Tarikh-i-Alfi* (hereafter *TB, TW, HN, TH, TR, QH, AN* and *Alfi* respectively).

23. The word seems to be Jannat-makani.
24. Zahir-ud-din Muhammad Babur, son of Umar Shaikh Mirza, was born on 6th Muharram A.H. 888/14th February, 1483 A.D. He succeeded his father as ruler of Farghana in Ramzan, A.H. 899/June, 1494 A.D., being then in his twelfth year. He conquered and founded his empire in Hindustan in 1526 A.D. He died on 26th December, 1530 A.D. in his forty-eighth year. For details see *TB, TW, HN, TH, QH* and *AN.*
25. Ahmad-al-Jami was one of the most respected saints of Nishapur. He died in A.H. 536/1141 A.D. *Nazhat-i-Jami,* 207. See also *Sadid-ud-din Muhammad Ghaznavi, Muqamat-Zindapil Ahmadi Jam,* ed. H. Moyyad, 1967.
26. The father of the human race.
27. Prophet Nuh lived for one hundred and fifty years, according to *The Old Testament Genesis,* chapter I, verse 21.
28. *Taj-ul-Maasir,* written by Sadruddin Muhammad bin Hasan al-Nizami, is a verbose, rhetorical and uninformative account, in prose and verses of the Sultans of Delhi, covering A.H. 587 to 613 (1191 to 1217 A.D.). For details see C.A. Storey, *Persian Literature,* Vol.I, part I, pp. 493-95. (hereafter Storey).
29. This is a history of Muzaffar (dynasty). They were the rulers of Kirman and Shiraz. For details see Rieu, *Catalogue of Perisan MSS in the British Museum, No. 28.*
30. Sharf-ud-din Ali Yazdi, the writer of *Zafar Nama-i-Taimuri* and Nadim Shah Rukh Mirza, son of Amir Timur died in A.H. 853/1449 A.D. For details see *Subah Sadiq* (hereafter *SS*), *Tarikh-i-Muhammadi* (*TM*), *Haft Iqlim* (*HI*) and *Tazkira-i-Daulat Shah.*
31. See *Zafar Nama'.*
32. The Persian Hercules.
33. A celebrated Persian king.
34. Verses quoted from the *Quran* have been omitted.

OCCURRENCE 2

Description of the Auspicious Birth of His Majesty of the Lofty Throne, Abu-al-Muzaffar Jalal-ud-Din Muhammad Akbar (May God Preserve and Perpetuate His Rule!) Victory Fly Over whose War Banners

The only way to attain height of pride and good luck was that His Majesty (Jannat Ashiani, Emperor Humayun), who adorned the most excellent throne (of Hindustan), endowed with the attributes of leadership and greatness got married, (it is only Allah who is giver of blessings, Creator of the best and gives us form in the mother's womb) was leading him to establish himself in the abode of wisdom. It was to establish and prepare the regulations of the country and the nation for the solution of the knotty problems (of the faith and state). The gift of all these appeared in the form of the birth of His Majesty (Akbar), who is of noble descent from both sides, mother as well as father. Most certainly and doubtlessly his birth is the reflection of the grace of God and an exhibition of beauty of nature and grandeur of personality. This is a gift which is a sign of the lofty status and success of the fortunate young prince.

Bait (*verse*)

O! my heart bear the happy news that such a person is born, who will revive the dead. I have worked out the auspicious *fal* (augury). There comes the person who listens to the entreaties of the poor.

The purpose of all this description is that on the 4th of Rabi II, A.H. 947 (August 9, 1540 A.D.) when the sun had obtained some of the beauty (of this person) and the moon of the 14th (i.e. full moon), had not seen even in its dream anything like unto its countenance, that blessed night of which the dignity and status are higher than the sun and stars, whereof they had lost their repose, His Majesty (Humayun), whose good fortune had woken up, at such a time when his clever mind moving far away from the din and bustle of government, had chosen to lay his proud head on the bed of repose, saw in his dream that God (*Allah Tala*) had bestowed on him a very lucky son and he had been christened Jalal-ud-Din Muhammad Akbar.[1] In fact his dream proved true after a period of two years.

Masnavi (*rhyme*)

In accordance with thy scheme, destiny is active in performing its assigned duty; although the king is asleep, his luck is awakened. It is not a mere dream but is the height of belief, because his noble objective is hidden inside his own sleeve. (p. 15)

On the morning of Sunday, 5th Rajab-ul-murajjab, A.H. 949/15th October, 1542 A.D. bearers of the happy and blessed news brought the joyful news to the king that the sun had risen from the horizon of success and triumph and God, opener of the gates of victory, made this soul preserving announcement that (if you are desirous of victory then you should feel delighted that it has come). The happy tiding is that the star of the enduring kingdom had risen, was given to His Majesty (Humayun) at the village of Umarkot, situated in Sindh; and that the Jupiter of good luck has begun to shine, and that the sun of blessed existence of him, the protector of Khilafat has risen out of the horizon of nativity, and the moon of good luck has risen in the east of success and good luck.[2]

Qita (*distich*)

When that planet saw the day of his (Akbar's) birth, it justly said that he is Saad Akbar.[3] The heaven proclaimed him the king of all the (*sic.*) directions (cardinal points) and the emperor of the seven regions by beating the drums throughout the four corners of the world.

The lights of rulership (kingship) are shining forth from his daily progressing family and the marks of success are written on his lucky forehead. The source of his noble virtues are established by the height of his grandeur. The rays of the kingdom are shining like the sun from the east of his forehead.

Bait (verse)

The bright planet rose on the noble sky; his wisdom is like the sun, while his face resembles the (planet) Zuhra (from Sans Shukra, Venus) and heart like Jupiter.

The chaste angels of the heaven are showering the oceans of blessings on him, men of high ranks make a present of the fruits and rewards of their prayers before (this) moon-like person. Old men have held their heads (in awe) at the sight of his joyous youth, and miserable get set itself right and happy by seeing his noble virtues. (p. 16) The angels who turn the rosary of beads, (i.e. repeat God's name) are reciting prayers for his reign and the denizens of the prayer halls of heaven, having made the prayer for the perpetuation of his reign are saying:-

Masnavi (rhyme)

May your flourishing head remain far from evil talk; may your broad mind become a new fountain; you are the master of lucky and progressive men of the age and you are the wise conqueror of countries!

At the moment when the heavenly blessings (grace) were covering him, and the sources of success and progress were becoming strong, the lights of the emperor were filling one-fourth of the world, the ray of God's greatness which illumines his forehead, has brightened the dark corners (regions) of the world. The star has risen to the zenith. The master of realm of the royal palace set his foot in it and the ruler of the rising fortune becomes perfectly victorious. The sun of the dome of his personal virtues turned his face, i.e.

moved towards the attainment of heights. The planet Zuhra (Shukr) proved worth of the assembly of the kingdom and the moon of the sky of pride rose out of its hiding.

Qita (*distich*)

His face is that sky which the sun has rendered golden. When through this happy tidings, the morning locked up its tongue. It should be known that until it received the wound of the eye of the star, he continued to read the prayer (*Fatiha*) of the morning, and kept gradually rising.

The illuminated mind of the sun applied the darkness of that night like antimony in the eye of the sky and adorned it with the rising clouds. The night filled with its fragrance the apron of Sumbul, and the day by means of its pearl-showering, filled the pocket of horizon with pearls and gems.

Bait (*verse*)

As his honour and grandeur grew side by side with the rising of the day, so his fame also spread. When his presence arrived in the world, it seemed as if a new world had entered the old. (p. 17)

The morning at once offered the golden sun, which sets in the west as an ablution or sacrifice, and the sky offered his precious bunch on a plate. The breeze of spring stood up to spread its matress in the royal palace; and the cloud came up to rain pearls in the palace courtyard for the world-protector. *Allah Tala,* who is the illuminer of these lamps, by His matchless power exhibited all the blessings at this auspicious hour of the king's birth; and made miserable and dishonoured (those jealous) of the everlasting government. (It is the grace of *Allah.* He gives to whomever He wishes. He is a great bestower.)

Masnavi (*rhyme*)

At the time of his birth, he kept his eye on the stars because the wise man keeps his eye fixed on them. He is able to make proper use of the astrolabe, and understands the auspicious time. When the star of victory arose out of the invisible, then good fortune showered gems from its store. The sun obtained respect from the sign of Aries (a sign of the Zodiac), he who leads from knowledge to action. In such an auspicious hour his light made debut. What should I say, only that my evil eye may not harm him.

The object of narrating all these things is that when in obedience to the illuminated *Shariat,* she (Hamida Banu Begum)[4] came to be tied in the bond of marriage, to the king, who possessed the prowess of Jamshed, then she was blessed with a son to whom the *Ayat-i-Karima* could be rightly applied, "He is not a man, he is an angel, who reflects the sublime attributes and beauty of Yusuf."[5]

Hamida's attributes, Nawab Mahdi Aliya (the pious lady) and great personality, who is equal to the noble lady, Sarah (wife of the Prophet Abraham), who can be compared to Asiah,[6] whose chastity and purity resemble those of Bilqis (wife of Solomon), whose dignity is like Khadijah (wife of Prophet Muhammad) and whose cradle exhibits pearls and the sun revolves in it.

Bait (*verse*)

Whose mighty arms are shining by the blessings and kindness of the emperor, whose lofty rank is full (to overflow) by God's liberality, viz. Rabia, the second.[7] Hamida Banu Begum (may God increase her chastity!) who is descended from Shaikh-ul-Islam entitled Ahmad al-Jami, who is the guide and leader of men (may God sanctify his heart!).

Qita (*distich*)

The arrow of her chastity will seal the eye of the day if it ventured to see the shadow of her crown. (p. 18) The guards remove the sun and its shadow from her cradle in the hope that in consequence of the universal respect that she commands the loftiness of her crown will attain the position of the moon.

Masnavi (*rhyme*)

Look and behold the Majesty of Allah. How brilliant is

this sun that it itself before him looks like an insignificant particle! When he rose high and spread on the kingdom, then from his face such a brilliant light emanated, that the whole world from east to west became filled with illumination, and such was the condition of the world as that of the garden in spring. The sun arose emitting such brilliant light that against its rays even the sun paled into hiding. The eye of His Majesty, Humayun, was illumined with a new sight and the advent of this Sahib-qiran became the source of his joy and delight. The park of the state was made green with the canal of richness, and the garden of his desire became fertile and enriched by the rain of the blessed fortune.

Bait (*verse*)

When the mother of the age was blessed with the birth of this moon, the heaven said with much love and affection: "May God bestow even more!"

He was the sun, who, when he rose, filled all corners (of the world) with the gift of light. He was the moon, who, when he raised his head with the spreading light, the gloom of misery scattered away. What can I say (about his immensity)? He was the lustre and glory of God's grace, so that when he looked, all sorrow and misery disappeared from the hearts of people. He was a ray of the divine kindness so that his appearance became a source of joy and freshness for all and sundry. He is such a king from whose brow is reflected the loftiness of the sky.

Masnavi (*rhyme*)

Son of a wise personality, he naturally achieved greatness for the pearl of high and noble luck is ever blessed. When the father found his son to be worthy and full of wisdom, he felt gratified that he begot a son, wise like unto himself. (p. 19)

One of his admirable qualities is that since the very start he was recording the story of his noble character in the book of greatness. Second, he was, since the time of his infancy, exhibiting the beauties of his excellent qualities. Third, it was quite evident from his countenance that he had, from his very cradle, set his foot on the royal throne. The lines of light on his forehead were announcing with brilliance, "We have from his very infancy endowed him with wisdom and thoughtfulness, and the Archangel (Gabriel) was reciting the verse of the *Quran* (which is read in order to ward off the evil-eye) so that no evil-eye should put a black mark on his noble personality. The priests of the hall of worship were earnestly praying that the step of his prowess may be firmly established on the zenith of great ranks.

Masnavi (*rhyme*)

May this tree planted by Humayun be ever flourishing and growing; his name may be high and his luck be luminous! May the world get fresh life from his crown and throne and the head of his foe adorn the door (lie on the sill of the entrance)!

Duaa (*prayer*) *for His Majesty*

It may be expected from *Allah Tala*, the Protector of this ruler of the men of the world, to keep him under the umbrella sheltering various people for years beyond count and on the garden of this frail and transitory world the grace and mercy of Him may remain together with the King's peace and that it may remain fragrant with his justice, by the grace of the Prophet and his progeny!

Qita (*distich*)

The four elements and the sky; one of them may become father and the other mother so that the line of progeny may continue forever, because, if the elements and the sky become family members of day and night, then the king would become the holy *Kaaba* of felicity and prosperity and the place of worship for the people.

NOTES

1. Gulbadan confirms the said dream in her *HN*, tr. A.S.Beveridge, p.145. Abul Fazl refers to the said dream. He however does not mention details. *AN*, I, p.13. See also *Nafais-ul-Maasir* (hereafter *NM*).
2. News of Akbar's birth at Umarkot was conveyed to Humayun when

he was encamping in a garden on the bank of a large tank, 30 miles south-west of Umarkot. The fort Umar or Omarkot was built by a chief of the Sumra tribe. It is situated in 25° 21″ north and 69° 46″ east, and is now a town in Sindh. Many Persian and English authors give the name erroneously as Amarkot, with various corruptions, as if it was derived from Hindi word 'amar', meaning immortal, a frequent element in Hindu names.

Abul Fazl gives the date as 1st Rajab-ul-Murajjab, A.H. 949/11th October, 1542 A.D. to suit the official birthday which is accepted. *AN* I, 389. The Ramzan/December date is given by Jauhar, and must be correct, but is, of course, inconsistent with the official birthday and Abul Fazl's account.

Arif's observation seems obviously based on reports that were current during the time in question. So it is not surprising that he forgot to mark that Humayun was far away from Umarkot at the time of Akbar's birth. See also *Alfi, TH, NM, TA, Muntakhab-ut-Tawarikh* (hereafter *MT*).

3. It is another name of Mushtari. the planet Jupiter (from Sans: Dyaus-Pitar).

4. 'Arif as usual reels out a long thread of the attributes of Hamida Begum, which for the sake of clarity and to avoid confusion, is relegated to the end of this passage. Gulbadan Begum calls her the daughter of Mir Baba Dost. Jauhar calls her the daughter of Hindal's Akhund. Mir Masum states that she was the daughter of Shaikh Ali Akbar Jami. Abul Fazl does not give the name of her father but calls him Muazzam, who was with her at Pat. It is probable that Mir Baba Dost may be a mere sobriquet of Shaikh Ali Akbar. Mrs. Beveridge does not feel sure and says that there is difficulty in making a precise statement about Hamida's family relations. See *HN*, tr. pp. 149, 237-39; *MT*, pp. 30, 31; *Tarikh-i-Masum* fols. 120(b) and 121(a) and *AN*, I, 364. (hereafter *TM*)

Hindal objected to the marriage. Jauhar's surmise that probably he wanted to marry her himself is incorrect for Gulbadan puts these words in the mouth of Hindal; "I look on this girl as a sister and child of my own. Your Majesty is a king, heaven forbid there should not be proper alimony, and that so a cause of annoyance should arise". At this Humayun took offence and left the place. The brothers were appeased by Dildar Begum. See *HN*, tr. pp. 150-51.

How Hamida agreed to marry Humayun is well described by Gulbadan Begum. When the young lady hesitated, Dildar advised her saying "After all you will marry someone. Better then a king, who is there"? "Oh yes, I shall marry someone; but he shall be a man whose collar my hand can touch, and not one whose skirt it does not reach". Dildar persisted in her endeavour and at last made her agree. *Ibid.*, p.152.

The date of marriage is given Rajab A.H. 948/October 1541 A.D. when Humayun was going to Bhakar. In short Hamida Begum married Humayun in A.H. 948/1541 A.D., which means that she must have been born some time in 1527 A.D. She accompanied her husband in his wanderings in Afghanistan and Persia. She died in 1604 A.D. at the age of eighty. See also *SS, Tarikh-i-Muhammadi, Maasir-i-Jahangiri, Tuzuk-i-Jahangiri* (hereafter *TM, MJ* and *TJ* respectively).

5. *Sura Yusuf,* 31.
6. It is rather amusing to note that in his endless pratter, Arif compares Hamida Begum with Asiah, wife of Pharaoh who had secretly become a follower of Moses and who was tortured to death by her husband.
7. Raba was a lady of Baghdad, renowned for her beauty and chastity. She being the fourth daughter of her father was called by the said name.

OCCURRENCE 3

Description of the Imprisonment of the Pearl of the Empire and Realm and His Despatch to Kabul by Nawab Mirza Askari

In the religion of politeness, brotherliness or fraternal obligations, and in the law of sons and particular relatives, (p. 20) this view is proper that on the declaration (*manshur*) of unity and seal of virtue (good name), the pen should not be used harshly (mercilessly) and brotherly obligations and promises ought to be respected, and the mirror of love should not be broken, and the blame of differences ought not be put on brothers, and one's step should not abandon the circle of loyalty to go into the wilderness of disloyalty, and should not go astray from the path of affection and unity and keep in view the saying that "one should be cautious against misunderstandings". If the writer will ignore these hints, he will certainly set fire to the grain-heap of confidence and self-respect. We (the authors) do not wish that our eye should become wounded and become forgetful or careless of the hostile wind and the mischief of incidents. On this earth greed and ambition are being prevalent and our lust wants to be nourished by the water of passionate desire. If you follow it then you will burn yourself unwillingly in the fire of death, and thereafter there would be no use of repenting and feeling ashamed nor would there be any means of obtaining pardon.

Bait (*verse*)

Steadiness and sobriety are better in everything. You should wait patiently till the sun shines on you.

The deceased Nawab Mirza Askari[1] is the example of the

above-mentioned statement. He was a subordinate to Mirza Kamran[2] (now dead) and the government of Qandhar was given to him. The imperial forces, according to the celestial signs, left for Qandhar from Sindh in A.H. 950/1543 A.D.[3] When it reached the towns of Shal and Poshakh[4], which are situated on the border of Qandhar, Nawab Mirza Askari came out of Qandhar with his entire army, fearing an attack of the imperial army while passing from there. He immediately sent his messengers hastily to Mirza Kamran to report to him that, "Humayun is advancing with a large force towards Qandhar. He intends to capture it and then will inevitably aspire to capture other regions. Consequently, the government of the land would be upset and its administration would suffer great damage and would be disrupted. It is therefore necessary to pay attention to it without any delay". He further prayed that, "the lord of the kingdom may please allow him to oppose the advancing force and prevent its entering the dominion". (p. 21)

Nawab Mirza Kamran believed the misguided men and he permitted Askari to fight it. Mirza Askari therefore advanced with the intention of fighting. Before the armies could come face to face, His Majesty diverted his route and he proceeded via Garmsir[5] and Qandhar to the dominion of Sistan, Khurasan and Iran. Its full account however will be given at its proper place.

Just at this time the prince (Khaqan Akbar), who was only two years[6] old and had not even attained the age of activity, fell into the hands of his unkind uncle and passed some time in unhappy custody.[7] When His Majesty (Akbar) became a captive in his infancy, the denizens of heaven began to wonder how that sun, for whose brilliance at noon even *Chemp de Mars* is insufficient and its gamestore are insignificant before his valour, will tolerate, being confined to an extremely small prison room of which the dimensions are smaller than the dimple in a chin? How is it possible that the victorious emperor under the shelter of whose merciful banner, one-fourth of the globe's inhabitants are about to come? How can that sun pass his time in a dark cell?

Masnavi (*rhyme*)

For the pearl, which illumines the night, oyster is not the proper place. It is not good that the sun should remain set in the day and for him whose destiny is to become the emperor, it is very strange to be imprisoned.

He (Mirza Kamran) killed the soldiers of imperial army and ill-treated those who were captured. Further, he summoned the Prince to Kabul in A.H. 951/1544 A.D., while it was happening, His Majesty came out flying from Iran to the vicinity of Qandhaṛ. Shah Tahmasp[8] provided reinforcement to him. (p. 22) Moreover, the Shah deputed his own young son, named Shah Murad[9] under the guardianship (leadership) of Dagh Khan with some amirs, commanders and a force, numbering about ten thousand for his help. The force came and laid siege to the fort of Qandhar.[10] Nawab Mirza Askari remained confined in the fort for six months. Thereafter, he prayed for peace, came out of the fort, and received the blessings by kissing the feet of His Majesty. As a matter of precaution, he was confined under custody for some time. Finally, he was released and proceeded towards Balkh, from where he left for pilgrimage. But he died on his way in between Sham (Syria) and Mecca.

The victory of His Majesty (Humayun) proved to be a guide for many victories in future. The emperor appointed Mirza Murad's vakils as the incharge of Qandhar and taking leave of Qazal Bashi nobles and chiefs marched to Sarband[11] which was at a distance of two stages from there.

By a mysterious coincidence of events news of the death of Shah Murad Mirza reached the emperor. Thereupon the emperor appointed some brave and gallant warriors, such as the deceased Ulugh Mirza,[12] Bairam Khan and Haji Muhammad Khan Kauki,[13] and sent them to take charge of Qandhar. Accordingly, the named valorous persons proceeded there immediately and taking into possession the fort of Qandhar, expelled Badagh Khan (from there). Despite the presence of princes of the royal blood, the emperor as a token of his generosity, appointed Nawab Bairam Khan its commandant and it triumphed. Soon his force conquered Kabul and released the imprisoned soldiers as well. (p. 23)

In any event, it is undeniable that when the sun, illuminiser of the world, shines over it, it has to go through a state of an eclipse, and if the moon intends to be full (*14th moon*), it cannot achieve its object without being passed through an eclipse.

Bait (verse)

The earth inside the pot has to endure acute headache (i.e. has to struggle hard), until it gets rid of the headache which appears in the form of a rose.

Duaa (prayer) for His Majesty

The Almighty has endowed Khaqan Akbar, with the admirable capabilities of governing the empire, with pleasing manners, so that he is the midday sun and pioneer of civility and excellent behaviour. He is the possessor of the power of assisting friends and melting foes, till the end of his life. He is also gifted with great prowess and superiority, by the grace of Prophet Muhammad and his progeny.

NOTES

1. Nawab Mirza Askari, the third son of Babur, was born to Gulrukh Begum in A.H. 922/1516 A.D. He always remained attached with his real elder brother Kamran. He died in A.H. 962/1555 A.D. in Syria. According to Farishta, he died in A.H. 961/1554 A.D. I, 240. For details see *TM, NM, AN, HI, SS, TA, IJ, MT* and *Tuhfa-i-Sami* (hereafter *TM*).
2. Mirza Kamran was also born to Gulrukh Begum in 1509 A.D. He also died on 11th Zi-hijja, A.H. 964/5th October 1556 A.D. while on his way to pilgrimage to Mecca. For details see *Ibid.*
3. Arif's date has been confirmed by other contemporary chronicles. For the conquest and other details see *AN*, I, 189 and 244; *NM* fol. 182-b and 185-a; *MT*, I, 477; *Tarikh-i-Shahi* (hereafter *TS*), 310 and *Farishta*, I, 237 and *Gulbadan*, 74.
4. Shal-o-Mastan; *NM*, fol. 182-b and *Gulbadan*, 65; Nizamuddin says Shal Mastan also. *TA, II*, 57 and *TS*, 168; Abul Fazl says Sal Zemastan. *AN*, I, 190. It is actually situated about three 'farsakh' (one farsakh is about 1800 feet in length) from Qandhar, *MT*, I, 442; Qasba-i-Shal Mashank, *Farishta*, I, 411.

5. Garmsirat is the centre of Qandhar. See also *AN*, I, 228; *NM*, fol. 183-a and *Gulbadan*, 68.
6. He was one year old. *TA*, II, 57; *MT*, I, 443 and *Zubda*, fol. 77-a while Abul Fazl says, he was one year and three months old. *AN*, I, 194.
7. According to Gulbadan Begum, "Askari handed over Akbar to his wife Sultan Begum who treated him as her own son." p. 66 and *AN*, I, 194. See also *TA*, *MT* and *TS*.
8. Shah Tahmasp, son of Ismail, son of Sultan Haider, was the second ruler of Safvi dynasty. He ascended the throne in A.H. 930/1523 A.D. and died in A.H. 984/1576 A.D. at the age of sixty-four. For details see *AN*, *MT*, *TA*, *NM*, *SS* and *MU*.
9. Arif does not mention that Humayun was provided assistance by the Shah of Iran, subject to his change of Shia faith. The strength given by Arif has been confirmed by others. See also *TA*, II, 64; *MT*, I, 445; *TS*, 306; *Zubda*, fol. 78; *Farishta*, I, 23 while Abul Fazl says 12,000. *AN*, I, 218.
10. Humayun came to Qandhar on Saturday, 8th Muharram, A.H. 952/22nd March, 1545 A.D. *MR*, I, 596. The siege started on 7th Muharram, A.H. 952/21st March 1545 A.D. and it ended on 28th Jamadi Akhir/7th September of the said year and accordingly within three months. *Zubda*, fol. 78-a; *AN*, I, 229 and *TA*, II, 61.
11. Abul Fazl says Chahar Bagh. *AN*, I, 336 and 339.
12. Ulugh Mirza was the son of Muhammad Sultan Mirza. He joined Ibrahim Husain against Akbar. He died in A.H. 975/1567 A.D. at Mandu. See *TM*, *AN*, *SS*, *IJ* and *MU*.
13. Haji Muhammad Khan Koki Sistani was a retainer of Bairam Khan in the beginning. He rose to the mansab of 1000. He died in A.H. 983/1575 A.D. in Bengal. *ZK*, 418 and *MU*, I, 548. See also *TM* and *AN*.

OCCURRENCE 4

Description of the Conquest of Kabul by Emperor Humayun, His Handing over it to Khaqan Akbar and the Invasion of Mirza Kamran on that Dominion

The luminous sentences and cherished stories given in respect of the emperor (late Humayun) would have made it clear that when he diverted his march towards Badakhshan, he nominated Khaqan Akbar as his successor in Kabul. Mirza Kamran on his return from Sindh, captured Kabul in A.H. 952/1545 A.D. and imprisoned him also. On receipt of information of the state of affairs, the emperor felt deeply grieved and became restless. Abandoning his plan in Badakhshan, he at once started for Kabul and laid siege to it. (p. 24) Mirza Kamran, realizing the situation, made Akbar his shield by avoiding gun, arrow and lance. Consequently fighting broke out on all sides which continued for some days. Brave soldiers came face to face and many of them were killed and wounded. The intensity of attack of the imperial army frightened the guards of the fort. Mirza Kamran also realised it. He came out of the fort and escaped after abandoning all his baggage and equipment. In short, he accepted defeat.[1]

Masnavi (*rhyme*)

When the enemy with a heart filled with agony and good sense, falls into misery and misfortune, some of them are drowned in the middle (i.e. are ruined).

Whoever could manage, escaped with Mirza Kamran towards Badakhshan, suffering all sorts of hardships. But a band of those who refused to move with him, were enlisted in the imperial retinue. Thereafter, the emperor entered into Kabul and started the administration of the region peacefully. He was inaffably delighted on meeting his son. He picked up Khaqan Akbar's arms with deep-seated affection and inquired from him about his imprisonment. The prince however consoled his father tactfully.

Bait (*verse*)

When the moon is hidden by eclipse, then the people say that gold is battered, because that is the test thereof.

When in A.H. 958/1551 A.D. Mirza Hindal[2] attained martyrdom (died) His Majesty had returned to Kabul and conferred upon Khaqan Akbar the province of Ghazni, which had been the capital of Sultan Mahmud of Ghazni and his descendants. Those who were under Mirza Hindal were placed under his command in addition. (p. 25) These events have been described in the course of the story (of Humayun). On the recapture of Hindustan, he took Akbar, his eldest son with him to Delhi, put him under the tutorship of the great Khan, Bairam Khan and despatched them to suppress Sikandar Khan Afghan.[3] During the same time, the fateful news of the sudden death of the emperor was received.[4] Therefore after performing the necessary obsequies, and transfer (of kingship) in the month of Rabi-us-Sani, A.H. 963/February, 1556 A.D.,[5] at the pargana of Kalanur,[6] he ascended the throne. Bairam Khan was given the title of Khan-i-Khanan and he discharged the state of affairs with absolute power. Shah Abu-al-Maali[7] who was among the great nobles of Humayun was imprisoned and sent to Lahore in chains because he had commenced rebellious activities. When Khaqan Akbar entered Nagarkot[8] Sikandar being frightened, fled away and took refuge in a hill near Pushkal.[9] Thereafter Emperor Akbar turned towards Jalandhar.[10] All these incidents will get a detailed description in the course of the history related to His Majesty.

Duaa (*Prayer*) *for His Majesty*

May the garden of the brilliant kingdom of government,

flourish like a rose garden! His Majesty, Khaqan Akbar, may ever remain fresh and blossoming with the cool breeze of the fulfilment of ambitions and everlasting greatness, and may he blossom forth (make progress) ever and ever! May the benevolent God protect the victorious Khaqan Akbar from all calamities and evils and be his guide, helper and supporter forever!

NOTES

1. Arif does not give the date of conquest of Kabul while it is given 10th Ramzan, A.H. 952/15th November, 1545 A.D. *TS,* 312 and *Farishta,* I, 238. Nizamuddin says in Ramzan, A.H. 952/November, 1548 A.D. TA, II, 65; Wednesday, 12th Ramzan, A.H. 952/17th November, 1545 A.D. *AN,* I, 244; *NM,* fols.128a and 185a; *TS,* 313. Akbar was eight years and four months old.
2. The real name of Prince Hindal was Muhammad Nasir or Abu-al-Nisar Muhammad. He died at the age of thirtythree and eight months on 21st Ziqada, A.H. 958/20th November, 1551 A.D. *Gulbadan,* p. 10. See also *ibid.*
3. Sikandar Khan, Ahmad Khan Sur was the nephew of Sher Shah Suri. He ascended the throne in A.H. 962/1555 A.D. He was defeated by Humayun in 1555 A.D. He took refuge in the mountains of Siwalik and died in A.H. 966/1558 A.D. in Bihar. For details see *AN, TM, Mt, TA* and *IJ.*
4. Arif does not give the date or details of the incident while the chronicles, as usual, differ about the exact dates. Abul Fazl's statement that some drops of blood issued from his right ear speaks of a fatal injury presumably a fracture of the base of the skull. *AN,* I, 654n. On the basis of this, Beveridge says that he died on Friday, January 24, 1556 A.D. For details see *NM, TS, MR, TA* etc.
5. The correct date of Akbar's enthronement seems to be Friday, 2nd Rabi II, A.H. 963/February 14, 1556 A.D. *AN,* I, 658.
6. Kalanaur, a small town, is fifteen miles west from Gurdaspur (town).
7. Shah Abu-al-Maali, born in a family of the Saiyeds of Tirmudh, was embellished with the qualities of beauty, dignity, intelligence and perception. Humayun had a particular regard for him, which helped him to nourish the idea of kingship. Though Bairam Khan wanted to put him to death, the emperor (Akbar) saved him by sending him behind the bars under the custody of Haq Wardi. Later, the emperor permitted him to go for pilgrimage. He returned after performing it. He killed Ahmad Beig in the presence of entire court and succeeded to escape Kabul. Mah Chuck Begum showed kindness, gave her daughter in marriage to him. But he killed the pious lady. He however was

arrested at the village of Charikaran by the Badakhshis and presented before Mirza Sulaiman. *ZK*, fols. 121-a, 126. See also *AN, TM, MT, NM* and *TA*.

8. Naghar Kot or Nagar Kot is an ancient city of Punjab which is famous as Kangra.
9. Pushkal or Pusha Kal.
10. "Due to the intensity of rain, the imperial forces had to stay at Jalandhar for five months." *Zubda*, fol. 96.

OCCURRENCE 5

Description of the Enthronement of His Majesty on the Throne of the Dominion of Hindustan and Happening some of Events

The formative aim of the Almighty which is a must for the management, regulation of creation and the element of all (p. 26) existence, is that when the morning of the fortune of the reign of a king approaches its end, then the sun of the fortune of one of his sons begins to shine. So whenever the star of good luck of some chief goes down, then someone of his relatives finds his star rising. The continuance of the existence or survival of a kingdom finds its support in this way that when the country begins to be deprived of the existence of the fortunate man of early ages then its wise successors come to its help and when the throne of the kingdom loses the protection of the royal ancestors then their progeny honours the vacant throne by stepping into it.

Musnavi (*rhyme*)

The world cannot remain without a king, the master of the country deserves crown and throne. The world cannot get peace without a ruler. A garden without gardener will be a playground of thorns. When a fruit bearing tree rises high, the circling sky begins to pour down troubles and misfortunes. When our foot slips from a place, it finds rest on some other placesth. Then he is entrusted with the guarding of flowers and leaves of garden; the spring season appears and lamps become illuminated.

The evidence of good luck is that the rose blossoms in shrub, and rainy cloud pours the precious water (pearls) which it has stored. Every young man of good luck whose difficulty solving or removing device, has the key to good fortune, when he attains age, does not close his door against his father (meaning he does not stop where his father left). And every such comfort giving and affluent person, who brings light to the people's eye, and a face shine forth. Such a person's eye of life never closes.

Even if the garden becomes a victim of hostile wind, though the flowers were in bloom, there is nothing to worry. If the garden be a victim of unlucky accidents, there is yet no cause for grief if the trees are fresh and flourishing.

Masnavi (*rhyme*)

The circles of misfortune of the world will get rotated in ever changing ways, from its creator. If he buries one end under the earth, he carries the other end to the skies too.

All these things, which have been covered in the preface, provide evidence for the information up to the death of Emperor Humayun (may God illumine his leadership!). (p. 27)

Bait (*verse*)

May his departure be bright and blessed; although he is dead his name is still alive! He vacated the assembly of his presence, and deprived the burden of rulership of the ornament of his sublime personality and alighting from his elevated rank chose to be under the floor of the earth (got buried in his tomb). Then His Majesty (Akbar) will ever preside over the everlasting kingdom. He will be its administrator, protector of the Khilafat, mighty as Sulaiman, leader of justice and fair play in the sphere of rulership of the world, stamp of the gem of the time of Sahib-qiran, pearl of the ring of the Sultanate of the world, sole support of the nucleus of administration, pivot of the circle of realm, king of the court of God's mercy, Sultan of the limitless canopy of land, sun of pride[1] and world protecting moon of greatness and prowess.

Qita (distich)

He is such a monarch that on the place of his excellences, the king of heavens places his golden crown every morning on the earth. The seal of his reign is the mark of helpfulness and dignity, and the banner of his empire is the mark of victorious ensign.

The great ruler (Akbar) of both east and west and (both) the ends of world; responsible for the cities of Allah, protector of the creatures of the Almighty, is His shadow on earth. He is the emperor of faith, master of length and breadth, who enjoys the grace of God's successor, Abu-al-Muzaffar Jalal-ud-Din Muhammad Akbar Badshah Ghazi. The flags of his greatness, virtues and helpfulness flew in the channels of beauty and the garden of his enduring blessed luck had become the rose bud of hope and the fruit bearing garden of whose rule had borne the desired (results) fruits of the throne. When the tree of Sultanate was uprooted by the wind of accident, then a fresh branch sprouted forth, and the diamond of whose kingdom was ascending like the sun on the beautiful hill from behind the curtain, and when by his great generosity the day was filled with light, he was the sun on height and was spreading light from the very beginning. (p. 28) He was the second morning so to say that he vindicated his true claim from the very start. He was such a sharp lance of the kingdom that so long its thirst (for blood) was not satisfied it would not stop its penetration. A call came from the four corners of the world that in the palace or hall of His Majesty, the drums would be beaten five times everyday and it was further heard from the directions that his empire would embrace all the seven-climes.

Bait (verse)

The sky beats the drum in all the four corners of the world to proclaim that he is the emperor of the six-directions and seven-climes.

[The shadow of *huma*[2] falls on that august personality as an evidence of virtue and grace, under whose light of government the crown of the state rests. Under his leadership the achievement constitutes such a brilliant guide which helps the world in maintaining peace and rest.] Though he is the only pearl in the oyster of kingship in the east, however, the jealous Afghans were waiting in their cells of retreat to muster their rancour against him with some illusions.

Bait (*verse*)

He who sits under the protection of God, he needs not fear even if the whole world becomes his enemy.

On Friday, Rabi-us-Sani, A.H. 963/February, 1556 A.D. Nawab Khan-i-Ali Shan, Muhammad Bairam Khan, known by the title of Khan-i-Khanan, and holding the high office of the tutor, together with other leading nobles of Emperor Humayun placed Khaqan Akbar, the eldest son who had completed fourteen years like the moon of 14th and had risen to the fourth sky, on the throne of kingdom, at the town of Kalanaur, which is a suburb of the capital city of Lahore, and made him the crown of the imperial throne. Thus the height of fortune, good luck and pride kissed the feet of the liberal king.

(p. 29), "I do not know whether it was the moon of 14th night, which graced the sky seen by the people or the 14 years old emperor who set foot on the throne. Those who have been engaged in search of truth and have knowledge of the five points of the book of wisdom, are well aware that the age of fourteen is equal to forty (i.e. just as the moon of 14th night is the full moon) even so the wit of man of forty attains perfection. The man of forty is gifted with such a state of mind that all his hidden qualities and perfection come up to view." Says Arif.

Bait (*verse*)

God has conferred upon him the blessed gift of the country and whatever is being presented suits him best and most.

For this reason the qualities and virtues of His Majesty resemble those of Prophet Muhammad (God's grace has reached its intended place). His lofty banner flew on the summit of the sky and the records of his victories were laid down on the world's books. The song suited to the time and circumstances was sung on the instruments and the star of his fortune appeared to be appropriate to the age.

Rubai (*a quatrain*)

His grandfather (Babur) had washed the blot of blood of tyranny from the page of age and the justice of his father smoothened its wrinkers. "O thou (king), the robe of kingdom fits you best and most. Thou performest as much good as thou canst because it is the turn of thy reign".

This emperor, substitute of Jamshed, inheritor of Sulaiman's prowess, stabilized the countries by infinite blessings of his administration. The equipment of Sardars or chiefs were established by the blessing of good luck. The throne of his kingdom matches the highest thrones, owing to its occupant. The pulpit (mimbar) of Islam stands shoulder to shoulder with stars on account of the revolution, brought by him.

Bait (*verse*)

The Almighty has decorated his head with the crown of kingship because He knows who is the deserving person. The coins of his dominions are shining more brilliantly than the sun on account of his name and these are giving the hint that if the stars of good luck were to sprinkle precious (p. 30) jewels, the time is appropriate for it. So on this happy news the men of knowledge and the denizens of the seven-climes, after saying the five prayers, may learn by heart the prayer for conquering of powerful empire, even then they would not be able to acquaint themselves adequately (summarised).

Abyat (*verses*)

It will be the fittest thing if Gabriel were to come down to see this magnificent sight, and read the *Khutba* in his name, defender of the faith, in all parts of the world and give rest to the seal and add to the currency, remove mischief and adorn the pulpit (of a mosque).

Without doubt he is such a king as the eye of heavens through all its movements had never seen in the noon time of kingdoms, and the eye of the age had never seen such a brave rider in the arena of kingship. He is capable of seething on fire the iron swords in the fields of battle and is the sun shining over the successful ambition.

Bait (*verse*)

Though in congregations he is a shining sun, in battle-field he is like a phantom which is burning the world.

The researchers of the acute and difficult points of Hindi, Turkish and Persian, place of quickness of resolution, and the moon having the grandeur of planets; the fire of the sharp tongue of the king burns the tongue of enemies like (the tongue of the) wick. The fear of your wrath has sunk into the heart of enemies like fire hidden in the heart of volcano.

Bait (*verse*)

When his sword revolves to spill blood, it forces stones to ooze fire and water. The brilliance of his sword resembles the brilliance of lightening while its cloud rewards equals the numberless rewards of rain-making cloud.

Bait (*verse*)

The sun of faith and kingdom, heaven of throne and destiny, the king of one-fourth of the world and descendant of Sahib-qiran.

He is the king who has collected together the virtues of his nature with the grandeur of his personality, and has polished his external behaviour to perfection with his intact qualities. (p. 31)

Masnavi (*rhyme*)

May the length of his age be merged with his safety and last till the Day of Judgement!

And everyday by the aid of the secret (holy) places, the ray of ever-fresh administration be flashed up and the whole time from the helpful horizon, the star of good luck would appear. When His Majesty moved his adventurous mind, the desired result itself came to welcome him. And in whatever direction his enlightened thoughts moved his good luck would cover all the stages of progress in no time, it is a matter for praise to the Almighty.

Bait (verse)

When I turned my eye towards his luck I say that his *Iqta*[3] would multiply to one thousand lives.

When His Majesty, whose army is innumerable like the stars, whose crown shines like the sun, whose court is as high as the sky, whose throne of honour and dignity is not only strong but durable, filled his mind with numerous engagements, lighted the garden of the court of kingdom with the rays of joy, i.e. the garden of young and lucky kingship, which possesses a thousand perfect qualities like the nightingale then his path was cleared of thorns of hostility and opposition. The garden of whose government which was seeking the touch of the cheeks of flowers, blossoming nursaries by the kisses of lips of buds, it brightened the appearance of the beautiful bud tree, and was increasing the stature of the cypress tree of courage, and was opening the eye of the narcissus of fate and placing a crest on the zenith of dignity.

Bait (verse)

So thou mayst understand that all this is the gift of God, and no one can snatch it by force. He diverted his attention immediately towards strengthening the affairs of administration and introduced the far-sighted policy to stabilize the very base of the centre of the kingdom. The angel of fate was announcing loudly behind the hidden world:

Bait (verse)

The throne of Jamshed and crown of Faridun are anxious to be on your feet and head. It was being proclaimed from Lahore. (p. 32)

Qita (*distich*)

Guide of leaders, keeper of victory, lover of goodness and friend of blessed fortune, whose obedient attendant is the sky, whose praises are sung by angels, whose worker or assistant is fate, and all these by the help of the army and weapons, loftiness of his crown and magnificence of his dress. The sun of adventure, riding on the horse of sky, set in motion the reins of government; and in the service of the victorious stirrup (may God ever keep this stirrup tied to good fortune and achieve honour and prowess!)

Khan Khanan Nawab Muhammad Bairam Khan started with certain other exalted amirs from there. From every side (being happy by the grace and mercy of Allah, faced no difficulty on their way) good news were heard and by and by the chiefs and nobles began to come under the flag of the government. They made the dust of the shoe of their horses of lightning speed, whose horse shoes were like the new moon, and whose speed competed with the sky — the collyrium of their eyes, and recognized the chief of valour. Finally the victorious army and its standards, whose number was written by the pen of God, arrived in the territory of Jalandhar. In this way, the promoter and protector of faith was honoured, then he commenced the management of the government affairs. The duty of the deputy (naib) was entrusted to Khan Khanan Bairam Khan. Therefore, so long as the latter's advice was sought, he had the sole authority of appointing, dismissing, imprisoning and asking explanation from anyone, or modifying any order related to spending, imprisoning and releasing anyone, etc. The emperor, however, realized that some merchants and travellers were feeling helpless and miserable on account of *Tamgha-tax*[4] and other demands on their incoming and outgoing of the country. Though the late emperor had promised to abolish all these unlawful taxes after his return to Hindustan, however it had to be done by His Majesty. (p. 33)

Meantime, Nawab Khan Khanan Bairam Khan presented himself before His Majesty and submitted that the graces of Divine Power are shining in our hearts, and the perfection of peace and contentment of the people depends on this that "all your subjects, who are a trust from Allah, may find happiness and prosperity under the care of your cradle, and more and more merchants and traders come into the land, without suffering any harm or damage on the way and they might also be settled under your protection free from fear and agony". We have passed orders that "in cities, parganas, qasbats and vilayats," *tamgha, jihat,*[5] *rahdari,*[6] *salamana,*[7] *peshkash* and *sarana,*[8] shall not be realized and no one on any excuse will be troubled and put under arrest". Thus all the people of the country as well as merchants, migrants and emigrants, filled with joy, expressed their happiness and gratitude most vociferously for the *Khalifa* (the king). In recognition of these humanitarian measures, the representatives of the empire and responsible officers of the preceding times, once again engaged themselves in establishing good administration and rehabilitation on a stable basis all affairs of government and adopted measures for the good and welfare of the people. And in this way, the symbol of the faith of Prophet Muhammad and the *Shariat*, as well as the brotherhood of Musalman, were advanced greatly.

Qita (*distich*)

The land was suffering much from want of necessities of life; at last the turn of time fulfilled its needs. All happiness and prosperity of which the people were deprived of in the past, were soon restored to them by the activity of the new age.[9]

Duaa (*prayer*) *for His Majesty*

O Lord, preserve in excellent condition, Khaqan Akbar, the emperor of the earth, giver of justice and good administration and maintain his crown of life till the end of the world and do not take away the hand of government from him till the last day of Judgement! (p. 34)

Bait (verse)

O Lord, may the emperor continue on the throne with all success and fulfilment of his object forever!

Notes

1. Arif refers to sun-rise.
2. It implies a bird of good or blessed fortune.
3. Iqta means land or dominion of the emperor. For detail see S. Nurul Hasan, Three Studies of the Zamindari System, A Miscellany, Vol.I, Aligarh, 1969.
4. It is a tax collected from merchants for export and import of goods. *Ain-i-Akbari*, 236 (hereafter *Ain*).
5. It implies local cesses. See Irfan Habib, *The Agrarian System of Mughal India (1556-1707)*, Asia Publishing House, Bombay, 1963 (hereafter op.cit.)
6. Tax for keeping watch and ward of roads. See N.A. Siddiqi, *Land Revenue Administration under the Mughals*, Munshiram Manoharlal (reprint), 1989.
7. Tribute offered to the high nobles as a mark of respect. See also H.H. Wilson, *A Glossary of Judicial and Revenue Terms*, London, 1885.
8. A kind of poll-tax. See P. Saran, *The Provincial Government of the Mughals*, Bombay, 1973 and I.H. Qureshi, *The Administration of the Mughal Empire*, Karachi, 1966.
9. See *Kuliyat-i-Anwari*, 71, published from Iran.

OCCURRENCE 6

Description of the Virtues and Deeds of the Blessed King, Exposition of Some Actions, Inventions and Proposals (promises) of the Ruler of the One-Fourth of the World, the Occupant of Happy Abode of Comfort by the Grace of the Almighty Who is without Second

Though, while describing his accession, some of the merits and good deeds of His Majesty have already been narrated briefly, it however seems proper to mention further (of them), by this most humble beggar, the observer of these lines, of the incidents that happened day to day as a result of his laudable character, and praiseworthy deeds and auspicious actions undertaken by him.

In short, a drop out of the ocean might be brought so that the world would be able to know and feel sure that its mention is not a mere formality.

Bait (*verse*)

The glory and brilliance of his own countenance is so great and beautiful that it does not need any artificial and ornamental description.

The most humble and poor beggar has written these lines because he has not gone through any book on history which contains the emperor's deeds and virtues. Certainly, he has marked out the boundaries of the empire and has also made its foundation stable and lasting.[1]

Bait (*verse*)

Everyone recited bravo (for you)! May the star of your fate ever be your friend!

Fiqra Awwal[2]

His Majesty gives expression to such humility and restraint in the assemblies that everybody feels no distinction between master and slave. Despite his towering status and prowess there seems no sign of vanity or snobbery ever on his face. (p. 35) He has illumined his throne so perfectly that even if the Qaisar of Rum and the King of China were to be present in his court, they would become so much overawed by his splendour and shrewd policy that they would stand (before him) with their hands behind their backs.

Bait (*verse*)

In the highest and choicest assemblies, there is none so successful in his objectives and none so victorious in the battle-field (than the emperor).

Fiqra Akhri[3]

He is such a resourceful emperor that at the time when he ascended the throne, in spite of a meagre force, he captured the vilayat (land) of Orissa, which extends from the coast of Sindh up to Persian gulf. He also made many a raja and Afghan chief to submit who were unrivalled in their time.

Qita (*distich*)

If your kindness and generosity were to assume visibility then it would have been moving like a living body; if your roar were to pervade the world, then the wolf would himself become the shepherd (a protector of sheep).

Fiqra Akhri

He is such a patron of his slaves (servants and people) that the leading chiefs and potentates are bowing their heads in submission before his throne. Even those who were vain and full of self-pride have become meek and humble and have submitted themselves before the royal seat. The dust of the imperial throne has become the sacred (worship) place of great and mighty men of the earth, and the floor of the auspicious court has become the place which the kings and chiefs of China and Hind come to kiss.

Qita (distich)

Wherever your mighty hand falls, it will be lips or mouths of kings, but your controlling hand falls on their heads. The servants of your palace are titled as Amir in Turkistan, and slaves of your gilded banner are called Rajas in Hindustan.

Fiqra Akhri

He is the ruler of the entire world. Therefore the keys of solution, entering into contracts or settlements and command of the whole of Hindustan from Kabul to the coast of the Persian gulf (Aman) and the territories of Sindh up to Bengal have come into the possession of his nobles and officials and have passed under their administration. (p. 36)

Bait (verse)

None except you can regulate and adorn the country with proper faith and administration.

Fiqra Akhri

He is the renowned ruler and weilder of such power that many of the powerful chiefs and sultans of the age wear his rings of obedience in their ears, and the emperors of the world cover the shoulders of their hearts with the sheet of submission to him.

Bait (verse)

The guidance of God and victory always march before him, wherever his victorious standards choose to move.

Fiqra Akhri

He is the most renowned emperor among the reputed kings of the world, who possessed maturity, and a combination of good luck of the young. Even the fast revolving sky has never seen such a state of the sun during its period of journey and the ears of the world in its experience of age have never heard such an excellent government.

Bait (verse)

He has won respect and obedience of the people by his justice and liberality; they are submissive while his sword is active.

Fiqra Akhri

He is the blessed emperor of great magnificence and dignity and he has made the *Jam-i-Jahan Numai* (of Jamshed's law and justice), the mirror of his life by his wisdom, in obedience to the laws of state, which is like that of Sikandar, who has summoned the life-giving water of justice.

Bait (verse)

By the force of his justice, tyranny and injustice have fled a hundred stages away into the forest of non-existence.

Fiqra Akhri

He is such a mighty horse rider that in the field of art and manner in which he sits his horse and in the skill of chaugan,[4] he takes away prize from the renowned horsemen and wrestlers of the world. (p. 37)

Bait (verse)

The heaven like chaugan that he plays throughout the year seems that such a horseman as he has never appeared in the field.

Fiqra Akhri

He is fond of games when he is full of delight in the forest. When he is engaged in hunting lions or stags and in releasing birds to fly, he exhibits great interest in gratifying hearts of hunters.[5]

Bait (verse)

When he comes out on an Arab (Tazi) horse, the forest becomes deplete of deer (because all these escape).

Fiqra Akhri

The emperor is such a destroyer of armies (one who tears through the enemy's ranks), that whether it is battlefield or an assembly of festivities, when he has to oppose the enemy or adorn a festive occasion, he has proved his prowess as well as his generosity and mercy to the kings of world.

Qita (distich)

The secret meaning of his mind is hidden in four things; time of action with farsightedness and wisdom; time of fighting of war; time of charity and time of hostility. He is the shining sun of conscience, full of good wit at the time of meeting and he is death himself when he holds a sword and an ocean of charity by his right hand.

Fiqra Akhri

He is such a paragon of justice that he has purified the whole country from the dirt and sin of drinking and adultery. In spite of the fact that the state gets a very substantial revenue from public shops (drinking-houses), serving light drinks, brothels and gambling-dens, he sacrificed this income once and for all which amounted to lakhs and crores of tankas. Spiritual happiness and consolation are a reward of his action.[6]

Bait (verse)

Mere joy and fun lead to ruin and nearness to God leads to the sunshine of royal favour. (p. 38)

Fiqra Akhri

He possesses such a magnificent and charitable heart that the sky seems to be dust in comparison with his boldness (in charity) and the sun looks dark before the brilliance of his wisdom. Even the charity of the sun is smaller than a particle in comparison with the charity of that blessed one. The waterpouring cloud is not even a drop by the side of the open handed liberality and charity of His Majesty. The merchants of neighbouring places were fortunate enough to be benefited by his unhesitating charities and assistances. His unbound charities and gifts have supported them under the shadow of the sun. During the journey travellers and thirsty-men were always benefited with all necessities, such as a supply of water and greenery. The emperor has already abolished various taxes throughout his empire such as *tamgha, baj, rahdari, peshkash, sarana* and *salamana.* No one was allowed to realize or receive in future even one dinar or one *man* (maund) of grain in accordance of the regulation.

Qita (*distich*)

I cannot, or do not say that you are like a cloud, because virtue does not come from mere wisdom, you cannot be compared to it, because when it gives (rain), it weeps, while you laugh (i.e. are happy) when you give.

Fiqra Akhri

He is hospitable. The merchants from foreign countries have started coming into Hindustan since the beginning of his rule. They engage themselves in buying and selling freely, and those who bring valuable booty or goods, are free from any fear and they safely return to their respective homelands.

Qita (*distich*)

There is no one on the earth (in the whole world) who does not make the dust of his court the collyrium of his eyes. His court is the *Kaaba* of the needs of all men, the rich and poor. Mendicants rub their foreheads on the door of His Majesty. The foreign merchants are busy extolling the virtues, (p. 39) expounding the goodness, relating to various kindnesses and giving thanks for many favours of the king of high dignity and sweet language. In the assembly, great and noble men of the time are found everywhere and on every side expositating the excellent attributes and broadcasting the obligations of His Majesty upon all men.

Bait (verse)

Thou shouldst exert to earn fame or good name and not diram because a good name is better than a thousand dynamic treasuries.

Fiqra Akhri

His Majesty is such a highly honoured and benign person that peace and prosperity in his kingdom are spreading so firmly that even mercury has acquired the stability and steadiness of a mountain. During his reign, the foundation of happiness of the people has been laid so strongly that even the wind is instrumental or helpful in lightning up the flames of shrivelled and dead lamps, and thereby the signs of miracles of *Masiah* (Christ) are becoming apparent.

Bait (verse)

Everybody is under the obligation of his favours during his rule; hostility and dominance have become unreal like dream (unqa) and enemies have fled away like the dead or non-existent alchemy.

Fiqra Akhri

He is the subjugator of the world and during his reign the command of Allah was promulgated that, throughout Hindustan, which is the centre of ensigns of the real men and women, young and old should not be imprisoned, concubines (girl-slaves) and slaves who belong to Hindustani families, if they do not agree to part with or sell their invaluable lives and low women of the Musalmans as also of the Kafirs (infidels), if they go astray from the right path and show inclination towards strangers, or if they earn notoriety in assemblies by making friendship with strangers so as to provoke people to point finger at (p. 40) them, the Kotwal put them on asses (donkeys') backs and take them around the city like Zohra, the adulteress and illicits were asked to get married because God has made marriage lawful and illicit connection a sin. Therefore men should marry and increase the population of the world which is a matter of pride for Prophet Muhammad. Consequently, those people who were enjoying illicit relations have come within the fold of married life, because men and women of good character are noble. Those tribes of the Muslims which were sunk in sin have come to the right path, and the pledge of repentance so as not to sin again has received acclamation and acceptance also.

Bait (*verse*)

If you give up sin and crime you will be rewarded in both the worlds, here and hereafter.

Fiqra Akhri

The King's crown is high during his own rule. He kept (grew) hair and a turban, tied on it, and when the powerful Turkish and Hindi youth tied the turban each one of its circles or rounds, was a trap and each of its wrinkles was so bright and beautiful that it was like a shackle for all those who were devoted to His Majesty.

Bait (*verse*)

If, thine heart is trapped in the brilliant halo (*aura*) of his *tura* (*chira*),[7] you should say that it is a fruit or result of blows of polo (the emperor), as the ball is hit about.

Fiqra Akhri

He is the shelter or patron of all the high qualities. When he is free from the affairs of state and administration, on the night of every Friday he invites men of all classes and of high rank and convenes an assembly[8] in the 'House of worship' (*Ibadat Khana*) and makes them sit in four-rows (because his mind is pure). Saiyeds, nobles, men of letters, scholars and righteous persons of all sects and beliefs, engage in debate or discussion. Thus they discuss the laws of *Shariat* (faith) as well as of reason and everyone of them is given prizes in cash and kind and is made happy. During these debates whenever acute and knotty problems crop up, His Majesty puts them on right path. He often (p. 41) brings out important questions from his memory. Many anecdotes, problems and memorable reminiscences are written on the tablet of his revered mind. Men of knowledge and informations are treated with due respect, regard and affection by him. He also extends the same patronage to the skilled and learned physicians, thinkers and philosophers who too are recipients of the highest honours.[9]

Qita (distich)

The time, which is spent in discussing learned topics, scholarly problems and reading the *Quran*, which is a source of removing sorrow and misfortune; and the time that is spent in receiving gifts from His Majesty, imparts perfection to mind of men. God only is everlasting and changeless.

For Those associated with the spiritual assembly the ritual on the Divine dinner table is like the superb wine of different topics, and resembles the soul refreshing motto.

Rubai (a quatrain)

O King! thy throne has become the seat of good luck; thy presence has given good administration to the affairs of the country. If thou desirest to earn fame and good name in both the worlds, then thou shouldst ever exert to promote and support men of knowledge and talents.

Fiqra Akhri

His Majesty is so proficient in discharging his duties, related to administration and in raising the dignity of royalty, that he is never in want, i.e. supply of information of families and tribes, or friendly groups (succour and numbers) or armies and regiments, slaves and attendants, or dinar and dirham (wealth) or any other equipment and provision, required for acquitting his kindly obligations.

Misraa (*a hemistich*)

He captured the country all alone, just as the sun spreads over the earth.

Fiqra Akhri

He is the world-taker, the depth of the moat of his forts and strongholds reach the earth's centre and the crenels (battlements) thereof reach the fourth-heaven from the constellation of Gemini; and the strong foundations of each is like the everlasting and as the strong foundations of domes in Egypt, called Harman[10] which are said to have been built by two great philosophers (p. 42) prior to the deluge of Hazrat Nuh and were not even damaged in any way by it (the deluge). These forts were so strong that the plan of their constructions never touched the minds of former kings, i.e. to conceive such edifices and the desire to get them free (to capture them) could never cross their minds also. And the sun of courage of the people vanished owing to the dreaded approach of the king. The length of lines or rows of the musclemen and wielders of heavy clubs which fell on the necks of enemies, opened wide the closely guarded forts. By the feet of the mountain like elephants, all the uncouth and inauspicious (execrable) were surrounded and destroyed by the wind of destruction. In short, the forts of the cities of Hindustan were conquered and held firmly. The help or pace of the people, having been invited, did come, but on hearing the sound of the imperial reinforcement, they fled.

Bait (*verse*)

To whichever fort he or his messenger proceeded, the owners themselves handed over the keys of their forts.

Fiqra Akhri

He is a founder (builder) who, dressed or adorned in a manner worth of pride, the buildings, beginning with the memorial houses of the saints in Ajmer,[11] constructed the great edifices in Fatehabad Sikri, and very strong and lasting forts of red stone in the capital city of Agra and the city of

Lahore with burnt-bricks, as also in many other towns of Hindustan.[12]

The foundations of these buildings were laid in such an unusual and wonder-striking manner, that those who had seen seven-climes, had not seen their match thereof; and these were made as strong as the foundation of kingdom itself and like the strength of these embankments of Sikandar himself. He had them arranged in such a perfect manner that the passage of time could not destroy them up to the end of the world. The city matches the city of Iran, full of buildings which had no parallel.

Bait (verse)

His lofty pillared-buildings point to the Zat-ul-Imad, and like paradise, canals flow in his palaces.

Fiqra Akhri

His Majesty is a great producer of amusement. He acquires a male deer to copulate with a black goat which comes from the Deccan (South) and looks like it as well. From it certain species of deer are produced which are very much unlike the ordinary deer, i.e. black, spotted and red. (p. 43)

Bait (verse)

Amazing or strange things are not produced from every species, but he makes every specie to produce a double (pair) from a single one.

Fiqra Akhri

He is a king, high placed and worth of reverence. He plans expeditions all the time, for which there are always in attendance before his court (palace) 500 elephants, a hundred rows of horses and camels (qatar), consisting of ten in a line, (followed by similar lines) to carry his baggages and camp equipments.[13] There are eighteen house tents of the same size, which are made of wooden-planks, consisting double storey and rooms (chambers) in his beautiful palace with attractive edifices, these are pitched and erected there. At the time of marching out all the planks are taken apart, loaded and carried. When the next stage for stopping or camping comes, the wooden planks are fastened by means of iron rings, on the inner side these chambers are covered with golden brocade and velvet from Europe (Farhang) and outside these are covered with woollenfelt or broad-cloth.

Bait (verse)

From the huge and lofty camp, you see as if it is the sun and sky, but the bright stars are always in the hills and wilderness.

Fiqra Akhri

He is such an expert in espionage that he keeps four thousand (4,000) foot-runers,[14] who in Hindi are called Meurah.[15] They are on His Majesty's service day and night so that news and reports reach regularly everyday from all sides of the world. This class of men run as fast as lion, so that within ten days news comes from Bengala which is at a distance of seven hundred karohs (kos) from Agra. His Majesty gets all information of good or bad and profit or loss.

Bait (verse)

O, thou excellent manager of the affairs of the world, who wears a wreath round the turban as a mark of delight of the world, by the beauty of thy solicitude and care for the country, it has acquired brightness, full of grace. (p. 44)

Fiqra Akhri

He is the ever-growing planner and has been able to capture the country by means of travelling through it, and has expanded his domains by relating or learning history and by destroying dreadful fighting forces, has put them to flight and made numberless soldiers happy.

Bait (verse)

O King! thy superior sword has set the conduct of the

people on the right path, like a straight-arrow, and by the flag of thy justice thou have brought about, as it were, the morning of truth.

Fiqra Akhri

He is one, who showers pearls and gems, that from necklaces of jewels, matchless pearls, vessels and vases of gold and silver, brilliant rubies, emeralds, topazes, famous cornelians, wealth and treasure in such quantities were stored in the imperial exchequer that even the belts were adorned with strings of pearls, and so also there are rings up to finger tips, so that such wealth had never been witnessed by the account helpers.

Masnavi (rhyme)

With jewels, gold and pearls, the imperial treasury is so full and all these come to it as a mark of righteous mind and beauty of his behaviour.

Bait (verse)

O' the best of brave and invincible soldiers, who have descended from the emperor of yore, O the superb pearl who has come from the progeny of Adam!

Fiqra Akhri

He is victorious, who warns and forbids (bad deeds) and therefore on all sides he keeps watchmen of high rank so that whenever their assistance in the administration of government is required, they may be summoned without delay. On the main roads, at every five kos, two speedy horsemen keep watch. Every messenger who carries the imperial farman, bearing the royal seal, is taken from among those horsemen. Whenever it is necessary the Khans and umara (i.e. guards of the frontiers) send information about the region; and the property of friends with their petitions bearing the seal of the emperor at the top, they send to the court and obey all orders and regulations. If the report is received that the message has to be reached urgently through those meurah (runners) who happen to be at the chauki (watchpost) they should be sent on horseback by relays. (p. 45) As such the order must reach Agra in seven days from Bengal (to Agra). It is known from experience that the messenger covers up to 150 karohs (kos) in a day and night. For instance from the capital of Gujarat to the imperial capital of Agra, they reach in five days, and from Tanda,[16] the headquarter of the province of Bengal, two meurah of the chauki run a distance of 100 karohs (in a day and night).

Bait (verse)

O thou whose enlightened mind is like the lance of a fountain of light from the sun; all the miscreants have hidden themselves in dark corners from dread of thy strong administration.

Fiqra Akhri

The king is an expert in dealing with and solving tough problems. He has invented new designs of *pashmina* (cloth made of the finest-wool), silk-cloth, brocade, rugs, carpets[17] (long and small) and he has provided training in the art to expert masters (ustads), consequently these craftsmen now produce such stuff, much superior to those of Iran and Europe (Firahangistan). They do the design works and colouring in such a manner that even if Mani (a great painter, who claimed prophethood) were present, he would put his fingers to his lips in amazement.[18]

Bait (verse)

Praise be to thy sweet speech to all men, and for thou being a model for the conduct of all men by setting an example.

Fiqra Akhri

The king's interest in the art of painting is unmatched.[19] There are three hundred and sixty episodes in the story of *Amir Hamza.*[20] He ordered that each one of those be painted together with its assembly. In the preparation (of this work) one hundred men, consisting of expert painters, gilders,[21] sketch-drawers and book-binders were engaged. The size of the book (album of these paintings) was half a yard Shara'e and its paper, made of cloth with a combination of colours and the border, decorated with floral pattern and there was cloth[22] in between two sheets of paper to make it durable.[23] All its plates were gilded. A farman was issued that the best of scholars who were matchless and known for their sweet voice, render the tables into musical prose, and the calligraphers, (p. 46) possessing the faculty of fancy writing in golden letters, must also help in its preparation. Despite all these equipments, each volume took two years in preparation, and an estimated amount of 10 lakh copper tankas (5 lakh silver tankas) was spent on each of the volumes.[24]

Bait (verse)

O thou inventor of new stories and unleasher of secrets, thine stories will form the top of the dignified diwan (book of poems).

Fiqra Akhri

The King is gifted with reason and faculty of showing the way; so he has built towers (minars) from the capital, Agra up to Ajmer, a distance of one hundred and forty Akbari karohs (kos) and at a distance of every ten kos, splendid rest houses have been built. On the road at every karohs,[25] minars are fixed with the horns of deer or stag all round which His Majesty has collected from the heads, hunted by him. There are three or four hundred of these horns round each of these minars. The reason is that travelling to and fro goes on day and night and these minars guide them from losing their way or getting off the route. Since the attention of His Majesty has been drawn to do the pilgrimage of the saint, the polestar of Saints, Khwaja Moin-ud-Din Chishti,[26] it is not necessary to carry the whole equipment of camp, tent and other necessary articles. Matchless buildings have been built in Ajmer. If a detailed description of these is given it will become too lengthy. The phrase gives the following date of the erected minars that is A.H. 981/1573 A.D.

Qita (*distich*)

The emperor has erected a minar at each karoh on the route from Ajmer to Agra, so that every traveller going on that route may be able to know the distance by each karoh. And because horns (taken during hunt) have been fixed on each; say that a milestone, contains the date thereof.

Fiqra Akhri

The elephant killer king when he decides to travel, riding on elephant or oxcart,[27] he sometimes takes the place of the driver (mahavat) and sits in the Chau-Khandi.[28] (p. 47) This quality of the emperor reveals the saying of the elders that a king ought not to give the reins of government into the hands of others, that is to say, the affairs of state should not be entirely left in the hands of other persons. So His Majesty has accepted this rule to follow in word and deed both.

Bait (*verse*)

As lofty as the mountains of *Alwand*[29] and *Judi*[30] when they are steady and are widely spread out as the revolving sky.

At present there are 5,000 select elephants[31] in the imperial stables, no king on earth has either seen or maintained such a number of them. The king turns his attention some time towards war-elephants and some other time towards uncharged (hot-headed) elephants near whom no one dares to go. He rides these elephants and makes them submissive and obedient. He has devised new methods of capturing elephants, which were neither known in earlier times nor practised.

Masnavi (*rhyme*)

On mighty elephants as high as Kohqaf (mountain) and when the lion of jungle goes into the field being struck by his whip, on the elephants side the riders, move on to the seventh heaven.

Fiqra Akhri

A man of perfect wisdom, the king quite often instructed the princes and rajas of Hindustan who, in the past possessed very strong and massive forts that, "there were about 320 rajas and zamindars and if he intended to subjugate them or to wipe them out, it would have required a very long time for the simple reason that the forts were very strong and even impregnable. If on each fort was to spend an average year and six months, at least a period of 230 years would have been required to compel them to agree or submit. So it was the reason why former rulers of Hindustan could not bring under their rule the whole country. For this reason the rajas of Hindustan too kept a thoughtful watch on them. (p. 48) This group of rajas wanted only friendly relations, came to attend the imperial court. And this is the reason why peace is being maintained on routes and robbers do not infest there. According to *Hadis*, a rebel (Kafir) should be first invited to submit peacefully and if he refuses then he should be attacked and killed.[32]

Bait (verse)

If the work is performed nicely and amicably, what is the need to use force for cutting the neck (throat) there.

Bait (verse)

The wise and perfect king carries out his righteous objects by means of words only, for such success cannot be achieved by great armies.

Fiqra Akhri

The lion-hearted king occasionally diverts his full attention towards chase and hunt of tiger, of dreadful attacking power and sharp claws, which is called 'chita' (leopard) in Hindi language. All alone, and without any assistance, by his lucky hand, the king pulls out one of them from the well of despondency and risks in keeping it engaged, gives it training. Each one is given a golden collar, beautiful winkers and covering quilts, made of velvet and European brocade,[33] by the occupant of the blessed throne, whose seat is in the sky. A large number of men are employed to look after and feed them. At present there are 550[34] collared chitas in the possession of His Majesty and the game caught by them counts about one lakh. Therefore, the actual condition is being described in the following musical strain:

Bait (verse)

If a wild animal will not avoid your trap of prey, then it will find rest and comfort by being a prisoner in your noose or lasso.

Fiqra Akhri

Sulaiman of his court, viz. the king maintains an expense of about fifty lakhs everyday on his elephants and other stables,[35] etc.

Nukta (a point)

The area (extent) of the empire of Hindustan, which is the nucleus of the heaven of the mighty state, which is the green-meadow, full of luck, the kingdom of His Majesty, the giver of justice, the area is confined to six months (p. 49) travel inevitably the fame of notable matters, the justice prudence and wisdom, regard for charity and adornment of the country by means of famous men, merchants, scholars, helpers and assistants has spread all round, throughout the world.

The reputation of King's great and excellent virtues has achieved such limit that even one line or part of it is enough to throw into shade or eclipse the memorials of the Qaisar of Rum, and of the dynasty of Nausherwan, the Khans of China, the Aqiyals[36] of Arabia, Tababiahs of Yamen,[37] Rayans of Hind,[38] rulers of the Saman dynasty[39] Al-i-Buiya[40] and Saljuq Sultans,[41] hence those virtues become all the more prominent or strengthened. The exposition of these long details has caused the writer to be drawn into them. And in accordance with the injunctions that the brief notice of a lengthy matter is enough to signify its worth. Some of these notices or descriptions of the excellent qualities of His Majesty have been stated in a few sentences only, so that thereby evidence máy be grasped not only of the extraordinary valour and courage, but exceptionally successful deeds also.

Duaa (prayer) for His Majesty

May the rays of light of the lofty portal, and the beams ot shining door-sill of the Almighty, between all sections of men of the world and of all the great men, spread, flourish and live for ever and ever! May the shadow of His Majesty's kindness and generosity extend over all the people till the end of time!

Notes

1. Arif does not mean any specific territorial division of these words which he goes on repeating in his characteristic and reckless style. It actually implies the country, which by then had come under the rule of Akbar.
2. The word '*Fiqra Awwal*' implies the first foremost or the highest praise to the emperor ever described for any emperor.
3. While the word '*Fiqra Akhri*' implies the last or the ultimate observation ever be described for any emperor.
4. Akbar built a city, called Nagar Chin, near the boundaries of Agra because he had profound love for Chaugan, a kind of polo. *MT*, II, 48, 69 and *Ain*, 174.
5. Abul Fazl confirms that Akbar had great love for pigeons and the art of their training was considered a love affair. *Ain*, 174.
6. Badauni says that liquor was only allowed for medicinal purposes. Those foreigners, who had settled in Hindustan, were rehabilitated outside the city and their abode was named Shaitanpura. *MT*, II, 301.
7. Chira, rounded turban, is known in Hindustan which is quite costly. *Ain*, 75. See also *Gulshan-i-Faiz*, 398 and *Farhang-i-Nizam*, II, 488.
8. The meeting of sincerity was to be held on Friday night and theologians, learned and nobles used to take part in it. *Ibid.*, II, 202. See also V.A. Smith, *Akbar's House of Worship or Ibadat Khana, Ind. Antiquiry*, 44 (1915), pp. 233-44.
9. According to Badauni, "The cell of Shaikh Abdullah Niazi Sirhandi, where he used to reside. Later its walls from all the four sides were expanded in A.H. 983/1575 A.D. and Anup Talao (tank) was added

with it. That cell was named Ibadat Khana which became (the house) of visiting of the sick with the passage of time". *MT*, II, 201.

10. Name of a fort situated on the confines of Egypt.
11. For the welfare of people during the year A.H. 978/1570 A.D. some of its edifices were renovated. *AN*, II, 25-b.
12. Abul Fazl confirms it. *Ibid.*, II, 246 and 365.
13. Abul Fazl says 100 elephants, 500 camels and 400 Arabi horses and 100 gallant warriors ready for action. *Ain*, 33.
14. Abul Fazl says one thousand while Farishta says that the number reached 4000 up to the death of Akbar. *Ibid* and *Farishta*, II, 272.
15. Abul Fazl also calls him Meurah. *Ain*, 147 while Khafi Khan says az bumi Mewat, known for fast running. *Muntakhab-al-Lubab*, I, 243 (hereafter *ML*).
16. Tanda is known as Saturat. Sultan Karami, the last ruler of Bengal, built this city in A.H. 972/1564-65 A.D. and made his capital. *Tarikh-i-Bengal*, 95.
17. Zilucha implies Qalicha (Ghalicha) (carpet). *Farhangi Rashidi*, 377.
18. See *Ain*, 39.
19. Abul Fazl describes Akbar's love for painting in the following words: "His Majesty, from his earliest youth, has shown a great predilection for this art and gives it every encouragement, as he looks upon it as a means both of study and amusement". *Ain* (tr), I, 107. He further says, according to Emperor Akbar, "There are many who dislike painting; but such men I dislike. It appears to me as if the painter had quite peculiar means of recognising God; for a painter in sketching anything that has life and in devising its limbs, one after the other, must come to feel that he cannot bestow individuality upon his work and is thus forced to think of God, the Giver of Life; and will thus increase his knowledge". *Ibid.* pp. 117-18.
20. The illustrations of *Dastan-i-Amir Hamza*, twelve volumes of one hundred folios and each folio was to contain an illustration, began under Humayun, when he returned to Hindustan and assigned this work to Khwaja Abu-s-Samad shirazi and Saiyed Ali Tabrizi. It however was completed in 1575 A.D. Brown, *Indian Paintings under the Mughals*, p.iii. See also Tasneem Ahmad, *Akbar's Love for Painting in the Light of His Doctrine of Sulah Kul*, pp. 73-80, Punjab History Congress, Twentieth Session, 1986.
21. It implies flower decoration.
22. 'Parch-i-Chutar', it is a kind of cloth which was prepared in the mansion of Saharanpur. *Balu Kaman*, I, 617.
23. According to Abul Fazl, "A school was opened in the palace wherein the Hirat painters were asked to train pupils". *Ain*, pp. 117-18. Though no documentary evidence is available whether the karkhana system was founded by Akbar, Bernier stands testimony to the fact that it existed during the time of Shah Jahan and Aurangzeb, though it had fallen on evil days due to the apathy of the rulers. *Travels in Mughal*

Empire. So it can be safely assumed that Akbar was the reguliser of karkhana system because it was necessary for such a huge number of employees and their execution of work. Tasneem Ahmad, *Nadir-ul-Asr,* Mansur, Indo-Iranica, Calcutta, 1972.

24. Arif gives the exact amount of money spent on the preparation of illustrations while other sources are silent.
25. Badauni says it was fixed at two karohs. *MT,* II, 173.
26. Khwaja Muin-ud-din, Muhammad, son of Ghayas-ud-din Hasan Al-Husaini-al-Sanjari, was a pious saint of Chishti order. He is widely known. He died on 6th Rajab, A.H. 627/21st May, 1230 A.D. at Ajmer. It is said that he died in the year A.H. 633/1236 A.D. while some say in A.H. 632/1235 A.D. There is variation in his age, some say he died when he was 96 years old or 97 or 90 or 104. For details see *Safinat-ul-Auliya, Shahjahan Nama* of Salih, *Arfat-ul-Ashiqui, Subah Sadiq, Gul-zar-i-Abrar* and *Haft Iqlim* (hereafter *HI*).
27. Bahal is known for riding mule in Hindustan. It is carried by two oxes. Arif does mean oxcart while it is known that Akbar never travelled by it.
28. Perhaps amari.
29. A mountain near Hamadan, north-west of Iran.
30. Mount Ararat in Armenia (Turkey).
31. Abul Fazl and Farishta confirm the number. *Ain,* pp. 101 and 124 and Farishta, I, 272. The number is given variously yet everyone has agreed that it is 5000. But it seems that the number of Khasa elephant was 101. These may be out of total number.
32. See also S. Nurul Hasan, *"The Mahzar of Akbar"*, *JUPHS,* I, pp. 125-37. S.R. Sharma, *"Akbar's Religious Policy"*, *IHQ,* 1937 (II), pp. 302-22. K.A. Nizami, *Akbar and Religion,* Delhi, 1989.
33. See also *Ain,* 167.
34. K.K. Says that at the time of Akbar's death one thousand chitas (leopards) were in imperial retinue. The number given by Arif does not seem appealing.
35. Fifty lakhs means fifty lakh dam. Forty dam was equal to one rupee. For details see *Ain,* II (39th R.Y. under the heading of expenditure).
36. Plural of Qail, who was the king of Himyar, a tribe of Arabia.
37. Plural of Taba, the title of the ruler of Yamen.
38. It implies the ruler of Hindustan.
39. Its founder was Ismail Samani while the last ruler was Abul Mulk Sani.
40. In Iran, Imad-ud-Daula's predecessors were under the Caliph of Baghdad.
41. Relation of Tughral Beig who died in A.H. 455/1063 A.D.

OCCURRENCE 7

Description of Battle with Hemu[1], the Accursed Rebel, His Defeat and Killing with Dishonourable Khans by the Wrath of Imperial Sword

As the reason for the continuation of this family which had continued like the Khilafat, was that the possession and control of the blessed emperor must be established fully. Therefore the Almighty took him within the circle of special care of His grace and brought him up. At the opportune time that priceless pearl was raised by the Almighty to the highest position and seated him on the throne of victory and his rule started. So the hordes of reclused took him under their protection against the evil-eye of time and the moon of the ability began to grow day by day. (p. 50)

Masnavi (*rhyme*)

The face of His Majesty emits the rays of light, I may say that I am wrong in my saying; it is even hundred times greater. If the clouds were to lift water from the ocean of the beauty of his face, then the whole earth would become full of suns everywhere.

As it has already been recorded in the foregoing pages at the time of his coronation the victorious army assembled at Jalandhar, and there in A.H. 963/1555-56 A.D. The news was received that Hemu, the commander of the army of the Afghans (Andali)[2] was anxiously preparing for action, had gathered an enormous army with the object that whenever there might be confrontation with the enemy (Mughals), they should be held back. Thus as soon as he heard the dreadful news of the death (of Humayun), he at once marched to

Delhi. On the other hand, His Majesty had settled at Sirhind. The chiefs and other officials like Tardi Beig Khan,[3] Sikandar Uzbek[4] and others who were at Delhi, were overpowered and defeated by Hemu after a brief encounter with them. When these accursed fellows began to gain their advancement, it disheartened the Mughal force which began to run for safety. The defeated nobles reached the imperial camp with a miserable remnant of 20 or 30 men only. This success naturally raised the pride of Hemu, who advanced and captured Delhi and became so bold that he proceeded in pursuit of the imperial army also. When he reached Panipat, he learnt that His Majesty was camping at Sirhind, having been thus taken by surprise, he stationed there and dared not to advance further. Thereafter, all those amirs and nobles who had escaped, presented themselves to kiss the royal feet, and thereby they felt as if, "they had been restored to life again". Ali Quli Khan Uzbek,[5] having been pushed away by Shadi Khan,[6] who had revolted, from Sambhal reached Sirhind. A separate contingent was placed under the command of Khizar Khwaja Khan[7] and he was despatched against Sikandar Afghan (Sur). Tardi Beig Khan, who had acted timidly against Hemu, with the consent of Naqi Pir Muhammad Khan Sherwani,[8] was put to death in the month of Zi-hijja of the said year (October 1556 A.D.) with all those who had behaved like him.[9] (p. 51) Thereafter, the Khans and amirs, who were under the command were appointed the vanguard and were ordered to proceed against Hemu, followed by him. Having come to know about it, Hemu also marched and both the armies met each other near the town (qasba) of Panipat.[10]

Nazm (*poem*)

The batallions of the imperial army rose one after another in successive waves as to present the swelling waves of a river after rains. Sounds of horns began to rise high and it seemed as if the Day of Judgement had come. Soldiers of both sides started shouting and challenging each other. The standards of armies began to fly on all sides, and the imperial streamer was fluttering so high as to show that it was even higher than the sky itself. Such a storm of clouds of dust and sand arose that the sun and the moon became dim (both the armies stood in line in battle array). Hemu, the accursed had elephants like a mighty shield. Swords and lances crossed which exhibited the scene of death itself.[11] All of a sudden such a dreadful onslaught was unleashed by the imperial army that the enemy force could not bear its brunt and started to fall back. Just at that time Ali Quli Khan, who was commanding the van, detaching a small party of soldiers, marched ahead and exhibited extraordinary valour and fearlessness. In the midst of confusion, killing and capturing, an arrow struck into the eye of Hemu, and he fell into the hands of Shah Quli Mahram.[12] All the rebels (Kafirs) disappeared. In short, the whole army of the enemy scattered and met with its destruction. All the elephants, which Hemu had collected from the various parts of the country, were captured and enrolled into the imperial corps. When Hemu was brought before His Majesty, Khan Khanan (Bairam Khan) prayed that he be killed by the emperor's sword. The king struck Hemu with his sword and he won the title of Ghazi.[13] As there was some life left in him, Khan Khanan, Bairam Khan killed him with his sword and finally sent him to hell.[14] (p. 52)

Nazm (poem)

When Hemu went to the fire of hell, the heaven (i.e. Allah Himself) destroyed his army. No one could escape alive from the field of battle that day. The enemy's day became dark night, and the night of allies turned into the day (of mirth and happiness). It happened on 2nd Muharram, A.H. 964/5th November, 1556 A.D. Mir Abdul Hai Sadar[15] wrote the date of this success:

Qita (distich)

Hemu, the rebel, took possession of Delhi, the capital, suddenly by means of trickery, cheating and deceit, such was the decree of fate. Jalal-ud-Din Muhammad Akbar whose magnificence touches skies, by the grace of God made this rebel, black faced one, a captive. The writer of destiny wrote on the tablet of life with the pen of fate the date of his death which is 'capture Hemu' 1556 A.D.

Later, His Majesty marched from Panipat to the capital of Delhi and established himself free from care and with perfect ease of mind there. He then proceeded to entrust the provinces (vilayat) and qasbas among his amirs and warriors. The country (khita) of Sambhal with its surrounding region was given to Ali Quli Khan. Jagirs and cash were conferred upon every deserving person.

Duaa (prayer) for His Majesty

May the eminence of the rank of His Majesty (Khaqan Akbar) become the asylum of hopes and wishes of people, and may the threshold of his greatness become a fountain of the Almighty's graciousness and mercy!

Notes

1. Hemu, born in Rewari, was a salt merchant by profession. By good luck he became one of the great amirs of Sher Khan and Salim Shah Sur. He deployed a large force under him and had with him famed elephants also. He assumed the power and title of Bikramjeet. *ZK*, fol. 13. See also *AN, TA, NM* and *Zafar al-Wali.*
2. Andali, Mubariz Khan entitled Sultan Muhammad Adil is famous. The justice of the son of Sultan was called (blind) by the people. He was killed in A.H. 964/1557 A.D. *Zubda,* fol. 96. See also *Duruj-al-Nafais,* fol. 75-b; *AN, MT* and *TM.*
3. Tardi Beig Khan was the person who gave Humayun the news of the birth of Akbar at Umarkot. When Bairam Khan formally proclaimed Akbar at Kalanaur as the emperor, Tardi Beig, an influential Turkman, who had been long in the service of Humayun, recognised the young prince's accession. and was granted the mansab of 5000 and was also appointed subedar of Delhi. When Hemu captured Delhi, Tardi Beig Khan fled to Sirhind where he met Akbar and Bairam Khan. *Zubda,* fol. 96. See also *AN, TA, NM* and *Subah Sadiq* (hereafter *SS*).
4. Sikandar Khan Uzbek belonged to the group of nobles of Kashghar who came from Persia with Humayun to Hindustan. The title of Khan-i-Alam was conferred on him. He died in A.H. 980/1572 A.D. at Lucknow *Zubda,* fol. 96-b. See also *MU,* I, 74; *TA, AN* and *SS.*
5. Ali Quli Khan Zaman belongs to the Shaibani tribe. He rose to the

high mansab and post during the reign of Akbar. *MU*, I, 622. See also *ibid.*

6. Shadi Khan Kakar, one of the exalted nobles of Afghans was killed in battle against Hemu by the imperial army on 2nd Muharram, A.H. 964/5th November, 1556 A.D. See *MT*, *AN*, and *TM*.
7. Khizr Khwaja Khan, the husband of Gulbadan Begum was the confidant of Humayun. When Hemu captured Delhi, Akbar and Bairam Khan persuaded him to follow Sikandar in the Punjab while they left for Delhi. *MU*, I, 613.
8. Pir Muhammad Khan Sherwani was in the beginning an academic (*talib-i-ilm*). Through the intermediary of Bairam Khan, he rose to the position of an amir and became the vakil of the former with absolute power. He held a mansab of 5000 and title of Nasir-ul-Mulk. He was appointed to pursue Bairam Khan after his rebellion. When his horse collided with a camel, he fell and drowned into the river Narbada in A.H. 969/1562 A.D. *ZK*, pp. 102-3. See also *AN*, *TA*, *NM*, *HI* and *MT*.
9. Tardi Beig Khan and other Khans, who had betrayed, were put to death in the month of Zi-hijja A.H. 963/October, 1556 A.D. *Zubda*, fol. 96 and *MU*, I, 466 and 484. See also *ibid* and S.K. Ray, *The Execution of Tardi Beig*, *JIH*, June 1952.
10. Panipat is situated forty and half karohs from Delhi towards north.
11. Though Arif has not given the number, force deployed under Hemu, "50,000 sawars, 1500 elephants and a huge park of artillery while Akbar had 10,000 persons out of it 5000 were armed". *Zubda*, fol. 97-a and *MR*, I, 651.
12. Shah Quli Khan Mahram was a retainer of Bairam Khan. Later he entered the (circle of) amirs and rose to the mansab of 5,000. He lived chiefly at Narnaul by virtue of its being his fief (jagir). He died in A.H. 1010/1601 A.D. *ZK*, p.182. See also *TM*, *AN*, *TA* and *Iqbal Nama-i-Jahangiri* (hereafter *IJ*).
13. For details see also *Tazkira Bayat*, 213, *Tarikh-i-Shahi*, 363 and *Makhzan-i-Afghani*, I, 401.
14. According to *ZK*, "Bairam Khan put him to death by the King's order. (Whatever) retinue and retainers, treasures, horses and elephants (of his) were in Mewat, Maulana Pir Muhammad Sherwani fetched and presented them before the august eyes. These were given to Bairam Khan". p. 13.
15. Abdul Hai Mashhadi was appointed Sadar by Humayun. He died in A.H. 980/1572 A.D. at Delhi. For details see *NM* and *MT*.

OCCURRENCE 8

Description of Posting of Khizr Khwaja Khan for the Suppression of the Menace of Sikandar (Sur), The Former's Defeat by the Accursed Surs, the Arrival of Khaqan Akbar and the Capture of Mankot Fort from the Ill-Starred, Sikandar

The knowledgeable persons would have realized that Sikandar (Sur), owing to his evil deeds, bad conduct and habitual mischief, accompanied by a horde of the Afghans, who had assembled under his banner from to and fro, was unleashing his (p. 53) tyranny and distress upon the helpless people which disturbed their peace and comfort. Soon it was felt that the hand of his tyranny and oppression was to be scrapped to the very traces of happiness from the people's hearts and minds. He was running for safety. He had neither shelter nor peace of mind. Realizing the intensity of situation, Khaqan Akbar appointed Khizr Khwaja Khan, who was one of the leading Khans among the nobles, to disperse Sikandar. Both the opposing forces faced each other and in the battle heap of corpses fell.[1]

In the thick of battle the vanquished Khwaja shut himself up in the fort of Lahore[2] and Sikandar pitched his camp in the vicinity of Kalanaur. As soon as the report of his defeat reached, His Majesty in order to put an end to the mischief of Sikandar marched against him in such a way that armies from every corner of the empire began to assemble like the waves of the sea.[3]

As soon as the news[4] of determination of the emperor spread all round, armies from all directions began to move and untold number of troops gathered, sent by officials, for his help.

Sikandar being perturbed, lost both his senses and peace of mind. The march of imperial forces sealed his luck as well as courage and he fled towards the fort of Mankot, which was built by Salim Shah Afghan[5] and was famous for its defences, and shut himself up there. (p. 54)

Masnavi (*rhyme*)

How can a fox face the lion, though it has nails as sharp as ten swords? When the earth is illumined by the light of sun, how can the lamp continue to burn?

Sikandar, thus closed himself in the fort of Mankot, maintained his defence from the imperial sword. The emperor laid a siege to it which continued for eight months and Pir Muhammad Khan Sherwani devised the plan of its capture.[6]

At the same time, report was received that fifty thousand Afghans while appearing there, had captured and taken away with them the young son of Hasan Khan Panchkoti[7] and Jalal Khan Sur.[8] In a vain bid to capture the provinces, they penetrated into the imperial territory also. Ali Quli Khan,[9] however, fought them in the vicinity of Lucknow, and with a show of valour overpowered them successfully. He annexed several provinces from them and brought them under his administration.

Bait (*verse*)

Universal kingdom is being bestowed by God Himself (Who has no equal) and everyone must respect the truth and justice of His Majesty.

In short the basis of this edifice (of saying) depends on the capture of the fort of Mankot. It woud be better if by any mean or comment a written sketch of the picture might be drawn so that whosoever is mentioned in course of narrating the incidents, may at once be identified. The fort is perched on such a mountain whose summit kisses the sky. If any philosopher were to see it he would be unable to say whether beyond the seventh sky there is empty space or if it is full. Even if heaven itself was to cast a glance towards its stronghold, then it would utter forth in all earnestness that 'Holy is My Creator' Who is high and lofty (meaning thereby that the heaven will utter forth a word of amazement).

Bait (*verse*)

From the height it is said that it is in the deep well. . . .

The circuit of its hill is surrounded by another hill. (p. 55) Therefore if the two hills are viewed together the first will look like the centre of them while some other hills looking like the domes of sky, which are situated opposite to it. In between there is a dangerous chasm to see it even the demons of forest by whose terror even a man of degraded character recites and takes shelter thereunder, and even then the devil is rendered unable to harm him, and even the white hobgoblin who commits all types of tyranny and oppression wished to reach there then he also utters that there is no power nor strength except in God and would escape by hook or crook. Each of the forts is known by a different name.

When the inhabitants of the region heard the fame of the blessed star (Akbar) their heart began to bleed and their face became pale like saffron with fear and dread, and the army of the fort sought shelter in its dark and dingy dungeons. Sikandar also realized that he had luckily escaped from the talons of a dreadful hawk and reached a palace of safety. The poor man did not imagine that he would be dragged out of his hiding place. Pir Muhammad Khan, who had been instructed by Khan Khanan (Bairam Khan), turned his attention towards it. He spent money lavishly to dig out trenches there. Eventually Sikandar Sur Afghan began to feel utterly helpless, and behaved with the greatest humility and supplication. He was therefore sent to the imperial court with a recommendation for pardon and he was there with the language of submission, saying:

Bait (*verse*)

Although my sins are as great as a mountain, the ocean of your mercy is also limitless.

As the river of mercy of Khaqan Akbar was immense, he scraped off the sins from his record by the pen of forget and forgiveness.[10]

He was however allowed to go out of the imperial dominion. (p. 56) He entrusted his son[11] to Ghazi Khan Tanawar[12] and left for Jaunpur. Soon after he died.[13]

Therefore, the emperor after the success marched towards Lahore. He finally reached the capital of Agra in A.H. 966/1558 A.D. via Delhi.[14]

During the same time, Khan Khanan (Bairam) sacked Pir Muhammad[15] (Khan) who was a high noble on the charge of disloyalty. He went to Gujarat and remained there till Bairam Khan himself became a victim of the same fate. Pir Muhammad Khan availed this opportunity to rejoin the imperial service and he obtained the honour of kissing the floor of throne. He was given the title of Khan, a banner (standard) and drum were also bestowed on him. I hope to be able to give some more details about Bairam Khan and Pir Muhammad Khan in the course of the following narrative.

Duaa (prayer) for His Majesty

The welfare and progress of the country and nation and proper observance of rules are adhered to by the emperor. May the blessings of God's grace remain with all His creatures for ever!

NOTES

1. *Masnavi* (rhyme) has been left. See p. 53.
2. Arif does not mention the defeat of the Khwaja by the Afghans while Badauni and *Zubda* categorically mention that the Khwaja was defeated at Chamyari, situated at a distance of 20 karohs from Lahore. Thereafter he escaped to Lahore. *MT*, II, 170 and *Zubda*, fol. 68a.
3. Akbar left himself with Bairam Khan in the month of Safar, A.H. 964/December, 1556 A.D. *AN*, II, 48. See also *MR*, I, 653 and *Zubda*, fol. 98b.
4. *Masnavi* (rhyme) has been left. See p. 55.
5. Salim Shah, Jalal Khan entitled Salim Shah and Islam Shah son of Sher Shah Suri ascended the throne in the year A.H. 952/1545 A.D. in the fort of Kalinjar. For details see also *AN*, *MR* and *Zubda*.
6. Abul Fazl confirms that Pir Mohammad Khan Sherwani was incharge

of the siege. *AN*, II, 58. While Badauni says that he was incharge of one of the Morchals while Muhammad Husain Khan, an experienced and elderly person was incharge of the whole expedition. *MT*, II, 18.

7. Badauni confirms as Panchkoti. *Ibid.*, I, 25 while Bajkoti is mentioned by Nihawandi. *MR*, I, 255.
8. Jalal Khan Sur was one of the leading Afghan nobles of Bengal and Bihar. He died fighting against Muzaffar Khan in A.H. 983/1575 A.D. See *AN* and *TM*.
9. Ali Quli Khan entitled Khan-i-Zaman, son of Haider Sultan Shaibani, was one of the exalted nobles of Humayun and Akbar. He held a mansab of 2000 and died in the month of Ziqad, A.H. 974/May, 1567 A.D. in the vicinity of Allahabad. *ZK*, fol. 365. See also *MU*, I, 622, *MT*, *TA*, *NM*, *AN*, and *HI*.
10. Abul Fazl confirms that on the recommendation of Bairam Khan not only Sikandar Khan but also Pir Muhammad Sherwani and Shamsuddin Atga Khan were pardoned. *AN*, II, 59. Masnavi has been left. See p. 55.
11. The name of his son was Abdur Rehman. *MR*, I, 656.
12. Ghazi Khan Tanawar commonly known as Shah Ghazi Turkman, held a mansab of 1000. *ZK*, fol. 424 while he is called Tanwari and Sur also. *MU*, I, 555 and 615. See also *AN*, II, 59; *MT*, II, 18 and *TR*, I, 655.
13. Sikandar never went to Lahore from the fort of Mankot (in Simmur hills) nor was it necessary for him to do so, as he was to go eastward to Bihar. Moreover, he did not go to Jaunpur. He surrendered the fort in May 24, 1557 A.D. and went to Gaur and died two years later in 1559 A.D. *AN*, II, 91. See also *TM*, *MT*, II, 18; *MR*, I, 655 and N.B. Roy, *Successors of Sher Shah*, p. 102.
14. Akbar reached Lahore on 2nd Shawwal, A.H. 964/29th July, 1557 A.D. He started for Delhi on Thursday, 15th Safar, A.H. 965/28th November, 1557 A.D. and reached there on 25th Jamadi II (of the said year) while left it in the month of Zilhijja, A.H. 965/September, 1558 A.D. and he finally reached Agra on Sunday, 17th Muharram, A.H. 966/31st October, 1558 A.D. See *AN*, II, 64 and 66; *MT*, II, 26; *MR*, I, 659 and *Zubda*, fol. 101-b.
15. Pir Muhammad Khan Sherwani achieved distinction due to the favour and kindness of Bairam Khan. With the passage of time, he nourished some ill-feelings against his patron which caused his sack. *MT*, II, 28; *Zubda*, fol. 103-a and *MU*, III, 182.

OCCURRENCE 9

Description of the Rise of Everlasting Empire by the Grace of Almighty, its set to March on Un-ceasing Progress and Success, Being Suspicious of His Majesty of Bairam Khan and Rushing of Victorious Standards towards the Capital, Hazrat-i-Delhi

Abiyat (*verses*)

The emperors rule by the grace and blessings of God Their actions are not like those of common folks. All their actions are most extraordinary and uncommon. If they decide to conquer and take possession of any country, they accomplish it in a single stroke.[1] (p. 57)

The proof of this statement is to be found in the fact, that when Khaqan Akbar[2] was residing in the capital of Agra, the great Khan (Bairam Khan) besides being the tutor of the young king was also functioning as vakil. While the latter was apparently acting for the good of his kingdom, some of (Bairam Khan's) acts were in fact not in the interest of state and he committed certain unmannerly and disrespectful acts. Such a behaviour naturally offended the emperor.[3] The Khan, who had intimate relations of loyalty and friendship with the emperor's family was not expected to forget all those favours by entering into a hostile conspiracy with some miscreants and trouble-makers against the emperor. Those mischief-mongers wanted that Khan Khanan be counted among them by following the accursed path of disloyalty so that he too be guilty of disobedience.

Masnavi (*rhyme*)

Everyone who has grown grey under the sky and ha

been friendly in all your affairs and whose affairs are properly managed by you, then if you become hostile (to his life) your attempt shall be futile.

During the time, that band (of rebels) committed certain deeds which gave much offence to the emperor. The course or decision adopted by the emperor can never be anything except the right and just way. It was resolved that the emperor ought to do away with the conspirators and he decided to be away from them. He, therefore, made use of his leisure (which he was enjoying at this time), and in the month of Jamadi-ul-Awwal, A.H. 967/January-February, 1560 A.D. started on a hunting expedition from Agra towards Delhi accompanied by a small body of nobles.[4]

The next day when Khan Khanan came to know about the departure of the emperor, he was perturbed and worried. (p. 58) Immediately, he sent several despatches to the emperor, praying that he too be included among his slaves (i.e. allow him to approach him) so that he might be able to rectify his mistakes that were committed by him. For this purpose he sent the emperor's relatives Khwaja Jahan[5] and Haji Muhammad Khan,[6] who was his vakil and Tarsum Muhammad Khan,[7] the keeper of his seal, to kiss the first feet. But his prayer was not accepted and his deputed persons never returned to him.

Bait (*verse*)

Thou should desist from wishing harm to others, for by doing so you will invite calamity on your own head.

The sardars (chiefs) and soldiers came continuously from Agra and submitted to the emperor, until all of them gathered under the victorious standard. Then Khaqan Akbar addressed the following letter to him:

My Dear Khan Baba,[8]

With my affectionate salutation and message of love, you may peruse this and know that on account of certain important matters, we have come to the capital of Delhi. We have also come to know that you intend to continue in the service of the court. So we are despatching Tarsum Beig to intimate you that we have certain complaints against you which have dissatisfied us. We (feel) that the heart of good persons will not reconcile to your continuance in service, holding your post and carrying on the work of the administration. If it were necessary we ourselves would go to perform it. You should, therefore, proceed to Gwalior and look after the affairs of its frontiers, and whenever we require, you should come to pay homage to us. We write to assure you to put your heart at rest. No doubt, certain unpleasant incidents might have occurred between father and son, but there can be no misunderstandings. You happen to be our Khan Baba and we in turn maintain due respect and regard for that relationshp. In spite of the recent painful events and of your improper and undesirable deeds, we still hold you in our affection and treat you with kindness and friendliness and we still follow the old custom of calling you 'Khan Baba'. We consider it fit and proper not to meet in near future. (p. 59) It is better you may proceed to holy Mecca according to your desire, for which you have prayed for our permission. You should further send someone to receive presents and cash, etc. left behind at Sirhind and Lahore so that all might be sent to you . . . written . . . the end."

The noble Khan felt awefully perturbed after the receipt of this letter. That very year, 9th Rajab-ul-Murajab, (A.H. 967/5th April, 1560 A.D.), he left Agra without waiting for Amir Najeeb-ud-Din Ḥabibullah[9] there. Like a lunatic, he proceeded towards Bayana. In short, when the hand of his courage failed to reach the branch of his ambition, he became the fruit of the tree of desire, who was biting the fingers of dependency with his teeth. In spite of the fact that on the road of deliverance, he says, "The moles of misfortune erupted and scattered under his feet, yet he at once decided to depart, and his retinue broke up and became scattered."

On hearing about these incidents the Khans and amirs, who had been appointed to besiege the fort of Mandu[10] and Ranthambhor,[11] marched back to the capital. They gathered at Bayana and mended their way post-haste towards the shelter of the universe. Thereafter, Khan Khanan released Shah Abu-al-Maali,[12] imprisoned in the fort of Bayana.[13]

Later Khan Khanan left Bayana for Alwar. The Khans and amirs who were accompanying him, left him by joining the imperial threshold. Khan-i-Saeed halted at Alwar, and from there he went to Hajipur, a pargana of Alwar. But the Khan's eyes were shedding like an afflicted one with grief and distress. That very night the eyes of clouds also began to tear out rain of grief for the remnants, and the eyes of time (or people) also created a waterfall by the floor of their tears. The proclaimer was announcing the following loudly: (p. 60)

Rubai (*a quatrain*)

The fate shed tears of blood and marched off; she wept over the government and *Khaniyat* (Khan's rank) and went away. Why thy fortune saw that, even the sky does not reward thy services, it too scratched its back and departed.

Resolution and peace of mind vanished and yielded to fear and despair. Eventually he (Khan Khanan) became humble and submissive. The reins of authority had passed out of his hands and the arrow of status was also separated from its hook. Therefore, he thought it wise to move towards Nagore. Many of Khans, amirs and old servants, who were still wandering with him, deserted (him) and joined the circle of His Majesty's faithful servants. They even did their best to destory his baggage, loaded on camels. But from among his relatives, Husain Quli Khan,[14] his father[15] and brothers, Shaikh Gadai[16] and Muzaffar Khan, the diwan of Khan Khanan, accompanied him. His Majesty, with victory and triumph, marched from Delhi[17] and encamped in the pargana Jajjhar.[18]

During the same time, Umdat-ul-Khwanin Pir Muhammad Khan, who had been expelled from service by the imperial command and had gone to Gujarat, returned and was the recipient of the honour of kissing the august feet at Jajjhar camp. Drum and standard were bestowed on him and the title of Khan was also conferred on him. Later, with some other Khans, he was sent in pursuit (of Bairam Khan). (p. 61)

It was further decided that Umdat-ul-Mulk Husain Quli Khan, be also provided standard, drums and war elephants and he be sent with a view to wipe out the dust of hatred and hostily which had erupted between the two parties. The Khans sent to the ears of (Bairam Khan) words of sound advice and sensible attitude (to be followed by him). They tried to persuade him to leave Nagore, where the two parties were arrayed against each other, and he should move away to the dominion (vilayat) of Bikaner. But the idea of dispute and battle ought not come to his mind at all. He should also realize that if he wished to adopt a course of shortsightedness and ignorance, and would act with vanity and complexed pride, then the imperial forces would inevitably be obliged to destroy him completely. In fact it would then be too late to exhibit the spirit of conciliation and humility.

Of necessity, the Khan accepted the advice and sent the possessed standards, drums and elephants, accompanied by Husain Quli Khan, to kiss the imperial threshold while he himself proceeded towards Bikaner from Nagore.[19]

Bait (verse)

Alas! he lost the capacity of peace and resolution, and except for running to and fro had no other alternative before him.

After passing some time there, the Khan, forgetting all that had happened, left for Firuzpur[20] and Tihara[21] which were situated in the jurisdiction of the Sarkar of Punjab. He kept some of his property, baggages and his relations in the fort of Tabrandha[22] in the charge of Sher Muhammad,[23] whom he had obliged by favours (it was in Bairam Khan's jagir). But the ungrateful fellow misused the wealth of the Khan and not only ill-treated his relations and employees, but inflicted on them all types of oppression also. Eventually he met his retribution. In short, the Khan while on his way thought it advisable and deputed Muzaffar Khan, who was in his train to Darvesh Uzbek,[24] his old favourite, the Hakim of Dipalpur[25] and requested for favour. Though it was an impossible favour any way the Khan could not think better.

Muzaffar Khan out of respect and regards (p. 62) left at once to meet that evil-minded Darvesh. That miscreant handed over the above-mentioned Khan to a band of his persons to be sent to the emperor. This incident will be fully narrated while discussing the account of Wazir Muzaffar Nishan. The despaired Khan left for Jalandhar.

When the emperor came to know that the Khan, turning his steps, had entered Punjab and was encamping in the foothills of the mountain range of Lahore, he boiled up with rage and the royal wrath came into motion.[26] He sent Umdat-ul-Khawanin-ul-Muazzam Shams-ud-Din Muhammad Atga, Khan-i-Azam[27] with a few other Khans for the suppression of sedition of the Khan (Bairam Khan). Both the forces came face to face and exhibited their valour but the Khan's army vanquished soon. It could not sustain the brunt of the imperial forces and took refuge in the mountains of Lahore (i.e. hills northward of Lahore).[28] Most of the rebellious were killed while others like Wali Beig Zul-Qader, Yaqub Hamdani and Murad, ignorant, unsuccessful, responsible for the sedition, were captured with much booty.[29] When the news of defeat of the Khan and the prayer of the inhabitants of the region of hills for protection reached the emperor, the imperial army was set to move once more and it marched off from Hazrat-i-Delhi to put an end to his mischief. As soon as the victorious army landed at the base of the hills,[30] the Khan was ashamed of his conduct. He deputed Jamal Khan,[31] who was his confident to the imperial court to convey his repentence and prayer for pardon.[32]

Misraa (a hemistich)

Whatever would be the command of His Majesty, I bow in respects. (p. 63)

The emperor accepted gracefully his prayer and deputed Shaikh-ul-Islam Maulana Abdullah Makhdum-ul-Mulk[33] (known for piety and wisdom). He came and impressed upon the Khan that the good of both consisted in strengthening unity and friendship and the cause of hostility be removed. Khan Khanan, fully satisfied, agreed to abide by pledges and promises and desired to pay his respects to His Majesty. So it was also decided if the Khan would like to seek permission (to present himself in the court), the emperor would send all his senior amirs and Khans to welcome him in a suitable manner and bestow on him the credit to reemployment with regards due to him.[34] Consequently, in Rabi II,[35] A.H. 968/December, 1560 A.D., the Khan, accompanied with some of his companions, came and received the honour of kissing His Majesty's feet. He mustered his courage and talked in a tone of humbleness and respect. The emperor pardoned all his faults and bestowed on him a special robe of honour and Rs. 50,000 in cash for his maintenance.[36]

Bait (*verse*)

Ever since the time of Hazrat Adam down to the period of His Majesty, the tradition has been that the elders and rulers forgive the faults of youngers and subordinates.

The very day Khaqan Akbar resolved to go out on hunting and reached Darul Sultanate, Lahore. He covered a distance of 200 karohs[37] from Lahore up to Hisar-Firoza in a day, riding on a fast running horse. Its commanding reins, great speed and flame like movement had no match. Like the morning breeze, piercing the lonely forests, crossing the country like a stag, and going from stage to stage without rest, finally reached Hisar-Firoza successfully. (p. 64) After finishing hunting, he returned to Hazrat-i-Delhi, had rest for a few days and then went to Darul Khilafa, Agra.[38] The victorious standards began to flutter on the centre of the empire and *Huma* (bird of good luck, mercy and favours) spread the shadow of kindness on the inhabitants of the place (vilayat).

During the same time, Nawab Munam Khan,[39] as per the imperial order (farman) came from Kabul and the emperor conferred on him the title of Khan-i-Khan. The imperial force skirted via the hills through Macchiwara[40] and Sirhind, turned towards Delhi and obtained the honour of kissing the royal feet. The exalted Nawab (Bairam Khan), taking permission for Haj, left for Mecca. He, abandoning the comfort of chiefship, got entrapped in the hardship of journey and scratching his dignified face by the nails of suppression, was entangled in fruit of his own actions. He proceeded to Gujarat via Nagore and Jodhpur. In Pattan, one of the provinces of Gujarat, (a haven) of the banished Afghan rebels, Bairam Khan, who was enjoying leisure, went to enjoy boat ride in the nearby Sahstralinga tank.[41] On 14th Jamadi-ul-Awwal,[42] A.H. 968/31st January, 1561 A.D., an irreligious among the Afghans,[43] killed him with his dagger. The palace of his existence became empty of its host, i.e. his soul, and the boatman of fates carried the boat of his life to the shore of death, his whole retinue and baggage were thoroughly devastated and ruined. The son of late Khan, Muhammad Rahim Mirza,[44] who was a young child, together with his relatives and companions, was somehow saved from being drowned in that storm of calamity, landed safely and they were brought to the border of freedom. The following quatrain (*rubai*) gives the date of martyrdom of Bairam Khan.[45]

Rubai (*a quatrain*)

When Bairam (Khan) made preparations to circumambulate the Kabah, he became a martyr on the way, Hatif, the mysterious related this incident in this way: it is said that Muhammad Bairam became a martyr.

The compiler of history, who was in the service of the great Khan, had also to suffer all these hardships.[46] But he (Arif) managed to save his own life and was sent to Ahmedabad with the infant (Abdur Rahim). (p. 65)

It had been my cherished desire to go on pilgrimage to the holy Mecca and Medina (Harmain Sharifain) and my heart used to circumambulate the Kabah, the object of my desire, and I used to say: "Turn my face towards the sacred place". I therefore boarded a ship at Khambhat,[47] in the hope of reaching the sacred land and started for Jeddah. The boatman released the anchor, which is lowered into the sea in order to stop the ship. It separated in the same way as lovers, who are thrown at a long distance from each other, lose their patience. Flags of those governments began to fly and the sails began to flutter. The travellers had to follow certain rules and instructions and the mercy of God was their faith with them. After a few days, whirlwinds in the opposite directions started blowing and the travellers got entrapped in it day and night and they became victim of the arrows of heaven. Everyone was helpless. We had to spend two days on the high sea, which seemed shoreless, and in the most dangerous conditions suffered all sorts of hardships. At last, after a long despair, the star of hope arose. My lost fate reconciled itself and returned to me, and the enemy of good luck himself welcomed me. The rower of happiness started rowing the boat of my desire in the sea of hope, until it reached me to my desired aim, and landed me on the side of Hurmuz[48] which became the source of relief for despondent people and they became to hum these verses:

Nazm (*poem*)

My dark night changed into the morning light, life was saved as if I got the reward of lakhs (of rupees). Dangers and difficulties overwhelmed me but by the grace of God all passed over, and I reached my destination.

Real luck favoured me, and by the land route I travelled and performed obeisance enroute to the tombs of great Shaikhs, whose tombs are situated on the road to Lar,[49] Baghdad, Basra and Turkey, in the company of the caravan of royal Hajis and was favoured with such good fortune, which is called the pilgrimage to holy places.

Duaa (*prayer*) *for His Majesty*

(p. 66) It is prayed that the gardens of the kingdom of the emperor be evergreen and flourishing by God's canals. And the fountain of the king's mercy and generosity may continue with ever-growing freshness and brightness, and the tree of the grandeur and brilliance of Khaqan Akbar, was and the fruit of exalted good luck may continue to flourish and bear fruit by the constant irrigating rain of God's grace!

NOTES

1. This is a gist of the verses.
2. Akbar assumed the title of Nasir-ul-Mulk after the conquest over Hemu. *MU,* III, 182 while Badauni says the title of Khan. *MT,* II, 28.
3. Though Bairam Khan had absolute power, he was sending farmans on behalf of Akbar also. *AN,* II, 108.
4. The date given by Arif has been confirmed by Abul Fazl, Badauni and Sadruddui Muhammad. *AN,* II, 94 *MT,* II, 36 & *NM,* fol. 25-a while Monday, 29th Jamadi Akhir (16th March) has been given by *Zubda,* fol. 102-a.
5. Khwaja Jahan, commonly known as Khwaja Aminuddin Muhammad, was one of the prominent nobles. He held the post of vakil also with full power and rose to the mansab of 2000. He died in the month of Shaban, A.H. 982/November, 1574 A.D. *ZK,* 373. See also *MU,* I, 630 and *AN, TA, SS* and *TM.*
6. Haji Muhammad Khan was vakil of Bairam Khan. See V.A. Smith, *Akbar the Great Mogul (1542-1605),* 1966, S. Chand & Co., Delhi. (hereafter op. cit.)
7. Tarsum Muhammad Khan was earlier a retainer of Bairam Khan. Later he rose to the position of Amir-ul-Umara. *ZK,* 336. See also *ibid.*
8. "My Dear Khan Baba" *MR,* I, 645 while Abul Fazl addresses him Khan Khanan. *AN,* II, 10 which does not seem proper.
9. Amir Najib-ud-Din Habibullah is probably Haji Habibullah, who was a famous person. He died in the month of Shaban, A.H. 1002/April, 1594 A.D. For details see *AN* and *TM.*
10. Mandu, the capital of Malwa.
11. Famous fort in the vicinity of Jaipur.
12. Shah Abu-al-Maali was imprisoned by Bairam Khan and later was released. See V.A. Smith (op. cit.).
13. Bayana means Bharatpur, which is situated in Rajasthan.
14. Husain Quli Khan, son of Wali Beig Zulqadar, was the nephew (sister's son) of Bairam Khan. He achieved a high mansab later. He, however, died on 19th Shawwal, A.H. 986/19th December, 1578 A.D. *MU,* I, 435. See also *TM, MT* and *TA.*
15. Wali Beig Zulqadar, brother-in-law of Bairam Khan was one of the leading nobles. After the battle at Jalandhar, he rose in rebellion and created sedition in the dominion of the country. For details see *MU,* I, 645; *AN, MT, MR, TA* and SS.
16. Shaikh Gadai, son of Shaikh Jamali Kanbu Delhvi; his real name was Abdur Rehman and became famous as Gadai. He was a learned man. On the recommendation of Bairam Khan, he was appointed Sadr-us-

Sudur. He died in A.H. 976/1568 A.D. For details see *NM, TM* and *MT.*

17. Arif has not mentioned the date of Akbar's departure from Delhi. According to Abul Fazl, "On Friday, 22nd Rajab, A.H. 967/18th April, 1560 A.D., he left Delhi. He reached Jajjhar on 26th of the same month/22nd April and returned to (Delhi) on 12th Shaban/8th May." *AN,* II, 104.
18. Jajjhar is the dependency of Punjab which is situated at a distance of thirty karohs in the South. *MR,* I, 673.
19. According to Badauni, "Bairam Khan himself separated most of his relations and companions and insisted they go to the emperor while he left for Nagore." *MT,* II, 38.
20. Firozepura, i.e. Firozepur Jharka which is the dependency of Gurgaon, Punjab.
21. Tahara. *MR,* II, 4. It is the operating part of Punjab.
22. Abul Fazl and Badauni call it Tabranda. *AN,* II, 109 and *MT,* II, 40 while Nizamuddin say Tabrandha. *TA,* II, 147, though it is Bhatinda. *MR,* I, 674.
23. Sher Muhammad Khan, one of the old servants of Bairam Khan, was his adopted son. In A.H. 973/1565 A.D, he was killed as a punishment for unleashing devastation and destruction. *AN,* II, 332, *Zubda,* fol. 104-b and *MT,* I, 40.
24. His name was Muhammad Uzbek. He died in A.H. 1001/1592 A.D. *TA,* II, 147.
25. Dipalpur is the centre of Mintgumri, a dependency of West Punjab.
26. The emperor had appointed Pir Muhammad Khan Sherwani to escort Bairam Khan out of the dominion to go on pilgrimage. *TA,* II, 146, *MT,* II, 39. *Zubda,* fol. 103-b and *MU,* I, 378.
27. Shamsuddin Muhammad Atga Khan defeated Bairam Khan at Jalandhar and got the title of Khan-i-Azam. See *NM* and *AN.*
28. It means Siwalik mountains near Jalandhar. *MR,* I. 677 and *Zubda,* fol. 104-b.
29. For details see *MR,* I, 676, *AN,* II and III, 113, and *TA,* II, 148.
30. On 20th Ziqada, A.H. 967/16th August, 1560 A.D., Akbar left Delhi while he reached Lahore, Tuesday, 26th Zi-hijja/18th September. *AN,* II, 111, 115, *MR,* I, 677.
31. Reference is not available about Jamal Khan in contemporary and near contemporary sources.
32. See also *MT,* II, 43 and *TA,* II, 149.
33. Maulana Abdullah, son of Shams-ud-din Ansari Sultanpuri, known as Shaikh-ul-Islam and Makhdum-ul-Mulk was a pious and learned alim

of Hindustan. After performing Haj, he died in A.H. 990/1582 A.D. in Ahmedabad. See *TA*, *AN* and *Gulzar-i-Abrar*.

34. According to Badauni, "Maulana Abdullah and Munim Khan with some nobles were sent to receive Bairam Khan. *MT*, II, 44, While Nahawandi says, "Bairam Khan said if Munim Khan comes, it will not satisfy him. So he requested that he may be permitted to present himself, which was accepted". *MR*, I, 668. See also *NM* fol. 89b.

35. The month is confirmed by Abul Fazl also. *AN*, II, 118. While Nihawandi says in the month of Muharram/January. *MR*, I, 679 and *MU*, I, 379.

36. Other sources are silent.

37. The distance between Lahore and Hisar Firoza is 100 Karohs (200 miles).

38. Akbar came to Delhi on 4th Rabi-ul-Awwal/23rd November while he left on Friday, 2nd Rabi II/21st December and reached Agra on 12th of the same month/31st December. *AN*, II, 122. *TA*, II, 150-1, *MT*, II, 44 and *MR*, I, 679.

39. Nawab Miyan Muhammad Khan Nayazi was one of the great nobles of Emperor Humayun. Among the Afghans, there were three nobles of long standing, but he was the greatest, best and most advanced in mansab and rank. For details see *ZK*, 239-50.

40. Maachiwara means Maachiwada which is situated in Ludhiana.

41. Kolab is the name of 1000 lingas. According to Nizamuddin "Sahas is attributed to 1000 in Hindi language which was the name of temple". As one thousand temples were in the pond, so it was famous. In the temples, the organ of Mahadeva was worshiped which were one thousand. *TA*, II, 150.

42. It was Friday. *AN*, II, 131. See also MR, I, 670 and II, 52.

43. Mubarak Khan was one of his assassins whose father was killed by Bairam Khan there. *Ibid*. See also S.N. Hasan, *New Light on the Relations of early Mughal Rulers with their Nobility* (Indian History Congress), Madras, 1944, p. 396; I.A. Khan, The Mughal Court Politics During Bairam Khan's Regency, *Medieval India: A Miscellany*, Vol.I, Deptt. of History, AMU, Aligarh and Qazi Mukhtar Ahmad, was Bairam Khan a rebel? Islamic Culture, June, 1947.

44. A thorny fruit of the size of pea with thorns, grown around it. Arif is using a pure Hindi word.

45. Here Arif is obviously condemning the emperor's action perhaps out of loyalty to his master Bairam Khan. Obviously he is doing so clandestinely so that the emperor may have no chance of knowing it.

46. Arif is making a peculiar combination of 'Shast' (the vice or line, attached to the hook for catching fish and arrows).

47. Khambat or Khambayat, situated near the bank of a river in Gujarat.

48. Harmuz or Harmaz, is a city situated near the bank of Persian Gulf.
49. It is the capital of Laristan.

OCCURRENCE 10

Description of Posting and March of Adham Khan and Pir Muhammad Khan Towards the Sarkar of Malwa and Mandu, Escape of Baz Bahadur and Finally His Capture After Great Chase

When His Majesty became free from dealing with the martyr (Bairam Khan), he cast his glance over all the corners of the country so that wherever he found the flag (reign) of injustice and oppression, he would bend down the head of oppressors. He appointed Kotwal of justice everywhere so that wherever they found the buildings of injustice rising high, they might at once pull them down. When the said policy was implemented, the attention of His Majesty was diverted to Baz Bahadur,[1] who had been the *mutasadi* of Malwa and Mandu since the time of Salim Shah Afghan and the administration of those regions had been somehow conferred on him, and he was carrying on the administration just as a donkey, employed to dig and carry mud. Due to the noble sentiments of the emperor in A.H. 968/20th September, 1560 A.D. Adham Khan[2] and Pir Muhammad Khan were despatched with a force of five or six thousand gallant soldiers to free the said province.[3] They accompanied by the soldiers who possessed the heart of lions, the strength of tigers, the courage of hawks and the sustenance of crocodiles. Victory was writ large on their faces, and the sky-rocking reputation of the state was constantly keeping them company.

Misra'a (*a hemistich*)

Victory or triumph is with them while success is their objective and the government is their friend. (p. 67)

When they reached the vicinity of Sarangpur[4] they did not realize that a great army of the enemy was present in that city. Immediately, the fire of battle blazed forth. The lances, though not strong enough, began to fight and the swords, even though thin and timid, started using sharp tongues, and the shields of steel began to bear the onslaught of clubs, the bows began to bend by the attacks of men, the mad armour shed tears of blood of bravemen and the bows started crying and wailing loudly, owing to separation.[5]

When the victorious khan brought out the bows and arrows which had been kept hidden till then and storm raising swords came out to Baz Bahadur Afghan, and both forces came face to face for battle, the brains of men became intoxicated and inflamed with draughts of old wines and the storm of riot which had been on fire for a long time, erupted into the form of a flame. Arrows began to rain from bows, spears from the stretched out hands of men with scattered locks and tall young men began to destroy lives ruthlessly. In a short time, brave soldiers of the enemy's army met their doom and those who survived began to flee for their dear lives. Baz Bahadur realized that nothing could be done to save the situation and in the midst of utter confusion and panic he, shedding tears of blood, fled away with a broken heart, to the Deccan.[6] The victorious standard (may the breeze of conquest be their helper and shelter!) of the state and good fortune beating the drum of triumph entered Sarangpur, and took into possession the areas of Ujjain and Mandu.[7]

On the receipt of news of success, His Majesty started on a joy trip, reached Mandu and that province which was among the best regions of Hindustan, was made the envy of paradise by his visit. He stayed there for some days and marched back to the capital of Agra (repeating that "return is better").[8]

(p. 68) During the same year the emperor went for hunting towards Kara and Manikpur. Ali Quli Khan, who was the hakim of Jaunpur, paid his respects by kissing the royal floor and the emperor allowed him to return to Jaunpur while he himself marched back to the capital.

In the year A.H. 969/1561-62 A.D. Adham Khan was summoned from Mandu. Pir Muhammad had cleared the entire land of Mandu from all enemies, and crossing the river Narbada, pushed them as far as Asir(garh) and Burhanpur and subjected those regions to ruthless destruction and killing. Meanwhile, Baz Bahadur who was running to save himself managed to collect a considerable force in complicity with the chiefs of Asir(garh) and Burhanpur, and advanced to challenge Pir Muhammad. The fellows of Pir Muhammad, who had been sick of his tyrannies, beastly conduct and intolerable behaviour, did not put their strength into battle and turning disloyal, surrendered to the enemy without any resistance. Pir Muhammad lost the battle and he tried to cross the Narbada with a row of camels, laden with baggages. His horse slipped, he fell into the water and was drowned.[9]

Misraa (*a hemistich*)

His entire pomp and grandeur went down into the water. Baz Bahadur considered it a great triumph and succeeded in re-establishing himself firmly there. When those chiefs, who had shown cowardice, returned to the imperial court, they were thoroughly humiliated and imprisoned. Thereupon, Abdullah Khan Uzbek,[10] the hakim (in charge) of Kalpi, was despatched to reconquer and subjugate Malwa and Mandu, and to uproot Baz Bahadur thoroughly. Khwaja Muin was given the title of Khan and was appointed the diwan and was sent with Abdullah Khan. (p. 69) As soon as Baz Bahadur received the news of the approach of the imperial army, being conscious of his inability, he escaped and the whole region fell into their hands. Thus Baz Bahadur was made cripple. Soon the bud of hope began to flower in the garden of government, and the face of victory began to glitter happily with the smile of imperial sword. Baz Bahadur ran from pillar to post and took refuge in jungles and hills. Eventually when no arrow was left in his quiver, he threw away his sword and winding sheet. He presented himself in the imperial court in A.H. 978/(5th June, 1570 A.D. to May 26, 1571 A.D.) and was enlisted in the ranks of royal servants and was taken under the shelter of the world conquering umbrella. Royal favour and kindness were conferred on him more and more everyday and his rank was gradually raised, so that his life came to an end at the imperial threshold.[11]

Duaa (prayer) for His Majesty

May progress rise which should remain unhampered and undying splendour and dignity, remain ever and ever with His Majesty! May the accidents and mishaps of time ever remain far away from the skirt of the king!

NOTES

1. After the death of Sher Khan and Salim Khan Sur, Baz Bahadur Afghan took upon himself the name of kingship in the government of Malwa and had the sermon read and coins struck in his name. His father Shujaet Khan, who was one of Khassa-Khail (special trooper) of Sher Khan and which, after the latter's death, was settled on his son. Baz Bahadur was unrivalled in his time in the art of music and varieties of Hindustani melodies and passed most of his time in the company of courtesans, dancing girls and frolic. *ZK*, 251. See also *MT*, II, 47.
2. Adham Khan, son of Nadim Khan Kokaltash, a faithful servant of Humayun, who shared with Shams-ud-Din and Khwaja Muazaam the honour of escorting Hamida Banu Begum and her infant son (Akbar) from Umarkot. *AN*, I, 135 and Gulbadan, p. 59.

   Blochman 12 seems mistaken in supposing Adham Khan to be 'a royal bastard'. His mother, Maham Anga was a wet nurse of Akbar also. He held a mansab of 5000. *ZK*, 124. See also *MT, NM, TA, AN* and *TM*.
3. Sadiq Muhammad Khan, Qiya Khan Gunj, Abdullah Khan Uzbek, Shah Muhammad Qandhari and other amirs were sent to assist him (Adham Khan). *ZK*, 251.
4. Sarangpur, the capital. *MU*, I, 389, *Zubda* fol. 106-1 and *MT*, II, 47.
5. Baz Bahadur woke up from the sleep of negligence when the imperial army reached within ten karohs of Sarangpur. Advancing (at a place) within two karohs (of his capital), he made a fortification and

encamped there. The battle took place on 12th Rajab/30th March. *ZK*, 251. See also *Zubda* fol. 106-a, *MT*, II, 47 and *MU*, I, 389.

6. He left towards Khandesh and Malwa. *MU*, I, 390 and *Farishta*, II, 274. According to Abul Fazl, "Neighbouring land". *AN*, II, 137. He came to Khandesh, marched towards Burhanpur hurriedly and the Raja of Baklana provided him asylum. *Makhzan-i-Afghani*, I, 407.

7. When the imperial army came and encircled his fortification, he arranged his army and hastened to give fight. The Afghan amirs who were vexed with him took to heel without giving fight. A Khwajasara of Baz Bahadur, under orders from him, struck a few blows at his consort, named Rupmati, in whose name he used to compose Hindi verses so that she was not taken alive. His entire possessions, servants and inmates of the harem fell into the hands of Adham Khan. In spite of the fact that Rupmati was wounded, Adham Khan with great craving (for her) summoned her to his private apartments. She at once took poison and died. Adham Khan reported the facts of the victory to the imperial court (but) retaining the property, courtesans, dancing girls and all inmates of the harem of Baz Bahadur, he sent only a few elephants through Sadiq Khan. *ZK*, 251.

8. On 21st Shaban, A.H. 968/27th April, 1561 A.D. When the emperor came to know the fact, related to Adham Khan, he set out in person to Malwa, reached Sarangpur and put up in the lodging of Adham Khan. He made an offering of whatever cash, goods, booty, etc. he had obtained, along with something more, to His Majesty, and was honoured. *Ibid.* 251, *MT*, II, 48 and *Zubda*, fol. 107-a, while Abul Fazl says on 28th Shaban/5th April and the emperor returned to Agra on 19th Ramzan/4th June. *AN*, II. 143-44.

9. Other sources are silent about it.

10. Abdullah Khan Uzbek was a great amir (and) held a mansab of 5000. *ZK*, 329. Khan-i-zaman and Bahadur Khan marched from Jaunpur. They performed the rites of respects (Taslim) and presented elephants and rarities. Khilats were bestowed upon them with horses. *AN*, II, 146-148 and *Zubda*, fol.107-a.

11. Baz Bahadur went to Rani Durgawati, stayed (there) for some time and in the year A.H. 978/1570 A.D., he presented himself at the royal court. He was granted a mansab of 3000 and horse and maintained (his) honour and dignity. His heart-alluring verses in Hindi language are widely known in Hindustan. The story of his love for Rupmati is well-known. *ZK*, 252. See also *TA*, II, 442 and III, 424; *MU*, I, 387; *AN*, II, 139 and 358; *Zubda*, fols. 106-a-b and *Farishta*, I, 25 and II, 273.

OCCURRENCE 11

Description of the Assassination of Khan-i-Azam Atga Khan and the Retribution of Adham Khan Forthwith

Khaqan Akbar showed exceptional kindness to Khan-i-Azam Atga Khan. A band of nobles (amirs and Khans) conspired with Adham Khan, who was his foster brother, and made him understand that it was very necessary to make an end of him. Adham Khan being carried away by the complaints of those jealous persons began to hate the Khan. Vipers of antagonism which were present in the circles of hospitality, were therefore talking aloud about the flood of that quarrel which had become full with the drops of cloud of enmity, began to flow and the plant of turmoil which had been irrigated by the canal of hatred (p. 70), the waves of hatred which were keeping quiet for long became restless, until on Saturday, the 12th of Ramazan, A.H. 969/16th May, 1562 A.D., having been instigated by those jealous men Adham Khan[1] s/o Maham Anga,[2] entered the office of Khan-i-Azam,[3] where many other nobles and amirs were also present, and ordered one of his attendants to kill him by his sword. The whole world knows that the consequence of quarrel is ruin and nothing else, and the retribution of violence and tyranny can only be in one's ruin. Wisdom was speaking the following with thousand tongues:

Bait (verse)

You will see that one moment of giving him pain makes the doer of wrong weak.

His Majesty (Khaqan Akbar) according to the Law of the Quran, viz. 'Life For Life', issued the farman that Adham

Khan be dragged up to the top of fort (Agra) and be hurled head down from there. This is how he lost his life.

Misraa (*a hemistich*)

The sky guffawed that this incident was the result of his deed and the fire of mischief was extinguished by the water of justice.

Bait (*verse*)

When thine have committed a serious fault do not sit at ease without caring for possible calamity, because nature must inevitably wrest vengeance.

A poet has described the date of the death of Adham Khan in a poem. (p. 71)

Abiyat (*verses*)

That fresh rose soon went to paradise. He could not enjoy life for long. His date of death is found in the words:

"The light of both eyes departed".

Duaa (*prayer*) *for His Majesty*

May the rules and regulations of the state and administration, the foundation of the prestige and success remain full with the blessings of justice and may the gracious shadow of the king ever cover his subjects!

NOTES

1. In A.H. 970/1562-63 A.D., Adham Khan Kokaltash who had no rival in propinquity and rank, out of haughtiness of position, youth and affluence, at the instigation of Shihabuddin Ahmad Khan, killed in the open court, Shamsuddin Muhammad Atga Khan, who was the vakil of the kingdom. Then due to pride and insolence and confidence he had in the protection of the emperor, he fled and remained standing at the door out of the inner royal apartments. His Majesty, having come out from within, managed to take away his sword, from his person by clever device, tied his neck and hands and threw him down from the terrace and (thus) punished him. He also punished the group of people who had taken part in this mischief. At that time, everybody had withdrawn to a corner. Of them, Munim Khan and Muhammad Qasim, Mir Bakhshi, having crossed the Jamuna, destroyed the bridge.

Shahabuddin Khan also went hiding. *ZK*, 125. See also *MU*, I, 67, *TA*, *MT*, *AN* and *NM*.

2. The Turki word Anga means 'nurse', and specially 'wetnurse'. She was one of the foster nurses of Akbar, wife of Nadim Khan. After the assasination of Adham Khan, she fell ill on account of grief and anguish. She died after forty days of her son's death. *Ibid*. See also R.P. Tripathy, *Maham Anga and Akbar*. IHC, 1922.

3. Shamsuddin (Muhammad Khan Atga) enjoyed the title of Khan Azam. He had risen to the position of an amir and a vakil and had become vakil, with absolute power. He was killed by Adham Khan. Two murders took place on the date (of his death) A.H. 970/1562-63 A.D. *ZK*, 80. See also *TA*, *MT*, *AN*, *NM* and *MU*, I, 67.

OCCURRENCE 12

Description of Posting and March of Mir Muhammad Khan and His Brothers for the Chastisement of Adam Khan Kakar and His Assassination with His Ill-Starred Son

In the year A.H. 970/1563 A.D., news reached the ears of the emperor that Adam Khan Kakar,[1] his son and followers, having abandoned the track of righteousness, have adopted the path of enmity, dispute and rebellion.[2] For admonition of the horde of mischief, which was destined ultimately to feel ashamed and earn a bad name, the emperor appointed Mir Muhammad Khan[3] and Atga nobles to uproot and destroy the said Kakars. Mir Muhammad Khan with his brothers left with this commission. The fast moving army with all its deadly equipment reached the land of Kakars and pitched its camp (may the guide of good luck bring the news of victory to the army!) there; it soon surrounded the regions which were their hideout, became the centres of the flags of Islam. The land which had become the hotbed of sedition and riot became the stable of horses of *Jehad* (holy war). All those persons who were assisting the rebels began to feel like a half-wounded cock(s) or like fish caught in a net. Soon the deadly fired arrows began to act as messengers and swords sending messages. So much noise started that its echo rocked the ears in a (p. 72) most frightful manner. The wailings of sufferers could even hike mountains from their seats. In a single onslaught, a large number of villages, hills and narrow places where even the air reached with difficulty, were captured. Heaps of property, cattle and prisoners, having been defeated and ruined, fell into the hands of the imperial army. The wealth which was collected by them was also taken into possession. Adam Khan, the chief or leader of the mischievous horde, fell down from the top of the hill and thus licked the dust of humiliation.[4] In short, being unable to face the world-burning wrath, he vanished into the air like a particle of dust and his sons too were killed. His companions when they saw that plight, started coming under the banner of protection. Victory came to the strong hand of state. The rest who survived fled away. A letter containing the details of happenings was sent to the emperor, who, keeping due consideration of deserving rewards, entrusted the land under the charge of Kamal Khan Kakar and made it a part of the province of Lahore and Punjab. Thereafter, the Khans returned to their respective jagirs and vilayats.[5]

Duaa (*prayer*) *for His Majesty*

May the stars of greatness, grandeur and victorious continue to flutter over the country of success, and may these illuminate the kingdom, rising from Khaqan Akbar!

NOTES

1. Abul Fazl also mentions Kakar. *AN*, II, 190 while Badauni says Khakar. *MT*, II, 54. "It is related to Gakhad which is the name of a tribe". *MU*, III, 144. For details see also *Zubda* and *Balukh Maun.*
2. For the earlier chastisement of Gakkars by Humayun and Akbar see *Zubda*, fol. 110-a.
3. Mir Muhammad Khan, Bahadur Atga Khan was (the elder brother of Shamsuddin Atga Khan) entitled exalted Khan was one of the great nobles. He was an expert poet in Persian and Turkish languages and had the title of Ghaznavi. He was an expert musician also. He died in Pattan, Gujarat in the month of Ramzan, A.H. 983/December, 1575 A.D. *MU*, I and III, 211 and *MT*, III, 287. See also *TM, TA, AN, NM,* and *HJ.*
4. *AN*, II, 194.
5. Kamal Khan, son of Sultan Sarang Khan was the Sardar of Gakkar tribe, who made peace with Sher Shah but the latter killed him and his son was imprisoned in the fort of Gwalior. Sultan Adam, brother of Sarang Khan, escaped. He offered to surrender and requested that the mansab of his father be granted to him. But Akbar did not agree to it. He however, was imprisoned in A.H. 972/1564 A.D. *A.N.*, II, 302. See also *Zubda*, fol. 110-b and *TA*, II, 437.

OCCURRENCE 13

Description of the Return of Shah Abu-al-Maàli from Madina Mukaram and Bait-ul-Haram to Hind via Gujarat, His Escape to Kabul, His Exercising Authority over There and Some Other Events, Occurred During the Time in Question (p. 73)

Because the Qazi of the department of destiny had written it, which was an everlasting fact, in the book (of destiny) that the power of kingdom should remain in the hands of Shah Abu-al-Maali, who was in prison in the fort of Bayana, when (Bairam Khan) reached thereafter being rebellious, he was released by him and sent to the capital. The unruly behaviour which he had exhibited, got him rearrested and he remained in prison for some more time. Realizing that even the intervention of amirs and Khans before whom he supplicated on his behalf, it was not easy for him to secure his release. Ultimately, his supplication reached the august ears and the tongue of his pen was repeating the following verse:

Bait (verse)

Separating from thou, O my beloved, is becoming unbearable more and more; Pray, be kind to this unblessed as this sort of life is torture!

The emperor's merciful heart moved and Abu-al-Maali was permitted to proceed to the Holy Mecca. Having performed his pilgrimage, he returned in A.H. 971/1564 A.D. and reached Gujarat.[1]

During the same time, Mirza Sharfuddin Husain,[2] owing to the ill-advice of certain evil-minded persons, turned rebellious and reached Gujarat. They met on the way. Mirza proposed that they should move to Nagore. Mirza put his troops[3] under the charge of Abu-al-Maali and they reached Nagore. They began to create trouble in the pargana of Dandwanah.[4] Husain Quli Khan entitled Khan-i-Jahan, in-charge over there was killed by them. (p. 74) Then they proceeded further and chanced to meet the uncle of the deceased Khan, Ahmad Sultan Zulqadar.[5] A skirmish followed, which resulted in his death. They entered into Narnol where they destroyed and plundered the property of Gesu Khan,[6] the *shiqdar*. They captured a large booty and left for Lahore along with Gesu Khan. The latter was allowed to go back from Lahore. Abu-al-Maali reached Kabul with lightning speed, but with safety, although Tatar Khan[7] and other chiefs did their best to check him. Thus he earned the merit of great bravery. During the same time, Nawab Muhammad Hakim Mirza,[8] who was still a child, was with his mother Mah Chuchak Begum,[9] wife of late Humayun, a very wise and clever lady, who was administering Kabul (Mirza Hakim's principality). She ruled very benevolently and maintained the welfare and happiness of her subjects. As Shah Abu-al-Maali reached Kabul, he solemnly assured loyalty to her and offered to abide by rules and regulations of the state. He submitted a petition that it was his firm resolve to serve under her, and it reads like this:

Bait (*verse*)

I have come to this door to obtain high dignity and status, but on account of bad state of affairs (in Hindustan), I have come to seek shelter.

In fact, Shah Abu-al-Maali had no equal in valour and cleverness. He had served under the late emperor (Humayun) for long and had given a good proof of his courage and bravery. In consequence, the mother of Hakim Mirza married her daughter[10] (sister of Hakim) to him. When he ascended the throne of Kabul, people were happy though his reign did not last long In the very beginning, he killed all those amirs whom he considered to be an obstacle in his way of capturing the throne, and paid no heed to the

Begum. Soon the insanity of power and position intoxicated his mind and he decided to punish some other amirs but suddenly he decided to kill the Begum. He entered the palace and (p. 75) slew the Begum with his sword in cold blood. This incident took place on 13th Shaban, A.H. 971/27th March, 1564 A.D.[11] Like all foolish people, he did not think of the consequences of this ghastly act. Next morning, the news of the murder of Begum spread and the people came to know of it. His action was naturally resented by all the amirs and they executed Haider Qasim Khan,[12] his brother[13] and all others who were suspected to be part of that nefarious deed. Then they pledged their loyalty with the deceased and decided to run the administration of the state themselves. Some of the amirs, such as Baqi Qaqshal,[14] Tardi Muhammad,[15] Hasan Khan[16] and Banda Ali Maidani[17] formed a group and attacked the capital after two or three days. A bloody battle ensued which resulted in the killing of many persons on both sides. Shah Abu-al-Maali however, acted with great courage and presence of mind and succeeded in bringing his men out of the fort. Thereafter, he sent Haji Muhammad Qasim, brother of late Qasim Khan, to Badakhshan to secure help from its ruler, Nawab Shah Sulaiman Mirza.[18] The emissaries of Shah Abu-al-Maali conveyed the fact to the Shah, i.e. misdeeds of the former, seen by them. They further entreated him to suppress (quench) by the water of his sword the fire of tumult and disturbance which was being fanned by the wind of overwhelming pride and vanity of Shah Abu-al-Maali. They prayed that there was no other solution of this storm except it. On their prayer the Nawab at once, without a moment's delay, marched from Badakhshan towards Kabul. He had such a numerous army with him that its grandeur even shook mountains there. On hearing of the coming of army to Badakhshan, shah Abu-al-Maali collected his troops and went out, although he knew well that the eye of the sun could not be covered (deceived) by cheating or flattery, and there was no sense in trying to dig mountains by means of nails. But when the mirror of a man's fate becomes blind and the eyes of hope are closed, every moment he invites the swords of misfortune by the magnet of his foolishness. (p. 76) The hordes of Badakhshan reached Kabul. The two forces came face to face, arranged their ranks in battle array and fighting started. All the faces were hidden behind the dark clouds of battle and a brisk struggle to capture the enemy was began. Abu-al-Maali gave evidence of such marvellous valour and practice of throwing the lances that watching it even the soul of Rustam had words of praise. The army of Badakhshan attacked with zeal like the waves of a sea and changed the map of the battle. Soon Shah Abu-al-Maali realized that the days of his power and might were turning against him and the night of misfortune had also come for him to face; he for one moment thought of fleeing the field, accompanied by a few companions, but his conveyance as well as all his plans failed. He was arrested and brought before His Majesty and the sun of his life slid down the limit of decline.

Bait (*verse*)

It is inevitable that he who does evil will suffer misfortune.

Those forces which are devoid of the sense of ministership and which consider matters of experience and wisdom as of no use and which without any forethought interfere in the affairs of administration and do not appreciate the evil resulting from hastiness (safety lies in going slow) and do not think before acting, in the end the waves of misfortune overwhelm them. Persons who are thus drowned in the sea of carelessness, begin to understand but the bate of their hopes are shattered and the wealth of their light which is the most precious possession is wasted in such a manner as in their youth. They run after the mirage only to find that their hopes are belied when they reach near it (those are the people in whose mind, eyes and ears, Allah has put a seal).

Duaa (*prayer*) *for His Majesty*

May the glory, grandeur and pride of His Majesty of the world continue to grow more and more every moment and may stars of his good luck rise higher and higher every hour! (p. 77)

NOTES

1. Abul Fazl confirms the date given by Arif. *AN*, II, 198 while Badauni says, "A.H. 970/1562 A.D." *MT*, II, 62.
2. Mirza Sharfuddin Husain, son of Khwaja Moinuddin, rose to the position of amir. He waged battle against the empire, but at last he was arrested and passed his quite time in custody. Later he was relesed on the recommendation of Muzaffar Khan, but he joined the band of rebels again. He was killed in A.H. 988/1580 A.D. by Masum Khan Kabuli. *Zubda,* fol. 112-b, *ZK*, 80 and *MU*, III, 308. See also *AN*, *SS* and *TM*.
3. According to Abul Fazl, "Three hundred personal servants". *AN*, II, 198.
4. Dandwana. *MU*, III, 164. It is situated near Sanbhar (Rajputana).
5. Ahmad Sultan, son of Shadi Beig Zulqadar, brother of Wali Beig Zulqadar, was a close friend of Bairam Khan. *AN*, II, 200.
6. Gesu Khan commonly known as Mir Gesu Khurasani, was one of the important nobles of Akbar. He was killed by his servants on the day of Id-ul-Fitr, A.H. 991/1583 A.D. at Meerut. *MU*, III, 249. See also *AN* and *TM*.
7. Tatar Khan, his real name was Khwaja Tahir Muhammad Khurasani, was one of the nobles of Akbari period and he reached to the position of Wazir. In A.H. 975/1567-68 A.D. he died in Delhi. *ZK*, 222 and *MU*, I, 471.
8. Muhammad Hakim Mirza was the step-brother of Emperor Akbar, born of Mah Chuchak Begum, wife of Humayun.
9. Badauni and Bihamad call her Mah Jau Jauk Begum. *MT*, II, 58 and *TM*. Abul Fazl says, "Mah Chu Chuk Begum". *AN*, II, 204 while Mah Chu Chak Begum. *TA*, II, 167 and *Tazkira Biyat*.
10. Her name was Fakhru-n-Nisa Begum. *AN*, II, 25.
11. *AN*, *TM* and *TA* confirm the said date while Badauni says in the month of Shaban, A.H. 971/March, 1564 A.D. *MT*, II, 58.
12. Haider Qasim Khan Kohkar, entitled Khan-i-Khanan, pseudonym Sabri was killed in the early days of *Shaban*. For details see *ibid*.
13. His brother's name was Muhammad Qasim. *MT*, II, 59 and *TA*, II, 168.
14. Nizamuddin says Baqi Qaqshal. *TA*, II, 168 while Baqi Muhammad Khan Qaqshal. *Zubda*, fol. 114.
15. Abul Fazl says, "Tardi Muhammad Khan Maidani". *AN*, II, 206 while Tardi Muhammad Khan, *TA*, II, 168. Tardi Muhammad. *Zubda*, fol. 114.

16. Hasan Khan. *Tazkira Bayat*, 261. Khuwesh Shahab Khan. *AN*, II, 187. Nizamuddin says that he was the brother of Shahabuddin Ahmad Khan. *TA*, II, 168.
17. Bande Ali Maidani was posted in the 9th Regnal year with Mirza Muhammad Hakim. He held a mansab of 350 and remained alive up to A.H. 995/1587 A.D. *AN*, II, 299 and III, 519.
18. He was the ruler of Badakhshan. (His account will be given in the foregoing pages).

OCCURRENCE 14

Description of His Majesty's Being Wounded, His Recovery after a Few Days and His March for Mandu Again

When His Majesty got the intelligence of the return of Shah Abu-al-Maali from Haj, he immediately started from Agra towards Delhi and sent few sardars with some force in pursuit of him as had already been recorded.[1]

The emperor passed a few days in Delhi. It seemed to be the intention of destiny to put the seal of perfection on the forehead of the emperor. It happened like this. One day the emperor, riding a fast moving horse, went out hunting. While he was returning and was nearing the city,[2] all of a sudden a man[3] hurled an arrow at him which wounded him in the back, i.e. to say on the back of that august person under which the whole world is sheltered. Because under all circumstances, God's blessings and prayers of pious persons and believers in Him are always with the incomparable personality of the king and because on account of the king and people of the world enjoy all necessities of peace and comfort, therefore the fruit of their prayer is in this:

Misraa (a hemistich)

The prayers of seclusionists prevent accidents and misfortunes.

The arrow did not prove very harmful, though the wound was deep. That wretched person along with his companions was cut to pieces and their heads were chopped off.[4]

Bait (verse)

The lance and sword which the enemy threw upon you

boomeranged and pierced the chest of the enemy himself. (p. 78)

Suddenly the prayers of the people rose up to the sky and there was a noise as to how such a thing had happened. The people came out of their houses and began to run. Nevertheless, His Majesty returned to the fort on his horse and allowed all the people to enter it. Immediately, physicians and surgeons began their treatment of the emperor. So his wound was healed soon. After four days His Majesty along with his close associates went back to Agra[5] by boat.[6] This frightful incident took place in the beginning of the month of Rajab (February, 1564 A.D.).[7] His Majesty, however, was all right after a few days because the might of his youth threw away the dust of indisposition from the apron of his blessed temperament. Though the saints and sufis continued to recite the following:

All the praise is due to the Almighty who takes away all our sorrows. Undoubtedly our God is the giver of comfort. The people continued their prayer with sincerity, humility and humbleness.

Qita (*distich*)

Thy body need not be beholden to the physicians, and your tender person may not have to suffer any ailment or pain.

On the 20th of Ziqada, A.H. 971/1st July, 1564 A.D.[8] the sun like personality of the emperor thought of going for elephant-hunting[9] and he left for the vilayat of Narwar.[10] Elephant-hunting had become a regular practice in the time of His Majesty (Akbar). He has imparted too much splendour to this art by inventing techniques for capturing elephants that were never known or practised before. The emperor went towards Malwa and Mandu in the course of his hunting expedition. When he reached the Qasba (town) of Sironj[11] and proceeded further the rainy season started and the passage was not felt fit for his movement, accompanied by a large army. Consequently every member of the party had to suffer much trouble. But when the emperor encamped at Mandu[12] all their fatigue disappeared due to the cool-refreshing air of the clean and wide open (p. 79) countryside and they felt greatly comforted. Undoubtedly the country or region of Mandu had no parallel in the entire Hindustan. By its wonderful buildings even the renowned architects were amazed at their magnificent sense. There is a palace resembling Shish Mahal in comparison to which even the reputation of the palace of Bahramgarh and others simply vanished. The bricks of its roof stand in comparison with the Moon and the Sun. The world is helpless in producing anything like it. It is rather impossible to find anything comparable to it either in actual existence or even in imagination.[13]

It is such a fort that in strength it can be compared to the palace of the Pahlavis[14] and the deep trench around it is full of fish. There is a hill on one side of Mandu where even the imagination of courageous men cannot reach its height and even the vision of farsighted persons is unable to assess its height and the lofty top of its hills which are always covered with the tents of cloud. And inside its walls the fireworks of swords are constantly playing.[15]

As Abdullah Khan Uzbek, one of the servants of the empire and incharge of the province of Malwa and Mandu, was extremely sad and sorrowful because he had been very cruel and tyrannical. He tried to draw a line on water, i.e. to harbour the thought of revolt. God, who is the correct guide, put in the heart of the emperor that it was absolutely necessary to put an end to the life of that mischievous person. He resolved to destroy him and he moved the victorious banner in the direction of Ujjain. (p. 80)

His Majesty, taking some of his selected soldiers, advanced further with the intention of launching an attack. Abdullah Khan saw the march of fortunate army in an auspicious moment and realized that the eyes of the people were filled with amazement at the dazzling rays of that horde, and they inquired from which forest "has this lion come to prey and from which nest has this Huma come flying". When he realized and satisfied himself fully that the incomer was the emperor and none else, he then found that there was no way out for his escape but to flee because his defeat was dead sure. What is the comparison between an elephant and a mosquito. A blade of grass cannot rival a mountain. He, therefore fled and took refuge in Gujarat. But the emperor went in his pursuit and took all his relatives and followers wherever they were found as prisoners. Finally, the emperor marched back after capturing his elephants.[16]

An other skirmish was awaiting him on his way. The emperor had to fight the Girasias[17] who were finally overpowered. When he eventually became free from all these tasks, he left in safety for the capital with the army and enormous spoils of wars. Thus the emperor returned to Agra and occupied the glorious throne.

During the same time, news arrived that Ali Quli Khan, Bahadur and Sikandar Khan Uzbek, leaving the right way, have adopted the path of hostility and rebellion. Therefore the emperor marched out against them in Shawwal, A.H. 972/May, 1565 A.D. He reached Jaunpur on 14th Zi-Hijja, A.H. 972 (Friday, 15th July, 1565 A.D.).[18]

Duaa (prayer) for His Majesty

May thy throne and palace remain full of prosperity and grace by the mercy and blessing of God for ever and ever, and may the evil-eye remain far away from the glory and grandeur of the emperor! (p. 81)

Notes

1. For details see *AN*, II, 20, *Zubda* fol. 113-b and *MT* II, 60.
2. He was near the Madarsa-i-Maham Anga. *NM*, fol. 190-a, *TA*, II, 167 and *MT*, II, 62.
3. Qatlaq Faulad, servant of Sharfuddin Mirza. *TA*, II, 167. Koka Faulad. *MT*, II, 62; Kudak Faulad. *Zubda* fol. 113-b.
4. He was killed immediately with a sharp sword. *TA*, II, 167 while he was burnt. *NM*, fol. 191-a.
5. On 6th Jamadi II/21st January he left for Agra and reached on 15th Jamadi/30th January of the said month A.H. 971/1564 A.D. *TA*, II, 167.

6. Abul Fazl also mentions by boat. *AN*, II, 203, *TA*, II, 167 and *MT*, II, 62 while Singhasan, *Zubda*, fol. 113-b.
7. Abul Fazl also says in the month of Rajab/February. *AN*, II, 201 while Badauni says in A.H. 970/1563 A.D. *MT*, II, 62.
8. Abul Fazl also mentions the same date. *AN*, II, 221 and *NM*, fol. 191-a while Badauni and Nizamuddin say 12th. *MT*, II, 67 and *TA*, II, 171.
9. Lakhna elephant was very dear to Akbar and it fell into the Narbada river and drowned. *Zubda*, fol. 116-b and *TA*, II, 171.
10. Narwar, a district, situated in Gwalior.
11. Saronj, earlier in Malwa.
12. He reached Mandu on Thursday, 2nd Muharram, A.H. 972/10th August, 1564 A.D. *AN*, II, 229 while Badauni and Nizamuddin say on close of the month Zi-Hijja, A.H. 971/July, 1564 A.D. *MT*, II, 67 and *TA*, II, 173.
13. Qita has been left. See p. 79.
14. A dynasty of kings of Persia.
15. Qita has been left. See p. 79.
16. Abdullah Khan Uzbek reached Sarangpur. For details see *MU*, II, 765, *Zubda*, fol. 116-a, *TA*, II, 172 and *MT*, II, 67.
17. A tribe or gang of persons whose profession is to live on robbery.
18. The emperor started from Agra on 3rd Rabi-ul-Awwal, A.H. 972/9th October, 1564 A.D. *AN*, II, 235, *MT*, II, 69 and *TA*, II, 274.

OCCURRENCE 15

Description of the Sedition of the Wretched Band of Ali Quli, Ill-Starred and Bahadur, the Mean and the March of Imperial Army for Their Suppression

When in the beginning of A.H. 972/August, 1564 A.D. Abdullah, the mischief-maker, fled away to save himself and Mandu was also conquered in the following year, Ali Quli and Bahadur,[1] who were hostile to the emperor, challenged the imperial forces and they spread the net of craft and fraud everywhere. Ali Quli was the ring leader and head of the rebels; he was like a python and occupied a place of honour among them. He was determined to upset the foundation of the government. He used the misguided Abdullah as a tool and encouraged him by means of his evil designs and strengthened his ungrateful plans by regulating them carefully. Alas! when the real flame of the soul is dead, it is useless to warm up parts of the body. When the garden becomes a victim of destructive wind or storm, then the cool breeze of morning cannot revive its refreshing beauty.

Bait (*verse*)

How can a weak and feeble person become strong by jealousy? How can a man, whose body is swelled up, be really called stout?

Being beguiled and misled by Satan, he began to be disloyal and following in the footsteps of *Iblis* (Satan) got entangled in the net of craftiness and deceit. He had a battalion fully equipped and ready to fight, and he therefore entered into an alliance with the army of ill-starred Sikandar, stationed with his horde in battle-array near the river Ganga, with the intention of starting battle. He hoped that the lofty sun of the empire would be eclipsed by his unleashing trouble, and that the sky of good luck would also fall a prey to chase and fear by the coming of clouds.

Bait (verse)

The spell of imagination of Pharoh (Firaun) has no power when Kalimullah (Moses) himself shows a miracle.

He forgot that the emperor wanted successful and skilful deeds and not deceitful and fraudulent practices. (p. 82)

Bait (verse)

It is destined by the spirit of age that to rule this country is the business of noble men.

Though the wisdom, proper guide, was proclaiming that these nonentities cannot match with Kai-Khusrau, only the sword of lightning can pierce the hill tops, and the shield of clouds can alone cover the disc of the sun.

Bait (verse)

Thy lion's paw resembles the wild animal of the cave, so that the stag has to submit humbly.

In short, his vision had become clouded and rendered him unable to see the right course. False ambition thus threw that band of mischief-mongers into misery. At last the emperor came to know that that ill-starred person was preparing and training a force consisting of Hindustanis, the Afghans and the Uzbek soldiers with the help of dirty Sikandar, who at that time happened to be in the region of Awadh for battle, and that there was nothing better in his head than creating sedition and chaos.

Bait (verse)

He had collected a number of stray and evil-minded persons, just as the water of a river collects dirty mud.

In the midst of such happenings, the emperor appointed the praiseworthy amir Ashraf Khan,[2] Mir Mal[3] to proceed against him. He was honoured with a special robe (*Khilat-i-*

Khasa) and studded sword with the requisite equipments. He was entrusted the charge to bring that group of mischief-mongers to the right path. Hence, keeping in view the emperor's advice and instructions, the just noble used restraint and politeness in his dealings.

Bait (*verse*)

Bad luck vanished from our head just as the mention of reckless drunkards rousth amusement. (p. 83)

It is sacred that the habit of disloyalty be weakened by good treatment and the movements of hostility and rebelliousness may be brought to an end by means of invitation or homage. In any circumstance the responsibility of the safety of life and property (of people) is the chief function and attribute of the administration and the duty of protecting the ambitions of people is the function and responsibility of kingly might.

Bait (*verse*)

We behold this ancient custom. You should not be disobedient so that you may not have to suffer.

When the above-mentioned Khan entered that territory, he tried to carry out the instructions of the emperor to the best of his ability and without compromising in any way the honour and obeisance due to him. While observing fully the imperial orders, he persuaded the rebels to surrender. But despite all his efforts, he failed to achieve his object.

Bait (*verse*)

The man whose words and intentions vary, deserves to be pierced (in the heart) by a scimitar.

In spite of these circumstances, Naqabat Panah was not allowed to return. When the emperor learnt the existing situation, in hot weather had set in full fury; wind was unable to give shelter from the sun, iron melted on the stones, sparks shot out even from stones in water, just as those that come from a magnet.[4] (p. 84) Although the emperor was requested to go to the western side where the climate was different and even in winter the season is not different from summer. The fire of kingly wrath and zeal burst forth and he made a firm resolve to march. The nobles and amirs prayed with great humility that His Majesty may postpone his pious determination for some time and suspend the despatch of imperial army till the end of the hot season. The emperor did not accept it and their efforts remained futile. The victorious army, though it had made no preparations, nor had the military officials, made proper arrangements for the stages of camping. That very day His Majesty mounted on his world-conquering horse and he marched out of the city (on Thursday, the 24th Shawwal,[5] A.H. 972/26th May, 1565 A.D.). The emperor passed a few days outside the city in order to give time to the soldiers to get themselves equipped with the requisite arrangements. Thereafter he moved away and the imperial army obeyed the royal command. When the notorious rebels heard about the expedition, they realized that the matter had slipped out of their hands and that they were lost. But they still continued to make a show of their bravery and grandeur. In short, when the royal army advanced in the said manner, and illumined the land with the lights of heaven, then the rebels felt that the hawk was about to fall into the king's trap and the ant was to roll in the dust at the feet of elephants, they gave up all their designs of battle and adopted means of cheating and deception. They desisted from fighting and closed themselves in mutual consultations. The imperial army crossed the river Ganga and advanced towards Jaunpur. Meanwhile, the ill-starred (p. 85) Sikandar and Ibrahim,[6] ignoble, approaching the vicinity of Lucknow,[7] laid a siege to the fort of Neemakara,[8] occupied by Umdat-ul-Ayab, Shah Badagh Khan.[9] Skirmishes took place several times between the two forces, because the courageous army had come well prepared. At last they (rebels) lost heart because they were in no position to face the imperial onslaught. Therefore, on the 2nd night, they lifted the siege, came and received the blessings by kissing the emperor's feet. His Majesty sent a force of amirs towards Awadh which was conferred on Sikandar as his jagir. To the command of the army he appointed Zafar Panah Naqabat Khan,[10] Amir Muizul Mulk and Zubdat-ul-Khwanin Lashkar Khan[11] was made mir bakhshi. As the amir entered the frontiers of Awadh, Muhammad Yaar,[12] the evil-doer, who was a close relative of Sikandar challenged them. Immediately, a clash started which turned into flames of battle. The imperial army crushed it and Muhammad Yaar was sent to hell.[13]

Bait (verse)

Who can resist your attack; how can a fox acquire the strength of a lion?

During the confusion, Bahadur the coward, began making much noise from the left side. Ali Quli received the news of the defeat of Bahadur's army while he was besieging Manikpur. He was also informed that the imperial army was approaching there fast so he visualized that a mosquito cannot have the courage to oppose an elephant, nor can a piece of straw dream of clashing against a mountain.[14] He therefore ran for safety towards Jaunpur.[15] Consequently, the emperor also decided to move in that direction and the reins of the army also turned towards Jaunpur. When the rebels realized the approach of the imperial army, they found no other way except flight from there. He handed over the fort of Jaunpur to his mother and Ashraf Khan, who had been deputed earlier to bring him to reason and sense, left for the district of Saidpur.[16] (p. 86) The people hearing of the presence of evil-mongers started moving to and fro in panic. But when His Majesty, with his natural benevolence and dignity reached the town of Jaunpur on Friday, the 14th Zi-hijja[17]/14th July (1565 A.D.) of the above-mentioned year, and settled himself there, the inhabitants of the place, who were expecting all sorts of favours and friendly relation, had a sigh of relief because the claws of tyranny were no more to scratch them.

Bait (*verse*)

The large-hearted emperor by his charitable deeds treated the people very generously.

When the rebels learnt of the advent of the imperial army in the region of Jaunpur, they ran to Ghazipur with all their property and equipment. After crossing the river Sarwal,[18] they escaped to Kandana[19] which was a pargana inhabited by the Afghan. Shaharyar Turkman[20] was a trusted friend of them. He helped them to cross the river course safely and led them in the fort of Kopa[21] which is also called Jeet(garh). During the same time, Asaf Khan[22] left for the vilayat of Rani (Durgawati).[23]

When the heavy rain stopped and the water course subsided, the exalted Majnun Khan,[24] who was with Nawab Khan Khanan at Buxar, was appointed the Sardar and was despatched with the army for the suppression of the evildoer, Shaharyar. During the same time Ali Quli, the mean and contemptible, passing the Ashura, i.e. 10th of Muharram, A.H. 973/8th August, 1566 A.D. crossed the river Sarwal, and landed in the village Tirmuhani. Majnun Khan inflicted a severe defeat on the worthless Shaharyar and destroyed all his camp and equipment completely. The wretched fellow, however managed to reach the bank of river Tirmuhani. As Ali Quli had maintained the possession of boats there, Shaharyar boarded a boat and thus escaped with his life. (p. 87) At this time Nawab Khan Khanan was at Buxar. Ali Quli expressed great penitence and begged forgiveness and he also came forward to the banks of the Ganga which was close to (Buxar). Through the Khan, he submitted his petition to the imperial court.

Now the battle which existed between fire and water was over; and the difference of parties had come to an end, and he had supplicated that he would come by boat from his side while Khan Khanan from the other and the two would meet in midstream and thus with the intervention and recommendation of the former his humble submission would be accepted as (good in his mutual agreement) has been said in the holy Quran, and this advice may be fulfilled for the emperor. And if the opposing parties intend to bring about reconciliation, then Allah helps them in their noble intentions. The benefits of such actions are soon expressed.

Bait (*verse*)

The emperor comprehended the recommendation of the good natured Khan and granted his blessed words. As it was considered advisable that the good of the country consisted in accepting the apology and fulfil the request of man. The king therefore like a man of charity, gave those enemies, prizes, rewards as well as *Khilat-i-Fakhra*, studded-swords, belts and horses. In spite of all the extended generosity and good treatment by the emperor, the enemy was always guilty, nervous and remained haunted with fears and suspicions. His lips smiled having attained his desire but his heart wept being always afraid of revenge (of his misdeeds). Although the emperor had bestowed on his mother and Mirza Arab,[25] his trusted friend, the territory of Jaunpur, and himself remained in the fort of Chunar.[26] The fact was that those people had nothing better in their mind except meanness and sedition. They abandoned the imperial shelter and brushing aside all the generous treatment given to them, they once again declared rebellion and disloyalty. (p. 88)

Bait (*verse*)

I knew that you would break your promises and oaths, but I did not know that you would do so soon.

During the same time it was decided that the exalted amir, Ashraf Khan should keep his mother under his shelter. The king proceeded from Chunar to Banaras and from there he led a campaign up to Ghazipur to arrest Ali Quli but the latter escaped that very night. The emperor chased him and expelled him beyond the river Narhind.[27] That shameless and imprudent fellow fled towards the hills beyond Bahraich.

At the same time Bahadur, Sikandar and Ibrahim, the wretched persons, were present in the boundaries of Awadh and Sarwal. When they came to know that the mother of Ali

Quli was being looked after properly, they felt free and took advantage of it by leading an expedition and entered the region of Jaunpur. On the same day they stormed entry from all sides in the fort of Jaunpur. Bahadur then carried his mother along with Ashraf and occupied it. Thereafter they left for Kara. He left that region for those ill-starred fellows and retreated towards the capital, and on Monday the 18th Shaban, A.H. 973/11th March, 1566 A.D., entered Kara[28] (Agra). Short-sighted fellows thought the retreat a bolt on the grandeur of the might of the emperor. They did not know that the return of moon and Jupiter could not bring any bolt on the sky. What fear is there to the river from ebb and tide (flood)? The emperor would have thought retreat to be good or advisable. The heavens had not fallen or the Day of Judgement had not dawn if the royal sun moved from one place to another. . . . God says "You are ever near Me and retreat is better at such a time which will be a blessing for you."[29] (p. 89)

Bait (verse)

Everything which is difficult in the beginning but fate brings happiness in the end.

NOTES

1. Bahadur, Muhammad Saeed entitled Bahadur Khan, son of Haider Sultan Uzbek Shaibani, was one of the great nobles of Humayun and Akbar. He joined his rebel brother and was arrested. According to imperial farman he was assassinated in Ziqada, A.H. 974/May, 1567 A.D. For details see *TM, MT, TA, NM, AN, SS* and *HI*.
2. Ashraf Khan was one of the accomplished men of the time. The name of that unique one was Muhammad Asghar. He was an Arab-Shahi Saiyed. He wrote seven styles of writing very well. He was well versed in the science of geomancy and practised it. He died in A.H. 983/1575 A.D. in the city of Gaur, situated in Bengal. Ganj-i-Fazl or Munshi Bemisal gives the date of his death. *ZK,* 339 and *MU,* I, 73. See also *TṂ, AN, SS, NM, HI* and *Tazkira-i-Gunahi* (hereafter *TG*).
3. The incharge of the royal revenue. For details see Irfan Habib.
4. Bait has been left. See p. 84.
5. Nizamuddin says in the month of Shawwal/May. *TA,* II, 182 while Thursday, 24th Shawwal/26th May as given above. *NM,* fol. 191-b.

6. Ibrahim Laim, Ibrahim Khan Shaibani was one of the servants of Humayun. After the conquest of Mankot fort, he was granted jagir in the dominion of Jaunpur. *MU*, I, 75.
7. He was already in Lucknow. But they started for Jaunpur after receiving the news of the emperor's march. *Zubda*, fol. 118-b.
8. Abul Fazl says, "Neema Kara." *AN*, II, 250 and *Tazkira Bayat* also mentions the same p. 285 while Neem Khar has been mentioned in *Zubda*, 118. Naimisaaranya is situated in the district of Hardoi (UP), a holy place where the sage Suta repeated the Mahabharata to the assembled people.
9. Shah Budagh Khan was one of the nobles of Humayun. In the 12th regnal year, when he did not assist Mirza Aziz in Pattan, he was imprisoned and remained in custody up to A.H. 984/1576 A.D. Later, he rose to the position of Amir-ul-Umara. During (his) subedari of Mandu, he constructed in the mountain valley a building facing south, of great pretensions and named it Nilkanth. After his death, he was buried in Sarangpur. *ZK*, 333, *MU*, II, 536 and *TA*, II, 431.
10. Muiz-ul-Mulk, Mir Muiz-ul-Mulk Husaini Rizvi Mashhadi, was a Saiyed of pure origin and was equipped with (i.e. was of) high lineage and lofty descent. He rose to a high mansab and was posted in the Deccan where he pulled on well with Khan Khanan Mirza Khan so much so that the daughter of the latter was married to his son, Mir Khalil. He was without an equal in religiosity, piety, asceticism and (orthodoxy in the) creed of twelve (Shiite) Imams. He was a mujtahid of the time. In A.H. 988/1580 A.D. he fell into the river Jun and drowned. *ZK*, 281 and *MU*, III, 227. See also *ibid.* and *AN*.
11. Lashkar Khan was from Mashhad and bore the name of Muhammad Husain. He was one of the great nobles of Akbar. He got wounded with Khan-i-Khanan in the battle against Daud. After the victory, he however died in Ziqada, A.H. 982/February, 1575 A.D. *MU*, III, 18 while Nizamuddin says that he died in A.H. 983/1576 A.D. See also *MT*, *AN*, *SS* and *TM*.
12. Badauni also says, "Muhammad Yaar". *MT*, II, 81. Abul Fazl says that he was the nephew and son-in-law of Sikandar. *AN*, II, 262; sister's son and son-in-law. *Tazkira Bayat*, 293, Nizamuddin says, he was only the son-in-law of Sikandar. *TA*, II, 189.
13. The battle took place near Khairabad. *Zubda*, fol. 120-a and Sultan Muhammad Yaar was killed in A.H. 973/1565 A.D. See also *AN*, *MT* and *TA*.
14. It implies the mountainous fort.
15. He was defeated. *AN*, II, 262 and *TA*, II, 190. It was given by Raja Todar Mal. *MT*, II, 79 and *NM*, fol. 191-b.
16. It is situated in Ghazipur, falls in the territory of Awadh. Badauni says that he passed from there, but did not stay. *MT*, II, 78.

17. The day and date are confirmed by Abul Fazl. *AN*, II, 253 and *NM*, fol. 191-b while Badauni says 12th July. *MT*, II, 76.
18. Saruwal. *NM*, fol. 191-a, *TA*, II, 188, *Tazkira*, 296, 297 and 335. Salwar, *MT*, II, 101 and Sar Nau. *MU*, I, 627.
19. Kandna. *Tazkira*, 286.
20. Shahr Yaar was killed in A.H. 974/1567 A.D., according to an imperial order.
21. Kopa fort could not be traced.
22. For details see *MU*, I, 77 and *TA*, II, 430.
23. Villayat-i-Rani means Rani Durgawati, daughter of Raja Sabahan who was killed in A.H. 971/1564 A.D. *MU*, I, 80. See also *AN*, *MT*, *TA* and *SS*.
24. Majnun Khan Qaqshal was one of the great nobles of Humayun and Akbar. He held a mansab of 5000 and died in A.H. 983/1575 A.D. at Gorghat, Bengal. *ZK*, 370 and *MU*, I, 80. See also *Ibid.*
25. Mirza Arab was the servant of Khan-i-Zaman. *Tazkira*, 239 and 288.
26. Situated in between Sarwar and the river Ganga. *AN*, II, 250. One of the conditions agreed was that, "as long as the emperor is there Ali Quli Khan will not cross the river Ganga. Their vakils will present their submission at Agra. *Ibid*, II, 260 and 65 and *TA*, II, 190, and *MU*, I, 627.
27. Badauni says "Narhind". *MT*, II, 83. See also *AN*, II, 267, *NM*, fol. 192-a, *TA*, III, 193 while *Farishta* says Narhan. I, 254.
28. This is obviously an error for Agra.
29. Arif does not maintain difference between province and sarkar because by the time such division was not made.

OCCURRENCE 16

Description of His Majesty's March to Chastise the Sedition and Menace of Mirza Muhammad Hakim, His Escape to Kabul and His Measures to Set Up the Administration of the Sarkar of Lahore

After the lion-like (king) horseman, had crossed the plains day and night and had crossed the whole earth many a time.

Bait (verse)

But the destination of His Majesty is the sky. How can he sit quiet at one place?

News was received that, "Mirza Muhammad Hakim has started from Kabul with his army to invade Lahore and a body of Baluchis, who reside near the river Sindh, have also joined him. In order to exhibit the great prowess of his army, Hakim is camping on the outskirts of Lahore, though he has gathered it with the false hope and foolish delusion of achieving success."[1]

As soon as the said news reached the ears (of the emperor), the fire of his wrath fanned out and his sense of honour was touched to the quick. He appointed Nawab Khan-i-Khanan, Jumdat-ul-Mulk Khwaja Jahan[2] and Umdat-ul-Wuzara Muzaffar Khan to look after and guard the capital. On Saturday the 3rd Jamadi-ul-Awwal, A.H. 974/16th November, 1566 A.D., he marched out to deal with that faithless brother. As soon as Mirza Hakim came to know the march of His Majesty with the imperial army, he struck his camp and ran away like lightning beyond Nilab (Indus).[3]

Misraa (*a hemistich*)

Everybody threw himself into the water (river) and ran to Kabul.

On 6th Rajab,[4] A.H. 974/18th January, 1567 A.D. the light of the bright sun (emperor) descended on the territory of the Punjab (p. 90) and the dust of the blessed horse (mount of the emperor) became the collyrium of the eyes of the inhabitants of Lahore.

The stars of grandeur and greatness sparked on the horizon of the emperor's glory so that owing to the splendid justice the subject who was sleeping peacefully was not disturbed and no fear or restlessness was roused in their heart and mind also. The inhabitants of the land were amazed to see the admirable temperament of the emperor, though he had brought such a strong army that even a mountain might have crushed thereby to powder and swept off in the wind and the earth owing to being plundered might become restless like water, and even the morning time owing to unlimited dust might become so thick that even breathing would become difficult, even then the emperor had passed through the territory of Lahore in such a way that ten grannies of wheat or barley remained intact like bushes of *sumbul* and not a single pomegranate became the acquisition of young lovers, and in spite of such marvellous things, he recited the following words from his pearl scattering tongue:

Masnavi (*rhyme*)

The darwesh and pious men of the land were surprised why the fountain of morality had not burst-forth on the spot where His Majesty's blessed steps had landed, and why the tongue of the lily in the garden did not get busy singing his praises, and why the awakened narcissus did not shower plates full of different jewels?[5] (p. 91)

As the king is always inclined to prey and hunt and his desire in that direction can be entitled to fulfilment only when he becomes *Jalal* (grandeur). Hunting and preying have been recognised as proper and good for the Muslims. Hunting which also provides worldly pleasure is allowed to the believers so that by eating delicious and nice things, their minds be inclined towards chastity of heart and purity of mind. The king whenever was thus inclined and felt free after having destroyed the enemies, turned his attention towards hunting with his natural royal valour. The pleasure of hunting imparted motions to his mind. The reason of it is that he had seen such a flourishing and green garden before which even the garden of Aram felt ashamed. Its dimensions were expansive like the heart of charitable persons, its width was broad like the mind of a farsighted man.[6]

Orders were issued that all the amirs, Khans, noblemen and public, whether weak or strong, must make necessary preparations and close in all beasts of prey in the fence and from an area of three karohs (six miles) should drive in all wild animals and cattle.[7] It was fully respected. The emperor in those days remained occupied in preying stags and capturing tigers while fellow-companions threw tags and sharp lances of sharpness were hurled on hordes of goats and sheep. He was sad to see the enacted cruelty and when the hunters drove beats near him, he became angry.[8] Thereafter, the lord of the world mounted a lofty horse which was as high as clouds from whose counters the wind flowed and its speed was like that of the water flowing the clouds.[9] (p. 92)

As a result of the blessed riding (of the emperor) the animals which had been caught emitted the scent of musk and the dust that rose added a scent to the musk and by the beautiful steps of his horse the grass of hunting ground acquired fragrance. By acquiring the blessing of touching the feet of the king's white horse the thorns of the jungle began to be proud of their flowers. The wild animals seemed to be fools; otherwise those would have stepped up to receive arrows of the emperor and would have quarrelled among themselves for a chance. The deer are devoid of sense or else those would have presented themselves as sacrifice to his arrow. The deer did not pay attention to the blessings of the emperor's arrow otherwise there was no reason why their sick eyes should have remained far off from his eye of benefaction.

Masnavi (rhyme)

When the emperor cast his lance over the hunting field,[10] the whole of it became worth, filled with the fragrance of its dust. Every deer that was born in that garden got several musk-pouches out of one.

During these days, by the blessed hand of the emperor (may it remain protected from the misfortunes and evil eye of the time!) thousands of deer,[11] other beasts (of prey) and some wild animals also had been shot, that the soul of Bahram Gor[12] feels amazed at his marvellous racing and hunting and congratulates him.

Bait (verse)

Whichever side the emperor turned his eye, he made the land empty of the wild ass and deer.

Thereafter, the imperial order was issued that all the servants, attendants and horsemen with their horses should assemble in the compound and none strong or weak, young or old should remain without his hope and desire not being fulfilled. Among them many achieved their desires without any exertion on their part.[13] (p. 93)

His Majesty killed such a large number of deer and other beasts that the soldiers were unable to carry them and hence they left many of them (there).

Bait (verse)

So many animals of every variety were captured that the hands of hunters became lifeless. (Consequently for a long time carnivorous animals and birds enjoyed the pleasure of eating them).

Bait (verse)

The heaven played host to the wild animals and birds by feeding them on the animals killed by the king.

When the attention of His Majesty was turned, he thought to confer on Muzaffar Khan a high office because the latter had no match in managing the complex and difficult affairs of the state and spared no efforts in strengthening the foundations of the empire. The emperor had issued orders to summon him before launching hunting expedition and had also prohibited that nothing should be released either from the royal-treasury (*Sarf-Khana*), or the parganas of Khalsa or jagirs or diwani before his arrival from the capital, Agra. Besides this recommendations for even a single dinar or a maund of grain or the request of any one heard (for grant) be accepted. The text of farman reads like this:

"You must immediately come and kiss the stirrup." If deprived of the grace of kissing the stirrup, even though forty days had passed no farman or government certified paper (*Sanad*) was issued for the expenses of the government or affairs of the kingdom. Umdat-ul-Mulk started from Agra towards Lahore, he presented himself in the hunting ground, and received the honour and royal favours by kissing the stirrup. In a very short time he brought under control the affairs of the Sarkar of Punjab and gave his decision which was also accepted. The emperor conferred on the ladies and sultans (i.e. amirs) of the Atga family the *Khilat-i-Fakhra* and jagirs, which they had held in the parganas of the above-mentioned Sarkar. He also bestowed upon everyone of them higher ranks, increased their jagirs with studded sword, belt and other gifts. (p. 94) A body of Khans consisting of Kamal Khan Gakkhar,[14] Saiyed Khan Barha[15] and Khurram Khan[16] were entrusted the charge of defending the Sarkar of Punjab and they were to assist the Khan of Atga Khail in its management. The subedari of Lahore was given to the exalted Khan, Mubariz-ud-Din Mir Muhammad Khan Bahadur.

On Friday 18th Shaban/1st March of the said year (1568 A.D.) which was the final day of hunting expedition, a strange incident took place. While the emperor was on his way towards Lahore from hunting ground and he was crossing the river of Lahore[17] (Ravi) on horse back. Khush Khabar Khan,[18] who was hiding there and Nur Muhammad Khan, son of Sher Muhammad Khan, the keeper of armoury and a band of his companions jumped into the river and they were all washed away (died).[19] But the emperor on whom the

Almighty has always been kind, passed over the water like air safely.

During the same time it was brought to the notice of His Majesty by some wellwishers that, "Ali Quli, Bahadur, the ungrateful and Sikandar, ill-starred, owing to their perpetual seditious nature, have again diverted their path of obedience and have also plundered and devastated some areas".[20] Therefore, the emperor started on 12th Ramzan,[21] A.H. 974/ 23rd March, 1567 A.D., to put an end to their mischief. The hawks of battle (flags) began to fly along with Huma (good luck). The emperor's zeal and presence was with the imperial army. He moved shoulder to shoulder with it, and his valorous resolve entrusted the covering of distance to the world-conquering conveyances. Everyday the sun of achievement covered a world and every night helped them cross a world of distance like moonlight, until in an auspicious hour on 10th Shawwal of the said year (1567 A.D.) 20th April, (may God bring this to a blessed end!), he entered the capital, Agra under the shadow of success. The inhabitants of it returned from the wilderness of sorrow to their homes happily and were relieved of great fear and pessimism. They were loudly (p. 95) singing the following *Tarana*:

Bait (*verse*)

We were all dead and our days had turned to misfortune but by your arrival we have come back to life and have begun to illumine the world.

NOTES

1. See *Zubda,* fol. 122-a, *AN,* II, 275 and *TA,* II, 201 while Farishta says that Mirza Muhammad Hakim requested help from Mirza Sulaiman, the ruler of Badakhshan before marching to Lahore, which was denied. The emperor sent Faridun Khan to give counsel to Hakim while the former misled him saying that the capture of Lahore is not difficult. I, 255.
2. Khwaja Jahan, Khwaja Amin-ud-din Mahmud entitled Khwaja Jahan. *Ibid.* II, 58 while his name is not given by others. See *MT,* II, 91, *TA,* II, 202 and *AN,* II, 272.
3. Nilab i.e. the river Sindh. *AN,* II, 277, *Farishta,* I, 256 and *Zubda,* fol. 123-b while Nizamuddin says, when the emperor started from Agra,

Mirza Hakim left Lahore and halted at Chanab. When the imperial force reached Sultanpur, he left from there also. *TA*, II, 203 and *NM*, fol. 191-a.

4. Nizamuddin says on 6th Rajab/18th January. *TA*, II, 202; in the month of Rajab/January. *MR*, I, 748 while Abul Fazl says in the middle of Rajab (January). *AN*, II, 177.
5. Qita has been left. See p. 90.
6. Bait has been left. See p. 91.
7. The emperor ordered that the nobles encircled an area of forty karohs and hunting be played within five karohs. *AN*, II, 281, *MR*, I, 750 and *MT*, II, 92 and *TA*, II, 92.
8. Arif gives strange recipe for stimulating the charity of heart and purity of mind. Later he contradicts his statement to mention the cruelty enacted there.
9. Bait has been left. See p. 92.
10. The hunting ground was fixed towards Sarwar. *NM*, fol. 192-a.
11. 1000 stags. *Ibid.*, fol. 192-a. See also *TA*, II, 206, *MT*, II, 96 and MR, I, 85. The details given by Arif have not been mentioned by the authors of above-mentioned works.
12. A famous king of Iraq.
13. Bait has been left. See p. 93.
14. Kamal Khan Gakkhar, son of Sultan Sarng, held a mansab of 5000. These people (Gakkhars) have been loyal from generation to generation. *ZK*, 357.
15. The word Baha means the twelve villages which are situated in the Ganga-Jamuna-Doab near the pargana of Sambhal. He was the head of his family, brave and manly. He was far more distinguished than his likes and equals in the entire (clan) of the Barha Saiyeds. He rose to the mansab of 5000, and made such a name in bravery and liberality that he became well known in the world. He died in A.H. 981/1573 A.D. *ZK*, 276-7 and *MU*, II, 375 while Nizamuddin says that he died in A.H. 982/1574 A.D. *TA*, II, 438. See also *AN*.
16. Khurram Khan held a mansab of 2000. *ZK*, 422 and *TA*, II, 449.
17. The river of Lahore implies Ravi.
18. Khush Khabar Khan. *AN*, II, 284 while Nizamuddin calls him Yasawal. *TA*, II, 201 and 204. See also *TM*, *MT* and *NM*.
19. With their companions. *NM*, fol. 192-a while Abul Fazl and others say only Khush Khabar Khan and Nur Muhammad died. *AN*, II, 284, *MT*, II, 92 and *TA*, II, 207.
20. Abul Fazl says some of the dominions. *AN*, II, 289 while Badauni says that Ali Quli Khan laid a siege to the fort of Shergarh where Mirza

Yusuf Khan Mashhadi was present. *MT,* II, 94. It was reported that Mirza Yusuf Khan had been killed. *NM,* fol. 192-b.

21. 12th Ramzan/23rd March. *Ibid.* For details see *Zubda,* fol. 124-b, *TA,* II, 207 and *MT,* II, 93.

OCCURRENCE 17

Description of the March of Imperial Army Against the Wretched Band of Ali Quli, the Cowardly and Bahadur, Ungrateful, Their Chastisement and Killing of Those Ill-Starred Persons while Absconding of Sikandar, Slovenly

The misdeeds of rebellious band, i.e. the ill-starred, Ali Quli, the cowardly, Bahadur and the slovenly, Sikandar[1] have already been recorded in the preceding pages, and in connection with every incident their reality has also been exposed, but because these fellows once more have raised the standard of rebellion, therefore a few facts about their early career are being mentioned. It is necessary to jot down the early condition of this group so that it may be known why the attitude of these wretched fellows is so despicable in spite of all the benevolence bestowed on them.

The real story is as follows: His Majesty (late Humayun) used to treat them with kindness, generosity and affection. After his death, the kingdom was illumined by His Majesty (Akbar) and these wretched fellows received the privilege of kissing his feet. They were always benefited by the dust of his doorsill and by the grace of the shower of imperial favours. The emperor granted benefits and rewards to everyone whether good or bad. Their ranks were raised high and they too became Khans. The titles and jagirs of the best regions, e.g. Sarkar of Jaunpur, Awadh and Sarwal in the eastern provinces, belonging to the Hindu Rajas, were conferred on them. But these wretched fellows always hide the sun of their loyalty under the cloud of insubordination and disloyalty and covered the pleasant fountain of happiness in the mirror of disobedience. (p. 96)

Bait (*verse*)

When evil-mindedness grips a person, it does not leave him until the end.

On the 6th of Rajab, A.H. 974/17th January, 1567 A.D. Punjab was being illumined by the Sun (Emperor Akbar) and the throne of empire had become elevated by his stay. At the same time, the news was received that these mean and notorious fellows have once again gone back on their promises, pledges and loyalty. The sparks of hostility, which had died in their hearts, once again erupted. That is to say the snake of opposition, nurtured by the drops of poison of enmity had begun to sneak again. The plant of mischief and sedition which had been nourished by the water of the canal of hatred had grown up. The wave which had been quiet for some time became active once again. The emperor went by invitation to the dirty Sikandar, who was in the territory of Awadh and thus attracted him by casting the grain of deceipt and fraud. He threw the trap of love and friendship round his neck and thus collared him tightly. Despite all his nefarious activities, he used to send petitions to the court continuously for favours. His Majesty as usual adopted the method of generosity and granted him the desired favours, as has been said.

Bait (*verse*)

Thou art like a pearl in an assembly, but like a sword in the battlefield; that is to say, thou never disappoint a desirous.

In the courtyard of their supplications he (the emperor) used to shower all sorts of gifts and rewards and by the pure and clean water of his obligations, he used to quench their thirst. He did it in the hope that they would stick to their pledges, assurances and promises and would not abandon the path of obedience and loyalty.

Misraa (*a hemistich*)

Everyone does not deserve good treatment. (p. 97)

If you put some drops of nectar (*ab-i-hayat*) into the

mouth of a snake it too becomes poison, and the Hindi sword, becomes more and more blood-thirsty if you add polish and shine on it. In other words vanity is the product of favours and rewards while arrogance and spirit of sedition come from sympathy. So these mean fellows tried to capture the imperial land and declared their independence by raising their own flags. The root-cause of it was the involvement of the emperor in various problems. They did not know that the sun even when red like gold, cannot become a goldcoin (*ashrafi*). If the stars are like shining pearls, these cannot be stringed. Wisdom and reason, the guide of far-sighted persons, always condemn such nasty ideas and actions. It advises that, "you should never go astray from the path of submission and faithfulness to the lord (master) who has nourished your life and body".[2]

But the door of their ears were sealed with the nails of disobedience. Therefore they did not listen to the advice of good fortune and strings of their hostility remained fastened. They were under delusion owing to their friendship with some Mughals and Afghans and their small band, which supported them, helped them to become a curse. They gathered around Shergarh,[3] and besieged Mirza Yusuf Khan,[4] the hakim of the place; and got themselves occupied in the preparations of battle near the bank of river Ganga. When the misguided go beyond limits then wherever they step they unleash ruin equally on farms and animals. Wherever they stay farms cannot be ploughed there so the peace of that place vanishes with their encampment. Wherever they muster their force, anxiety follows and the territories through which they happen to pass, disappear. (p. 98) The whole world knows that the consequence of fighting and oppression mean nothing but destruction and the result of jealousy is also nothing but ruin. Common sense says it with a thousand tongues.

Bait (verse)

They do not realize that it does not only disturb the living of most persons but makes the foodstuff also dear (scarce).

Whoever possesses farsightedness knows well that the end of tyranny is like the flash of lightning which is not lasting, and that delight which brings sorrow (to others) is like the autumn grass which is temporary.

Bait (verse)

Old or weak persons feel miserable on account of their jealousy and its wound goes deep and deep.

When the emperor came to know of it, he at once ordered the victorious warriors to go across the river Jamuna on Saturday, the 26th Shawwal[5] (7th May, 1567 A.D.) where they should remain in camp for four days and then proceed on the last Saturday of the month. The imperial camp was laid in its vicinity of Saket,[6] three more days[7] were spent in the arrival of imperial artillery and the remaining force. In short the badges of various forces moved stage by stage like the waves of sea and reached Qannauj. The enemy was encamping on the other side of the river and some of his fellows being frightened submitted.

The victorious standards moved forward and the side of river which had become impure by the rebel's presence, began to be purified then on Saturday, the 16th Ziqada,[8] A.H. 974/26th May, 1567 A.D. after the emperor's arrival at the bank of the said river. (p. 99) Immediately a farman was issued that, "the Bakhshis, detaching themselves from the imperial army, a troop which looks like a green mountain should go through the arch of heaven, and it should present a spectacle of a red iron in the fire of battle. These persons should mount mountain like elephants, each of it be as high as a mountain, as fast as the wind and should give the sight of the wall of Sikandar in opposition to the unblessed enemy; they should cross the river Ganga without a hitch.[9]

Just at this time[10] the star of bravery and leadership, Abul Qasim Mirza,[11] son of late Mirza Kamran, imprisoned in the fort of Gwalior, was executed by Raja Bahar Mal.[12] Thus he achieved martyrdom.[13]

His Majesty, mounting on a fast running elephant himself, crossed the river Ganga even before the other imperial troops had done so and the wisdom described his valour: (p. 100)

Misraa (*a hemistich*)

I have never seen such a bone which could swim over the water.

The emperor exhibited such extraordinary bravery, the like of which could not even be imagined either by Rustam or Isfandiyar. As his luminary illumined the face of the river Ganga the entire army of rebels drowned in amazement. They began to run helter-skelter in utter confusion and fright. The wretched Ali Quli ran towards the accursed, Bahadur (brother) who was present in the neighbourhood of Kara and Manikpur, and was besieging Majnun Khan in the fort of Manikpur so that after meeting him, he may escape via Chausi[14] and Prayag[15] towards Kalpi[16] and its environs. Asaf Khan[17] fought with Bahadur Khan and having been wounded badly, returned to the emperor.

Bait (*verse*)

The heaven made the pledge with you that whoever would dare to raise his head against you, his head would be presented to you quickly, covered with dust.

That slovenly Sikandar and the accursed Ibrahim ran towards Awadh. This was known to the imperial army after its crossing over the river. Next day it reached Mau-Mahal[18] and then left for Muhan.[19] The imperial farman was issued that a company of Khans and amirs, particularly Umdat-ul-Mulk Muhammad Quli Khan Barlas,[20] Wazir Muzaffar Khan, Shuja-uddin Qaba Khan[21] and Haji Nizamuddin Khan Sistani should set out with numerous army in pursuit of them and should try to capture them (alive).[22] (p. 101)

They should exert themselves with manliness and bravery to wipe out the very existence of that ungrateful band of men. The victorious army was, however, given leave.

Misraa (a hemistich)

The king himself along with an innumerable force remained encamped there.[23] Later he marched in the direction of Ali Quli and Bahadur, the accursed, with the army.[24]

When Sahib-qiran[25] (Akbar) made the pargana Rai Bareli,[26] the envy of paradise, many Khans of Manikpur and Kara, specially the gallant, Nizamuddin Majnun Khan sent the report that the rebels were probably planning to cross Manikpur by ferry and then viz. Jhansi, Chausi and Prayag to reach Bidar.[27] If His Majesty turned his attention that very day towards it, it would illumine not only the eyes of the inhabitants of that post by the light of his banners, but they would very soon be saved from their tyranny and oppression and the whole band of the wretched would also be crushed under the giant feet of wild elephants. The population of Muslims and well-wishers of the kindgom would also be set free from their sedition and the world would also be purified from their shameful actions. (p. 102)

Bait (verse)

These regions from the mischief of rebels became the abode of peace and happiness while the name of the emperor became exalted and the heaven also got honoured.

Although the Khans were not willing to launch an aggressive and fast campaign, the emperor decided to march towards Manikpur in the wake of the blessings of God after a part of night.[28] By the time the golden sword of the emperor appeared in the East, the rebels marched away towards the West. The emperor however, reached the environs of Manikpur by the afternoon. At the same time Asaf Khan, Majnun Khan and all other brave Khans and amirs, assembled at Manikpur and Kara around the throne to earn the pride and honour of serving the emperor. Without wait, they were ordered to cross the river at Manikpur by ferry. Avoiding all differences at Manikpur according to imperial orders Khwaja Jahan and Tahir Muhammad Khan (chiefs of the private apartment) were required to remain in the fort. A large number of soldiers were left behind on account of long distance, scarcity of water and heat, though some of them had fully equipped presented themselves to accompany him.[29] The emperor, relying on God, mounted an army destroying elephant, whose speed was like the wind, and armed with a studded-sword[30] (p. 103) marched forth.

From the river Ganga the pure and sparkling flow seemed to be unfathomed, particularly as there had been by the heavenly generosity a very heavy downpour, there was no limit to the length and breadth thereof, the elephant was in the hand but his feet were in deep-water, like a mosquito caught in the claws of the wind and therefore in much trouble, and the thunder of the sky and the wind full of frightful noise of the cotton like clouds was impinging on the ears.[31]

Bait (verse)

As the wind due to its fast-speed, the fire due to its heat, the snake owing to its poison and the lion due to its roar are known.

On the morning when the king of the planet was about to enter into the battlefield and the Sultan of noon had cast his plundering hand on the advance troop of the bright stars (that is, the morning had dawned).[32]

From the different directions (armies) began to marshal and an imperial farman was issued that the Khans of Manikpur and Kara should be the vanguard of the victorious army while the army was praying with a thousand tongues that the help of Allah and victory are close at hand.

The emperor himself resolved to launch the attack because fate and destiny had made the ears of the rebels deaf. In spite of the presence of the imperial army within five karohs (ten miles), they remained unaware. The king's awe and might took possession of them. They were lost in the forest as it were to be. (p. 104) So much so that when they saw the advance-guard of the Khans of Manikpur they remained under a delusion that it was not being followed by any other force and the emperor himself was not coming. Thus, they prepared to fight under such an impression. The two armies therefore joined in battle . . . soon the lances and swords began to strike and Hindi swords began to slaughter rebels in their armoured dresses.[33]

Bait (verse)

Soon the restless and heartless seekers of men's hearts began to beat their chests.[34]

In the very first attack the royal bud started to flourish with the breeze of victory and the plant of good fortune began to decorate it. The wind of blessed luck of the emperor began to blow dust on the face of rebel. The rain of the clouds of victory started driving the flood of misery towards the enemy. Then they realized that the only safe course would be to accept defeat and to withdraw gradually. The emperor pursued the luckless horde and within a short distance some of the prominent rebels were taken prisoners. One of the slaves arrested Bahadur,[35] brought him before the emperor and severed his head. (p. 105)

In the mean time some of the soldiers advised Ali Quli to escape, but the feet of his horse were tied down by startle of death and his ungratefulness had also become a wall of obstruction in the way of his escape. His neck was cut off by a sharp sword and his head was thrown at the feet of a horse.[36] Their rebellious heads were carried round all the countries (regions) in order to exhibit that persons might take a lesson from their fate. Those foolish persons who had the ambition of kingship and crown became the clown at stake.

Abiyat (verses)

A poet has recorded the date of the execution of these unfortunate persons A.H. 974/1567 A.D.

Qasim Arsalan recorded the killing of both ungrateful and faithless fellows as A.H. 975/1568 A.D.[37]

Misraa (a hemistich)

Therefore, the emperor offered profound thanks to the Almighty and despatched the imperial army towards

Banaras. In anticipation of the imperial procession, the rebels strengthened the defences of the fort. (p. 106) Umdat-ul-Ayan, Hasan Ali Khan,[38] the hakim of the fort of Chunar was besieging the fort and the battle was about to commence. In the meanwhile, the news of the imperial army's march frightened the enemy. They came out of the fort with all humility, kissed the feet of the emperor and handed over their chiefs to him.

Muhammad Quli Khan and Ali Dost Khan[39] appointed Ishaque Aqa with other braves to capture the escaped Sultan Sulaiman and the relations of Ali Quli and Bahadur. Nizamuddin, Lashkar Khan and Tawaji Beig Khan were instructed to march with the requisite force to arrest all others. They arrested all of them and presented them before the exalted personage. Thereafter, the imperial entourage proceeded for Jaunpur (may God protect it from all calamities!) The ferry of the government was free from any hardships or difficulties and the robe of the kingdom was also free from enemies. By the good luck of the emperor all trouble was brought under control while peace and happiness of the people was restored.[40]

By the blessings of God, the emperor laid camp in Jaunpur and then by the rays of the justice of his sun scattered the clouds of tyranny and oppression from that area and the darkness and misrule ended there.[41]

The affairs of the nation which had been corrupted like the eyes of idols became beautiful like the faces of the beloveds. (p. 107) The condition of the inhabitants which had become very unbearable stabilized once more. The draught of misfortunes which were stuck in their throats transformed into the drafts of achievements of their desires. The cups which were full of anxities were changed into happiness. The emperor left Naqabat Panah Shahabuddin Ahmad Khan[42] with the company of other Khans to look after the affairs of Jaunpur till the arrival of Khan Khanan, its administrator-designate. Thereafter, he left for Kara and Manikpur, which became the envy of paradise by his presence and he stayed there for sixteen days.

The real purpose of the stay was to investigate the misdeeds and crimes of those who had been made captives. Some of them, responsible for serious crimes were executed, while others, not much involved in sedition were pardoned.[43] After four days Nawab Khan Khanan presented himself before the exalted personage and congratulated him on his splendid victory. The territory of Jaunpur, Banaras and Ghazipur, which had been under Ali Quli, Bahadur and Ibrahim, besides some other portions, were given in jagir to him and an imperial farman, bearing the seal and signature of the emperor, was also issued in this regard. Some of the Khans and amirs who held jagirs on this side of the Ganga, were also placed under his command.

During the same time, the petitions (arizas), sent by those army chiefs who had been deputed against Sikandar and Ibrahim were received, stating that those accursed on account of the fear of imperial army, had gone across the river Sarwal. There they erected a fortress and were hiding with an armed force in the fort of Awadh. As one of its gates is opposite the river, it could not be besieged. However, about fifty boats, armed with garrison, were keeping watch on them. The imperial army was confident that the world conquering sword had at last reached their neck and the spring of their lives was set on decay. The devious Sikandar was in luck due to the presence of river, which provided him an escape route.[44] Farsighted wisdom uttered forth loudly. (p. 108)

Misraa (*a hemistich*)

When one's sense goes deaf what is the use of giving good advice (to him).

At last the water went over his head and there was no way left for him to stay. So he became despondent. All those ambitions and desires which he had nourished were shattered by the world conquering sword of the king. Some of his trustworthy soldiers along with the chief, Ahmad Khan, came out of the fort, made their submission and pledged their loyalty. Soon the fighting mood of Sikandar was destroyed because the building, which he had been banking upon, was not lasting as its foundations were laid in water, it washed away like the river itself. In short, Haji Ughlan was deputed to assure the Khans that if they were to submit, they would be pardoned by the emperor. As a result the fighting stopped and Sikandar vacated the fort. He conveyed his intention of submission and joined as a well-wisher of the emperor. His plan was first to have a talk with the imperial servants because he wanted to be assured by them of the manner in which his submission would be executed. From his side Sikandar and Ibrahim with a few companions would proceed by boat and from other side a few in the same way. Then at first Haji Ughlan would be set at liberty. Thereafter, he (Sikandar) would go and receive the honour of kissing the imperial threshold. On their return to camp, they received the news of the execution of Ali Quli and Bahadur which made those misguided fellows awefully terrified and they began to run helter-skelter and at last reached the fort of Gorakhpur. Immediately, an imperial farman was issued that those ill-starred be pursued and the army should not return without the captors. (p. 109) Therefore, the Khans crossed the river Sarwal and succeeded in driving them out of the imperial domain. After a few days, they returned to the imperial camp and kissed the royal feet. His Majesty after achieving the victory marched towards the capital (Agra) on Thursday, 20th Zi-hijja, A.H. 974/29th June, 1567 A.D.[45]

Bait (*verse*)

Wherever you go, success kisses your feet.

On Saturday, the 11th Muharram,[46] A.H. 975/17th July, 1567 A.D. he reached Agra.

Duaa (*prayer*) *for His Majesty*

May God preserve the king and keep him under His protection and in the same way he may keep within his grace the people of the country as well!

NOTES

1. Sikandar revolted in the 10th regnal year of Akbar and later in the 12th year and he joined hands with Ali Quli Khan. *MU*, I, 85.
2. Bait has been left. See p. 97.
3. Shairgarh is a qasba (district), situated at a distance of six karohs from Qannauj. *Zubda*, fol. 125-b and *TA*, II, 209. while four karohs, says *MU*, I, 627.
4. Mirza Yusuf Khan Rizavi is from the Saiyeds of pure descent from Mashhad. He achieved prominence in the service of Humayun and rose to the rank of 5000. He held Kashmir in fief while his brother's son Yadgar Mirza, used to govern on his behalf. He died in the last part of Jamadi Akhir, A.H. 1010/October, 1601 A.D. in the Deccan. *ZK*. 255 to 259 and *MU*, III, 314. See also *AN*, *TM*, *TA* and *SS*.
5. Abul Fazal says, "Abkar started for their suppression on the said date from Agra". *AN*, II, 290, *TA*, II, 209, *Zubda*, fol. 125-b, *MT*, II, 94 and *NM*, fol. 192-b.
6. Saketah. *Zubda*, fol. 125-b and *AN*, II, 290 while Badauni and Nizamuddin say, "Saktiha." *MT*, II, 94 and *TA*, II, 209. It is situated in Eta (UP).
7. Number of days i.e. (three) is only mentioned by Arif while other sources are silent.
8. The date as mentioned by Arif has not been recorded by others.
9. Badauni says that a badge of troops was despatched. *MT*, II, 94. While Nizamuddin says that, "the emperor despatched six thousand sawars from Qasba-i-Bhujpur under the command of Muhammad Quli Khan Barlas, Muzaffar Khan and Raja Todar Mal against Sikandar towards Awadh. Qiya Khan was posted as the van of army. *TA*, II, 209 while Abul Fazl says that the force was despatched from Qasba-i-Muhan. *AN*, II, 290 and Qasba-i-Mahavan, says, *NM*, fol. 192-b.
10. The date is given 15th Zi-hijja/24th June. *NM*, fol. 230-b.
11. Abul Qasim Mirza, son of Mirza Kamran, son of Babur was assassinated as per imperial orders on 17th Zi-hijja, A.H. 973/26th June 1566 A.D. in the fort of Gwalior where he was imprisoned. He was fifteen years old. See *TM*, *SS* and *NM*.
12. Son of Raja Bihar Mal, most probably Bhagwan Das. *Farishta*, I, 241.
13. Wahshati, Jau Shaqai Kashi, a poet of Golconda, died in A.H. 1012/1603 A.D. For details see *SS*. (verses have been left. See p. 99).
14. Chausi is the centre of Allahabad.
15. Pa-yak and Payak both imply Allahabad. *NM*, fol. 192-b.
16. How could anyone go to Kalpi which is about fifty miles south-west of Kanpur on the right bank of Jamuna, (in district Jalam) via Jhansi and Payag, situated on Ganga, opposite Allahabad.
17. Asaf Khan was earliar with Quli Khan. In A.H. 974/1566 A.D. he came

to Bakkar and joined the imperial service on the recommendation of Muzaffar Khan Turbati, he was granted a mansab also. *MU*, I, 82 and *AN*, II, 283.

18. Mau is the centre of Banda, three karohs from Allahabad near the river Jamuna.
19. According to Abul Fazl, "Mauhan". *AN*, II, 29 while it is written Mahavan. *NM*, fol. 192-b. According to Badauni, "The emperor sent the above-mentioned amir after Sikandar Uzbek." *MT*, II, 94.
20. Muhammad Quli Khan Barlas was in the service of Humayun. He was first posted at Multan and later at Nagpur. He died at Midnapur (Bengal) in A.H. 982/1574 A.D. *MU*, 204 and *ZK*, 326. see also *AN*, *TA*, *SS* and *MT*.
21. Qiya Khan Gung was one of the exalted nobles of Akbar. In the early year of A.H. 988/February, 1580 A.D. he died fighting against Qatlu Afghan. *MU*, III, 54 and *ZK*, 330. See also *ibid*.
22. Masnavi has been left. See p. 101.
23. A large force numbering six thousand persons is also given by Badauni. *MT*, II, 94 while the strength of the force which was sent against Sikandar has not been mentioned. *NM*, fol. 192-b.
24. Masnavi has been left. See p. 101.
25. Arif calls Akbar Sahib-qiran (probably in its literal sense of master of the twin stars). It was the title of Amir Timur.
26. Rai Barailli. *NM*, fol. 192-b and *TA*, II, 209. It is one of the famous and old cities of UP.
27. According to Abul Fazl, "Ali Quli Khan and his brother wanted to go to Gwalior". *AN*, II, 290 while Kalpi is mentioned by others. *Zubda*, fol. 125-b, *MT*, II, 95 and *TA*, II, 29.
28. In the night of 29th Ziqadda, A.H. 974/8th June, 1567 A.D. *AN*, II, 290 while others say next day 30th Ziqadda (9th June). See *Zubda*, fol. 125-a and *TA*, II, 209.
29. The word Aghraq is not found in any dictionary and the meaning of this sentence is not clear.
30. According to Badauni, "Due to the intensity of heat even the brain of the animals was melting in the skull". The emperor covered fifteen or sixteen karohs. *MT*, II, 94 and 95 while Nizamuddin says not more than one hundred. *TA*, II, 209. But *Zubda* says one hundred and fifty. fol. 125-b. See also *NM*, fol. 192-b.
31. The river Ganga was crossed by the emperor with Shaikhan (nobles) and reached Manikpur. *AN*, II, 291 while Nizamuddin says that only the emperor passed it. *TA*, II, 209. Bait has been left. See p. 103.
32. The emperor reached with one half of the amirs. *NM*, fol. 192-b while Nizamuddin says Asaf Khan and Majnum Khan were also there. *TA*, II, 29. Bait has been left. See p. 104.

33. The battle took place on Sunday, Zi-hijja, A.H. 974/June, 1567 A.D. in the centre of Mangarwal or Mangrawal. *Ibid.*, II, 211, *MT*, II, 98 and *Zubda*, fol. 126-b but Abul Fazl says in mauza-i-Sakrawal. *AN*, II, 296. See also *NM*, fol. 192-b. Nazm has been left. See p. 104.
34. Bait has been left. See *Ibid.*, p. 104.
35. One of the slaves and his name was Nazar Bahadur. *AN*, II, 211. Bait has been left. See p. 104.
36. His head was chopped off. *NM*, fol. 192-b while Nizamuddin says that he was killed by an imperial order. *TA*, II, 211. Masnavi and Abiyat have been left. See p. 105.

    He was attacked by a sharp sword. *MT*, II, 97 and *AN*, II, 295. But Nizamuddin says that second arrow hit his horse which lost balance and Khan-i-Zaman fell on the ground. Though the Khan pleaded for life, the elephant driver crushed him under its feet. *TA*, II, 210.
37. Qasim Mashhadi entitled Arsalan was a reputed poet in composing historical lyrics. He died in A.H. 995/1586 A.D. at Lahore. For details see *MT*, *NM*, *HI* and *TM*. Abiyat have been left. See p. 105.
38. Abul Fazl has mentioned him Tarkan. *AN*, II, 15. According to Jahangir, he was alive up to the 11th regnal year. *Tuzuk-i-Jahangiri*, 308.
39. Ali Dost Khan Barbegi was one of the nobles, who held a mansab of 1000 and died in Lahore. *ZK*, 414 and *TA*, II, 448.
40. Bait has been left. See p. 106.
41. Bait has been left. See *ibid.*
42. Shaihabud-Din Ahmad Khan Nishapuri belonged to the Saiyed family of Nishapur. He assisted Maham Anga in the downfall of Bairam Khan. He held a mansab of 5000. He held the subedari of Gujarat and later Malwa. He died there in A.H. 999/1590 A.D. *ZK*, 149 and *MU*, II, 567. See also *TM*, *AN*, *MT*, *TA* and *SS*.
43. They were killed. *MU*, fol. 193-a. Badauni and Nizamuddin say that some of the captured were crushed under the feet of elephants while the rest who were not much involved were pardoned. *MT*, II, 100 and *TA*, II, 212.
44. Sikandar escaped in a boat from Gorakhpur and reached Bengal. *AN*, II, 30. See also *Zubda*, fol. 127-a, *TA*, II, 214 and *Farishta*, I, 257.
45. Abul Fazl says Friday. *AN*, II, 298 while the month is only mentioned by Badauni and Nizamuddin. *MT*, II, 101 and *TA*, II, 213. See also *Zubda*, fol. 126-b.
46. Friday, 12th/18th July. *AN*, II, 298. The name of the month is given. *TA*, II, 213 and *MT*, II, 108.

OCCURRENCE 18

Description of His Majesty's March Towards Chittor Fort, Its Conquest by the Grace of Almighty and Slaughtering of Condemned Infidels by the Wrath of Arrows, Swords and Guns

His Majesty felt free from setting the affairs of administration by making the finest arrangements for the governance of the people which set up his banners of justice in all parts of the empire. It was also decided that wherever there was oppression or tyranny it should be wiped out. Therefore he posted kotwals to deliver justice and save the people from oppression.

At the same time it was submitted to the emperor that the fort of Chittor[1] in its height touches the sky. (p. 110) It is mentioned in history books also. The new moon looks like a bangle in front of it, while Zohra (Venus) presents only like a shining granite in comparison with the size of its domes. The sword of its mountains is compared to the sword of Behram. The kings of the whole world failed to conquer it so they became despondant by their inability to capture the bird *unqa*.[2] The bravest persons of Hindustan are so despaired of capturing it as they are unable to capture the fort of Sipahar.[3]

Jaimal,[4] who was a shrewd rebel (Kafir) was also near relative of the Rana,[5] one of the famous rajas, was the commandant of the fort and the administrator of its nearby areas. The commandant, considering its height and fortifications, considered it to be independent. The emperor cast his shadow of kindness on it which made it blessed. Though the accursed rebel raised all sorts of obstacles including the preparation of battle, the emperor remained unmoved from his cherished desire. (Jaimal) because of his satanic (evil) principles became proud and refused to carry out the imperial orders. The bird of his baseless dream began to fly and he started entertaining all sorts of foolish ideas. Consequently, being rebellious, he started flying like a hawk on its mountains. This was brought to the notice of the emperor who therefore resolved firmly to subjugate it.[6] (p. 111)

In the month of Rabi-us-Sani, A.H. 975/October, 1567 A.D.[7] the emperor decided to march along with the army for the conquest of the said fort. The imperial tent of the world protector was more magnificent than the sun and the moon. The exalted nobles and Khans of the army surrounded the fort and the bakhshis posted the soldiers firmly on the requisite points. The siege continued for seven months, though there was fierce fighting day and night. The speedy arrows were constantly hitting the target from bows and the stones hurled from catapults were all presenting the scene of the Day of Judgement.[8] The noise produced did frighten even the bravest men, but it further encouraged the zeal of bravery among them. The sound of guns seemed to remind the sound of angel Israphil's[9] horn while the noise of battle seemed to have filled or gripped the whole world.[10]

The besiegers and miners marked out a proper place for dynamiting the wall to make a breach. They made a big hole in that place which was filled up with gun-powder and set on fire. Though the brave soldiers of the fort did (p. 112) their level best to extinguish the fire, they were enveloped into it which resulted in a big massacre. But the shrewd Jaimal was still full of snobbery of his power and the rebels were wearing sacred thread.[11] The emperor prayed to the Almighty in the month of Ramzan/March of the same year saying "O God thou should come to the help of the army of Muslims". He further desired that the army should launch a sudden attack on the fort from all sides. The army came up like a huge pack of pigeons and, entered the fort by slaughtering those soldiers, who were guarding its gate. They pierced a group of enemy by their arrows and killed them. Then they scaled the wall of the fort with much courage and jumped into it. Naturally the fire of battle blazed forth.[12]

On both sides the arrows and bows were rendered useless while the famous Kshatriya soldiers resorted to fighting with swords and lances. The imperial army thrust forward, shouting the sound of victory which made the old and young of the enemy shriek with fear. The clouds of swords arose and the lightning of scimitars began to shine.[13]

The emperor himself entered the battle and picking up a gun he aimed a shot which luckily hit Jaimal and he was killed.[14] (p. 113) He (the emperor) performed feats of such amazing courage which could only be performed by the grace of God. His soldiers too performed similar acts of bravery which made the past deeds of the braves alive.[15]

Thus the emperor became the owner of the flag of battle, i.e. victorious and the rebels (Kafirs) became the prey of arrows. The breeze of the grace of God began to blow. The heart of enemy began to wreathe in pain. By the time of prayer the full volume of sound was blown and delivered the final attack on the Satans. Realizing their helpless condition that wretched race began to slaughter their women and children with their own hands, and set fire to them, reducing (them) to ashes.[16]

Despite all,[17] there was only one victorious army and the vanquished one were thousands.[18] In short, many of the misguided persons were killed by swords. The number of the dead was about thirty thousands.[19]

As a result of this victory,[20] most of the persons of the army became rich, and under the emperor's government (or in his kingdom) (p. 114) they became men of substance. Everyone achieved the desired object. Everybody got in his army his cherished ambition. Men of sport enjoyed the beautiful ladies. Those who were covetous of hoarding property, benefited themselves fully. Every one was very happy over the success and every soul got a fresh lease of life by this triumph.

In short the awe and splendour of the emperor increased a thousand times more and the rulers and kings of the different countries started correspondence and exchanged presents and gifts with him.[21]

If proper attention is to be paid to understand the exceptional qualities and graces of the character of His Majesty, then it would become clear that the feelings and mind inside and outside are the mirror of Divine injunctions (p. 115) because on that day an extraordinary effect appeared from the limbs and organs of his body which is beyond comprehension. His pure heart and noble mind were turned inwards and in consequence of this purity he made a pilgrimage to the tomb of Qutb-ul-Qutabi Khwaja Muinuddin Chishti in his dream[22] and he paid full attention and due reverence to that paradise like tomb.[23] On Sunday, 26th of Ramazan/15th March, of the aforesaid year he went for the pilgrimage. He stayed there for ten days and then left for Agra.

After staying there for ten months he besieged the fort of Ranthambhor.[24] Then he offered prayers for a son which was the object of his dream. When the saint appeared in his dream he was assured that his cherished desire would be fulfilled. So in an auspicious hour, on Wednesday the 17th Rabi-ul-Awwal, A.H. 977/31st August, 1569 A.D. the blessed Prince Muhammad Salim Mirza was born in the town of Fatehpur Sikri.[25]

Duaa (prayer) for the long life of the prince

May God grant him long life! Some account of the events after his birth and other matters concerning the Prince would be recorded in its proper place.

NOTES

1. Chitor implies Chittor, which is situated in Udaipur (Rajasthan). It is situated on a mountain. Its height is one karoh and mountains adjacent prevailed to be captured by any earlier rulers. Its circle is three karohs while its length is nine karohs. *TA*, II, 216.
2. The phoenix which is hard to find.
3. *Nazm* has been left. See p. 110.
4. Jaimal, one of the great (Rajput) nobles of Rana Udai Singh, was the

commandant of Chittor fort. He was a reputed brave warrior. *MT,* II, 102 and *TA,* II, 216.

5. Actually it implies Rana Udai Singh, son of Rana Sanga, was the ruler. He died in A.H. 979-80/1572 A.D. at Golconda. *AN,* II, 202 and *TA,* II, 214.
6. Qita has been left. See p. 111.
7. Abul Fazl says, "The emperor left for Chittor in the middle of Rabi-ul-Awwal, A.H. 975/September, 1567 A.D. and conquered it on Thursday, 19th Rabi-ul-Akhir/23rd October, 1567." *AN,* II, 302 and 314 and *NM,* fol. 193-a.
8. Gun-powder was being thrown from the fort. It was ordered on Thursday, in the month of Rajab of the said year (January, 1568 A.D.) that channels be prepared by Hasan Khan Chaghtai in the centre of the fort, filled with gun-powder be fired. Some of its portions were blown up. A second one was fired but it did not show the desired results. Therefore, the soldiers were ordered to climb up the wall which resulted in the killing of one hundred persons. *NM,* fol. 193a. Abul Fazl says that two hundred warriors perished. *AN,* II, 317 while Badauni and Nizamuddin say about five hundred. *MT,* II, 104 and *TA,* II, 218.
9. Name of an angel who will sound the last trumpet on the day of Resurrection.
10. *Masnavi* has been left. See p. 111.
11. *Bait* has been left. See p. 112.
12. *Bait* has been left. See *Ibid.*
13. By the blessed hand of the emperor in A.H. 975/1567 A.D. *N.M.* fol. 193-b, *TA,* II, 218 and *MT,* II, 102. For details see also *AN, SS* and *IJ.*
14. *Masnavi* has been left. See p. 113.
15. They killed their wives and sons. *NM,* fol. 193-b while Badauni says that they burnt their relations and performed jauhar. *MT,* II, 104.
16. *Bait* has been left. See p. 113.
17. *Bait* has been left. See *Ibid.*
18. "Six thousand." *Zubda,* fol. 128-a while Nizamuddin and Badauni say more than eight thousand. *MT,* II, 104 and *TA,* II, 219.
19. Bait has been left. See p. 114.
20. It took about six months. *MT,* II, 104 while Abul Fazl says, "The siege started on 19th Rabi-us-Sani/19th October and conquest came on 25th Shaaban/24th February. So the time span seems to be four months and few days. *AN,* II, 314. See also *NM,* fol. 193-b and *TA,* II, 218.
21. For details See *Ibid.*
22. Abul Fazl says 7th Ramzan/13th February. *AN,* II, 324. See also *ibid.*

23. On Sunday, 15th Ramzan/21st February he left Ajmer and reached Agra on 15th Shawwal/3rd April. *AN*, II, 328.
24. After four months. *NM*, fol. 193-b. See also *TA*, II, 221.
25. Arif seems to be ignorant as the town or village of Sikri had not till then been named Fatehpur.

OCCURRENCE 19

Description of His Majesty's March Towards Ranthambhore Fort, Its Conquest on 10th Shawwal by the Grace of God and His Departure for Ajmer (to Pay Homage at the Shrine)

Let it be known to the brave that in accordance with the injunction of Quran, viz. that whomever Allah helps, becomes victorious. The flowing winds of victory over the flags of the empire are all dependant on the mercy of God. To have a numerous army is only in name; real victory entirely depends on the grace of God. To have a great war preparation is only a pretence. "You O God, confers dignity and honour on whomever you wish and misery and dishonour on whomever you please. Benevolence is in Thy power, Thou hast power over everything." (p. 116)

Whatever has been described as mentioned above is exemplified by the fact that when the report[2] reached the exalted ears that "Raja Surjan[3] is determined to defy the imperial orders and he has unleashed the fire of his rebellion which has blazed forth, and the flames of his sedition (Kufr) and his evil-intentions are touching the height (of sky)." It forced the imperial dignity to quench that fire by means of the water of the sword, and that the wrath of turbulence and disobedience be extinguished by the lances of the victorious army. Consequently, the emperor on the 1st of Rajjab-ul Murajjab,[4] A.H. 977/10th December, 1569 A.D. put his blessed foot in the stirrup and marched to lay a siege to the fort of Ranthambhore.[5]

When the fast moving imperial army arrived within sight of the vicinity of the fort on 24th (13th January 1570) of the aforesaid month,[6] it pitched its camps in the village of Khaljipur while the house (tent) of the emperor excelled in loftiness to the camps of sun and moon, and the great Khans and nobles and the brave (of Marikh Mars) or fire-brand warriors, who by their numbers and strength were spread over more than three karohs, surrounded the fort.[7]

The next day the emperor inspected the surroundings of the fort. In spite of the fact that former kings, who had gone to (p. 117) conquer it, had found it very difficult to encircle its sides due to the impregnable hilly passages and narrow gorges protecting it, the emperor got cauldrons installed at the bottom of its walls. Umdat-ul-Mulk Muhammad Qasim Khan,[8] the chief of artillery and navy, was appointed to prepare a tunnel leading into the fort. The artillery was placed on a high platform and those persons who were experts in hurling stones were ordered to commence rain of stones into the fort. It destroyed many bastions and battlements of the fort. All passages for the escape of the garrison of the fort were sealed. They were seeing their death in the mirror of their mind. Some of the besieged prayed for mercy through the worshipers of God. On account of the fright of the emperor the inmates of the fort were overwhelmed with fear and it paralysed their hands also. The mighty fort was so impregnable that the height and strength of its crenelles were like a mountain, and the trench surrounding it was like an ocean, deep and wide, so that even a hawk was unable to cross it. Nor the coned eye could reach its top from its bottom.[9]

In short all the efforts and struggles of the rebels to defend proved futile and the iron like fort could not stand before the mountain splitting warriors of the battle. (p. 118) Although the capture of fort seemed very surprising and its conquest seemed to be most difficult due to its great strength and massiveness, by the grace of God, the auspicious bird (Huma) of victory cast its shadow on the head of the emperor and the sun of good luck rose from the foreheads of the supporters of just cause.[10]

Raja Surjan, who was flying the banner of horror and evil

and was filled with vanity on the impregnability of his fort, soon found himself drowned in the slope of despondency when he saw the emperor and the grandeur of the army of Islam. He felt helpless in the narrow lane of terror and found that the day of his fate changed into dark night.

Whichever way the Raja turned his eyes in order to get released from his bad luck, he found his way barred by bloody swords and murderous lances. He felt that his fleeing feet were broken. (p. 119) He realized that there was none except His Majesty who could grant pardon and forgive him. From the high pedestal of pride he came down to the low level e.g. humility and meekness and submitted the petition of loyalty and faithfulness through the trustworthy persons.[11] The emperor on his part, in accordance with his usual kindness, treated him with mark of courtesy and goodness.[12] The capture of the fort which could have taken very long was conquered even by men of great skill and experience within just thirty-six days.[13]

The conquest of the fort has been described by Mir Farghi[14] A.H. 977/1569 A.D.

Mihtar Khan[15] one of the trusted nobles amongst the servants of late emperor (Humayun) was appointed the Kotwal of the fort and all its equipment such as artillery and financial management etc., were also placed under the command of the great nobles and Khans. The emperor himself left for Ajmer to pay a visit to the tomb of Qutb-ul-Waslin Khwaja Muinuddin Chishti. The time was reciting the following verse of Firdausi of Tusi.

Masnavi (*rhyme*)

Nought may remain with you except your good luck; and thy enemy may remain far from your sight. (p. 120) You may enjoy all good fortune, and may return (to the capital) with victory! On the 24th Ziqada, A.H. 977/10th May, 1570 A.D., the emperor returned to the capital, Agra.

(It may be recalled that) when the emperor was busy in besieging the fort of Ranthambhore and was delivering a shocking onslaught to uproot or devastate the nefarious activities of rebels, which were worth of exemplary punishment, Umdat-ul-Mulk Majnun Khan Qaqshal at the same time with some other Khans was laying siege to the fort of Kalinger.[16] As a matter of fact it is also one of the strongest and highest forts of Hindustan. Its edifices too were the envy of paradise, its balconies were likewise the envy thereof, its crenelles excelled the constellation plebeians (in Turus) and the depth of its moat was greater than even the very bottom of the earth. The breeze, carrying the clouds trembles to touch its courtyards, and the world covering lightning too genuflects its knee in its depth.[17]

After the victory of the emperor over Ranthambhore, the Raja[18] of the fort, who was its commandant also realized that he should not fight with death because all his efforts would go waste against it. He prayed for mercy and adopted the path of submission. The aforesaid Khan pardoned his faults and fulfilled his desire by forwarding his supplication to His Majesty. It was accepted. (p. 121) A gracious epistle, pardoning him was issued in the name of the Raja and he was also admitted among the protector of Islam.[19] The imperial generosity and charitable attitude evinced by the emperor was such that he neither touched his buried-wealth and treasure nor made any inquiry about his valuables, wealth and possessions.[20]

Indeed the blessings of the emperor's noble temper is to be seen in the fact that the knots (difficult situations) which cannot be solved by the world, become easy by the trouble-resolving keys of the emperor and every mystery which other persons are unable to unravel become easy even by his momentary attention.[21]

NOTES

1. Abul Fazl mentions Ranthabore. *AN*, II, 235. The actual name was Ranthpur. Ran is for its lofty place. So it became famous as Ranthambhore.
2. The army was sent on 10th Shawwal/29th March. *Ibid*, II, 238. Badauni says, on Tuesday, 3rd Shawwal/22nd March. *MT*, II, 108. Nizamuddin says on Wednesday, 3rd Shawwal (22nd March). *TA*, II, 224.
3. Raja Surjan Hada was one of the nobles of Rana Udai Singh, the ruler

of Chittor. He was the commandant of fort and held it out against the imperial cavalcade.

4. In the month of Rajab/December. *NM*, fol. 193-b, *AN*, II, 334 and *TA*, II, 223 while Badauni says that the emperor reached Delhi on the said date. *MT*, II, 107.
5. *Bait* has been left. See p. 116.
6. Abul Fazl says that Akbar reached Ranthambhore on 1st Shaban/9th January. *AN*, II, 335, while Badauni and Nizamuddin say that the emperor reached the fort in the last of Shaban. *MT*, II, 107, and *TA*, II, 223. See also *Zubda* fol. 130-b.
7. *Bait* has been left. See p. 116.
8. Muhammad Qasim Khan, Mir-bahar was one of the old amirs of this line. He held a mansab of 3000. *ZK* 371.
9. *Qita* has been left. See p. 117.
10. *Qita* and *Bait* have been left. See p. 118.
11. *Bait* and *Qita* have been left. See p. 119.
12. When the circumstances straitened for the inmates of the fort, Rai Surjan, having come down to the nadir of humility from the zenith of haughtiness and disobedience, begged for quarter by sending out of the fort his sons, Rai Duda and Bhoj. The emperor honoured both of them with royal favours (and) sent Husain Quli Khan and Khan-i-Jahan inside the fort. He brought Rai Surjan (to the royal presence) after giving him assurances. He received a mansab, fief and honour. The emperor inspected it and appointed Mihtar Khan its commandant. Rai Surjan rose to great distinction and remained alive up to 28th regnal year, i.e. A.H. 991/1583 A.D. *ZK* 401. See also *AN*, III, 404. *MU*, II, 113 and *TA*, II, 446.
13. See also *TA*, II, 224, *MT*, II, 108 while three months. *NM* fol. 193-b.
14. Farghi was the brother of Amir Fatah-ullah Shirazi. He came to Hindustan during Bairam Khan's time. After his death, he left for Iraq. Later he became court poet. See also *NM*, fol. 116-a, *MT*, III, 292 and *TA*, II, 502.
15. Mihtar Khan Khasa Khail, taken captive, came from Kara-Manikpur, served as a gate-keeper of the harem of His Majesty. Whenever the emperor left Akbarabad, he would leave him as its incharge (governor). He held a mansab of 3000. He died in the last days of A.H. 1017/1608 A.D. *ZK*, 384-85 and *MU*, III, 344.
16. Kalinger fort situated on a mountainous track in Banda, in (UP).
17. *Qita* has been left. See p. 120.
18. For details see also *TA*, II, 226, *MT*, II, 120, *AN*, II, 340 and *Zubda* fol. 132-a. His name was Raja Ram Chand.
19. The Raja surrendered the fort on 29th Safar, A.H. 977/14th August, 1569 A.D. For details see also *ibid*.

20. Pargana Arbal near Chausi was given in jagir to him. *MT*, II, 120. *Bait* has been left. See p. 121.
21. *Masnavi* has been left. See *ibid.*

OCCURRENCE 20

Description of the Birth of Prince Sultan Muhammad Salim Mirza Entitled Mirza Shaikhu

During the same year by the grace of the Giver of all gifts, a new rose blossomed in the garden of the realm. In the precious necklace of the empress, luster and beauty were added by the birth of a priceless pearl. On wednesday, 17th Rabi-ul-Awwal, A.H. 977/31st August, 1569 A.D., a son was born at Fatehpur Sikri to the emperor. The expectant eyes of the emperor became illumined by the sight of the son, named Mirza Muhammad Salim.[2] (p. 122)

The emperor's delight and happiness at the sight of this light were unabounded. All the people, irrespective of their class, brought and presented suitable gifts to join the auspicious occasion. Men of letters brought offerings in the plate of supplications. Men of science, out of their gifted wisdom displayed all sorts of meticulous feats. Festivities were celebrated and musicians and singers with their splendid art made all and sundry happy and they forget their sorrows. For full one week, the festivities marked the occasion and the people enjoyed.[3]

The culinary-experts of the imperial threshold prepared all sorts of varieties and feasted old and young, rich and poor. It was God's wish that the new born of the emperor be a source of comfort and well-being of mankind till eternity by the blessings of the Prophet and his progeny and your (the king's) family as well. A poet of the time has described the date of birth of the Prince in a distitch (A.H. 977/1569 A.D.[4]

Notes

1. Shaikhu Jiu. *NM,* fol. 194-a while Jahangir in his Tuzuk writes Shaikhu Baba.
2. See also *MT,* I, 120, *AN,* II, 345, *TA,* II, 226, *Zubda,* fol. 132-b, *NM,* fol. 194-b and *Tuzuk. Nazm* has been left. See p. 122.
3. *Bait* has been left. See *ibid.*
4. *Qita* has been left but date of birth is derived out of its *Misraa.* See p. 123.

OCCURRENCE 21

Description of His Majesty's Walking on Foot up to the Tomb of Hazrat Khwaja Muinuddin Chishti to Pay Homage There (p. 123)

The high and noble determination of the emperor is a proof of his profound faith. He arranges his programme of activities in such a perfect manner that the absolution of sins might be automatically done. So the king, the hunter of lions, decided to cover stages of distance on foot,[1] starting from his abode. He is endowed with unique qualities, capabilities and resourcefulness. (p. 124)

So on Thursday,[2] 18th Shaban, A.H. 977/26th January, 1570 A.D. he fulfilled his resolve and set out from Agra towards Ajmer for the pilgrimage of the Shrine of Khwaja Moinuddin Chishti.[3] The distance from Agra to Ajmer is one hundred and forty karohs (200 miles). The emperor covered it on foot. There it was brought to the notice of the emperor that a dispute was going on among the shaikhs who claimed to be among the descendants of the Khwaja. Thereupon he dismissed them all and appointed Shaikh Muhammad Bukhari,[4] a wise and respectable saint, its keeper and entrusted its management also to him.[5]

(p. 125) As the obvious fact is that none occupying a high position ever achieved such blessings and grace. Everyday he used to walk seven or eight karohs. He thus completed the journey in about a month's time, and reached his destination.[6]

All the time infinite Divine grace descended on him, because there was no other object of his journey except charity and good work. "God forgives all sins". In accordance with this verse, the grace of God is always available to him.

Nothing else except blessings and goodness come from a person who is an embodiment of benefaction. Be of good cheer therefore that the final one would also be blessed.

The Misdeed of the Unfaithful, Shafi against Muzaffar Khan (Wazir) and his Death

The description of the auspicious event in brief is that when the emperor with the blessed Prince, Sultan Muhammad Salim Mirza[7] (may God grant him long life!) and some members of his harem (Bilqis Makani) finished his homage and pilgrimage at the shrine, where he had kept himself occupied in prayers, submission and in showering all sorts of gifts and charities on the denizens of that place; after a few days he started back and left for the capital Hazrat-i-Delhi.[8] When he reached the town of Palam,[9] which is one of the suburbs of Delhi, he encamped there. A foolish and ill-starred person named Shafi complained against the appointment of Muzaffar Nishan Wazir. (p. 126) His hidden wrath against him became evident. Farsighted and wise men feared lest he might be given a high mansab. If such a thing did happen, that wretched person's foot might reach to a rank, then surely he would cause great sorrow, misery and anguish.[10]

The philosophers have said disloyal and evil-doers ought not to be relied upon. The actions of Shafi, the rebel are designed to create differences and he is full of all sorts of mischief and evils. In spite of the fact that he had attained the high position of Jumdat-ul-Mulk and was looking after the personal expenses of the emperor, simply on account of the support and favour of (Muzaffar Khan). Yet owing to his meanness and jealousy, he had become so bold that he began to entertain in his swollen head the belief that he could permanently hold and manage the affairs of the department of the wazir. He was under the impression that it was quite an easy and simple work.

So he, leaving aside all shame and forgetting all the bestowed favours, started behaving most unabashedly, i.e. began to show such ungratefulness and misbehaviour which could not be atoned for a hundred thousand years. He set ablaze such fire of trouble which could not be extinguished even by the ocean. He complained with his stupid mouth that there had been a careless frittering away of fifty crores of rupees[11] which he was prepared to prove. When the emperor heard his submission, he enquired, "By what means and in what way had you ascertained what you said regarding that sum and that if you were having a detailed account of income of the realm you should at once show him, or else all your statements were false and not worth or credence." Owing to the deep concern about the affairs of his subject, the emperor ordered that the son of Raja Baharmal[12] to keep him under his custody as a prisoner so that it might be a lesson to mischief-mongers and ruinous fellows. (p. 127) He reaped the fruit of his disloyalty, ingratitude and fraud. He himself became a prisoner by the hand that he had raised to create trouble. He gained nothing from the foot which he had moved in the faithless way.[13]

Some persons of the opposing group who had been in alignment with him, when they witnessed his fate, became dumb, and began to condemn his unworthy actions. They then carefully thought over the consequences of such things "Whoever kept quite, remained safe." So they acted upon this proverb. They bore in mind that anyone who turned his face of uncivility towards Muzaffar Khan, would not get good name. So long as he would try to hide his hostility, he would be deprived of the benefits of friendliness. Whenever anyone ventures to quarrel with him, he himself gets into a trap and whoever keeps hidden his envy can never remain happy.[14]

In short, that stupid fellow became confounded and subsided into the corner of anxiety and degradation, and in consequence of his great lie, had to feel thoroughly ashamed and overwhelmed with distant fears and worries. He then repented how foolishly, "I have acted and thus entangled myself in bad luck? Why have I behaved so rudely and talked so wildly in spite of having the diwani of Bayutat?"[15]

(p. 128) The wise says that respect those who shut their mouths in silence than those who talk nonsense.

Bait (verse)

Animals are tongue-tied (do not speak) but man talks; who is better, the talkative man or silent animals?

The gist of all this description is that the foolish Shafi was suffering in prison, bound in chains and his eyes were trickling blood in anger, and was pointing his own finger towards himself on his boldness in maligning the subordinates of Muzaffar Khan. On 20th Ziqada, A.H. 977/26th April, 1570 A.D., the emperor started with the imperial army and that ungrateful fellow was deprived of his jagir as well as rank and no one therefore heard or saw him. He bore the consequence of his misdeeds and for a period of six months or more and he kept weeping and wailing in prison. It is sheer ill-luck for anyone to compete with the fortunate and to talk loose and undesirably against one's highly placed master is surely a sign of misfortune.[16]

In short, the emperor decided to have mercy on that accursed Shafi and despatched him enchained to Jamdal-ul-Mulk Muzaffar Khan to whom he had been very kind. The object was that Muzaffar Khan should deal with Shafi as would please him. When that fellow with hands and neck tied was brought before Muzaffar Khan, he prayed to his master saying, (p. 129) "My lord, you are my master and your decision and command should be carried out on my life as a result of my misconduct, and you would be justified to shed my blood, but it would be more pious if you pardoned me. God has made you the chief of all those who can grant forgiveness, just as He has made me the leader of sinners. It will certainly be doing justice if you inflict on me due and deserving punishment, but if you decide to pardon me, it will be a great generosity and favour of yours".[17]

Qita (hemistich)

The noble wazir, Muzaffar Khan melted into tears at the entreaty of Shafi, he pardoned his misconduct and imagined as if all his doings were forgotten and gone. However, in the month of Rabi-ul-Awwal, A.H. 980/July, 1572 A.D., Shafi passed away.

NOTES

1. The emperor as a mark of respect and gratitude undertook the journey on foot. See also *NM*, fol. 194-a, *MT*, II, 123, *AN*, II, 349, *Zubda* fol. 132-b and *TA*, II, 227.
2. On Friday, 12th/20th January. *TA*, II, 227. *NM* fol. 149-a, *AN*, II, 350 and *MT*, II, 123.
3. Bait has been left. See p. 123.
4. Shaikh Muhammad Bukhari Dehlvi was one of the nobles of Akbar. He died fighting against Sher Khan Fauladi and Muhammad Husain Mirza with Khan-i-Azam at Pattan, Gujrat in A.H. 980/1572 A.D. See also *TM*, *TA*, *AN*, *NM* and *SS*, while the date is given A.H. 979/1571 A.D. *MU*, II, 542.
5. Ghazal of Maulana Tariqi, who belonged to Sawa, a unique imperial court poet, who died in Iraq, has been left. It covers four lines of p. 123, 124 and two lines of p. 125. It contains the praises of the emperor on his walking the whole distance and thus paying his homage there.
6. Six or seven karohs. *Zubda*, fol. 132-b, *TA*, II, 227 and *MT*, II, 124, while Abul Fazl says that the emperor covered about ten or twelve karohs. *AN*, II, 350. *Bait* has been left. See p. 125.
7. Sultan Muhammad Salim. *Ibid* and *Zubda*, while Nizamuddin says, "Prince Salim". *TA*, II, 227.
8. The emperor reached Delhi in the month of Ramzan, A.H. 977/February, 1569-70 A.D. See also *AN*, II, 351. *MT*, II, 124 and *TA*, II, 228 and *Zubda*. fol. 133-a.
9. Palam, situated at a distance of seven or eight karohs from Delhi.
10. *Bait* has been left. See p. 126.
11. Fifteen crores perhaps fifty crore dam.
12. His name was Bhagwan Das. Both father and son were among the great nobles of Akbar and held a mansab of 5000 each. Among his charitable works is the Jami mosque at Lahore in which a large number of people gather till now to offer Juma (Friday) prayers. *ZK*, 152-3. See also *MU*, II, 111.
13. *Masnavi* and *Bait* have been left. See p. 127.
14. *Bait* has been left. See *ibid*.
15. *Bait* has been left. See p. 128.
16. On Wednesday, 26th Ziqada/3rd May the emperor undertook the journey to Agra. *AN*, II, 352 and *NM*, fol. 194-a.

17. This incident of Shafi has not been given by other contemporary and near contemporary sources.

OCCURRENCE 22

Description of the Birth of Mirza Shah Murad and Certain Other Happenings which Occurred in That Year

Prince Mirza Shah Murad, surnamed Mirza Pahadi, was born at Fatehabad Sikri on 3rd Muharram,[1] A.H. 978/8th June, 1570 A.D. The emperor was profoundly delighted to see the lucky child. So the gates of festivities and ceremonies were thrown open. (p. 130) The giver of good luck and happiness gave the news of the fulfilment of his object.

The star of Murad rose from the horizon of the graciousness of God. The star of success appeared on the horizon out of its rising place by Divine Command. Maulana Qasim Arsalan composed a couplet to narrate the dates of birth of both princes. The first verse contains the date of birth of Salim while the second of Murad.[2]

Qita (*hemistich*)

The second son of the emperor resembles Emperor Babur in facial cut and countenance. When I inquired from wisdom the date of his birth, wisdom said: Sani Babur Bahadur,[3] this gives his date (of birth).

Duaa (*prayer*)

It is expected from the infinite kindness and benevolence of the Almighty that whenever the desire of heart is reflected in the mirror of the heart, every high rank rises higher.

NOTES

1. Mirza Pahadi, Sultan Murad was born at Ajmer. The emperor used to call him Pahadi out of love. He died in the prime youth at Jalnapur (Deccan) on 15th Shawwal, A.H. 1007/2nd May, 1599 A.D. See also

TM; AN, SS and *NM*. Abiyat have been left but their gist is given. See p. 129.

2. Prince Salim's date of birth is given A.H. 977/1569 A.D. while that of Prince Murad A.H. 978/1570-71 A.D. *Diwan-i-Arsalan,* fol. 34-b. See also *NM,* fol. 196-b, *TA,* II, 228 and *MT,* II, 132.
3. Replica of Babur is born A.H. 978/1570 A.D.

OCCURRENCE 23

Description of the Fourth Pilgrimage of Hazrat Khaqan Akbar Jahangir to the Shrine at Ajmer and the Happenings of Certain Other Events

His Majesty, who resembles the sun, having stayed long in Virgo and Libra (signs of Zodiac) was fed up owing to heat, turned towards Sagittarius and the summer season having passed the air became cool, decided to move from Agra on 20th Rabi-ul-Awwal,[1] A.H. 978/23rd August, 1570 A.D. He passed twelve days at Fatehabad Sikri and on 7th Jamadi-ul-Awwal/8th October of the said year, marching slowly this village, reached Ajmer and made it the envy of paradise. (p. 131) He once more paid homage to the shrine of Khwaja Moinuddin Chishti. The keepers of the shrine were asked to read the *Fatiah* and they received many gifts and presents. The emperor stayed there for a few days. Thereafter on 4th[2] of Jamadi-ul-Akhir/3rd November of the said year, the emperor left for Nagore. In the month of Shaban/December[3] he adorned the town of Nagore with the imperial flags.

As the pond of Nagore was running short of water, the emperor ordered the army to dig it deep. The Bakhshis carried the orders by assigning the task to the soldiers, who performed the work accordingly.[4]

The emperor bestowed unbound favours on Mubariz-ud-Din Mir Muhammad Khan Bahadur, who had no match in intelligence, manliness, good manners and courteous behaviour. The administration of Nagore, Ajmer, Jodhpur and up to the frontiers of Gujarat was entrusted to him. Thus the emperor made all efforts to organise the administration of the country around.[5] After completing it to his satisfaction, he turned his steps in the direction of (Pak) Pattan to pay homage at the shrine of Shaikh Farid-ud-Din Ganj-i-Shakar.[6] (p. 132) The emperor prayed for success and endorsement of his actions at the shrine.[7] By the hand of supplication, the emperor obtained treasure (mercy and grace of God) and stores of unlimited conquests. He distributed gifts, presents and other awards among the keepers of the tomb and others.

From the paradise-like place the emperor left for Lahore which was like the mother of the cities of Hind. On the way on Tuesday, 20th Ziqada[8]/16th April he arrived at the pargana of Dipalpur which is one of the parganas of Punjab and belonged to his dear kith, Mirza Aziz Koka entitled Khan-i-Azam.[9] The Mirza, one of the supporters of the state, was known for his might, wealth, achievements and nobleness all over the country and abroad. (p. 133)

The emperor stopped in the mauza and accepted presents and offerings of the Mirza. It included numerous gifts such as gems, magnificent pearls, beautiful dresses, all types of valuable articles, fine utensils, gold, silver and jewellery plates, full of ashrafis and rupees. Yet in a mood of modesty, he was murmuring (blushing). Shaikh Muhammad Ghaznavi in his line of a verse gives the date of the emperor's visit.[10]

The sky kissing banner with fish-emblem entered Lahore on 22nd Zi-hijja/17th May (of the said year).[11]

Amir Husain Quli Khan on whom the emperor had conferred the title 'very wise' and was the hakim of the Sarkar of Punjab, received the honour of kissing the royal feet and rubbed his cheeks (face) in front of the throne. The imperial army in Zi-hijja, A.H. 978/April-May, 1571 A.D., reached the village of Malakpur which was situated at a distance of five karohs from Lahore. The imperial party, however entered the fort of Lahore and the above-mentioned Khan performed the ceremony of spreading red-carpets for receiving the emperor and offered presents and numerous varieties of gifts and dresses, five pieces of pashmina, zarbaft, Kamkhwab of bright colours, atlas, velvet and thereby obtained blessings and happiness. (p. 134)

The above-mentioned Khan decorated every corner of his

house for the auspicious occasion. Wall to wall carpets of various colours and dining sheets were spread. Then the emperor entered it.

On 23rd/19th April of the said month, he began his march for Lahore and covered the stages Batala and Jalandhar passing time in hunting and excursion.[12]

In short, on 1st Safar, A.H. 979/25th June, 1571 A.D., the imperial camp was pitched in the vicinity of Hisar-Firuza safely. (p. 135) On 11th Safar/6th July (it so happened) that Lashkar Khan,[13] who was a Twaji Begi, Mir Bakhshi and Mir Arze and beside these offices was very close to the emperor, intoxicated (of wine), his fame, power and position came in the said state of nature and he forgot that God is there to inflict retribution. So riding high he desired to pay his respects to the emperor. Shahbaz Khan,[14] Mir Bakshi and one of the principal *hajibs* of the court was aware of the former's madness. He immediately informed the emperor that the dead-drunk Lashkar Khan had come to pay his respects to him. It sparked the emperor's wrath and he ordered that he be imprisoned and the charge of Mir Bakhshi was also given to Shahbaz Khan. The reality is that the emperor was opposed to all those things which were against or forbidden by the Shariat. For a long time he had been reflecting the secrecy of his heart and he always condemned those who acted against the law, and has also expressed his disgust against wine.

Suppliant for God's mercy was announcing, "We have changed the bad into good. He said, "I am ready and accepted it." (p. 136)

Qita (*hemistich*)

Indulging in intoxicants and being reckless is not the habit of the emperors. It is best for them to be always wide awake and watchful; the king is the guardian and watchman of the realm. Wantonness or intoxication is a dream; it does not behove one who is guardian or custodian; it behoves him to remain alert and cautious.[15]

During this delightful weather when the wine cups are

shimmering like the eyes of lovers, the emperor smashed the maddening wine cups on stones and in these times where the roses were blossoming forth like the cheeks of the beloved, he adopted the path of purity and piety.

Bait (*verse*)

He is the king who has escaped wine in obedience to God's command; he respects the Law (Shariat) and has turned away from the farce of drink. The troublous protests and noises of those to give up drinking has been transformed into the praise of God, and to the prayers of pious men. Those who indulged in forbidden acts or deeds lost their respect and whoever set his foot into forbidden things was severely admonished.

In short the victorious standards started from Hisar-Firuza to go to Ajmer.

On 1st Rabi-ul-Awwal, A.H.[16] 979/25th June, 1571 A.D. the emperor reached the holy shrine of the Shariat, Khwaja Muinuddin Chishti (p. 137) and again earned the blessing of paying homage there. From there he started for Agra. On Monday, 21st[17]/16th July of the said month by the mercy and kindness of God, he adorned Agra just as if the soul had returned to the body. He enjoyed festivities for some time and then left for Fatehabad. He reached there on Thursday the 17th Rabi-ul-Awwal/12th July. He turned his attention to the construction of that city and it would be described at a proper place. On 10th Jamadi-ul-Awwal/1st October, he pardoned and set free Lashkar Khan. But a fine of rupees fifty thousand was imposed and collected from him. It was deposited in the imperial treasury. It was in addition to that money which had been confiscated at the time when he was imprisoned[18]

NOTES

1. Badauni and Nizamuddin say on 20th Rabi-ul-Akhir/2nd October. *MT*, II, 133 and *TA*, II, 229. While Abul Fazl says Saturday, 22nd Rabi-us-Sani/21st September. *AN*, II, 356 which is confirmed by *NM* fol. 197-a also.
2. Friday, 4th (3rd November). *Ibid.*

3. On 16th Jamadi-ul-Akhir/15th November the emperor reached there. *AN*, II, 357, *NM*, fol. 197-a, *TA*, II, 229 and *MT*, II, 133. *Bait* has been left. See p. 131.
4. The emperor named it Shakar Talaoo (Hauz-i-Shireen). See *ibid.*
5. They remained encamped in Nagore for about fifty days. *TA*, II, 230.
6. Shaikh Farid-ud-Din Masud, son of Jamal-ud-Din Salman, son of Shuib Qureshi, is one of the most respected saints of Hindustan. For details see also *Gulzar-i-Abrar, Akbar-ul-Akhyar, Jawahar-i-Faridi, Kalmat-us-Sadiqin, MT, SS* and *TM*.
7. Mir Ala-ud-Daula entitled Ba Kami was the second son of Mir Yahya Qazvini and younger brother of Mir Abul Latif Qazvini. During the time of Akbar, he came to Hindustan and he died in A.H. 982/1574 A.D. *MT*, III, 97 and 316 and Rauz-i-Roshan, 570. Rubai, *Masnavi* and *Qita* have been left. See p. 132.
8. On Monday, 29th/25th April. *Zubda* fol. 35-a and *NM*, fol. 197-b.
9. Mirza Aziz Koka entitled Khan-i-Azam, son of Shams-ud-Din Muhammad Atga, entitled Khan Ghaznavi was one of the great nobles of Akbar and Jahangir. He held a mansab of 5000. He died at the age of 76 in A.H. 1033/1624 A.D. in Gujarat. For details see also *ZK*, 129-46, and *MU*, I, 675. *TA, MT, SS, HI, NM* and *Tuzuk*. *Bait* has been left. See p. 133.
10. *Masnavi* and *Bait* have left. See p. 134.
11. The emperor undertook his march from Lahore in the early days of Muharram, A.H. 979/May, 1571 A.D. *AN*, II, 364 and *NM*, fol. 197. *Ghazal* has been left. See p. 134.
12. It is situated in the midst of Gurdaspur (Punjab).
13. Lashkar Khan was from Mashhad and bore the name of Abul Hasan. He held a high mansab in the time of Akbar. For details see also *ZK*, pp. 322-23 and *MU*, III, 161.
14. Shahbaz Khan Kanbu was one of the great nobles of Akbar. He died on 4th Jamadi-ul-Awwal, A.H. 1008/12th November, 1599 A.D. at Ajmer. He lived for more than 70 years. *MU*, II, 590. *Bait* has been left. See p. 135.
15. *Bait* has been left. See p. 136.
16. Wednesday. *AN*, II, 364 and *NM*, fol. 197.
17. On 15th Rabi-ul-Awwal/10th July. *NM*, fol. 197-b.
18. The other contemporary and near contemporary sources do not contain the above-mentioned happening.

OCCURRENCE 24

Description of Hoisting Splendid Banquet in Honour of His Majesty by Asaf Jah, Muzaffar Nishan and His Enjoyment in the Grand Assembly, Presenting the Sight of Paradise

The king's heart has ever been inclined towards seeking pleasure and sometimes these sentiments assume brightness in the mind of the fortunate one. So once he thought of adorning the abode of Muzaffar Nishan and making it the envy of paradise of China by setting his foot on his door. So he started from Fatehabad Sikri and came to the capital.

Misraa (*a hemistich*)

The eagle came to the city of sparrow. (p. 138)

On 17th Shaban, A.H. 979/24th September, 1572 A.D. the emperor in the wake of great delight, coupled with magnificent arrangements made by that able wazir, reached there. Every possible equipment for the grand celebration in all manners of festivities and enjoyment was affixed. The entire passage, measuring two thousand yards, from the royal palace up to his residence was decorated with various cloths such as zarbaft, Chinese silk, European velvet, atlas and Kamkhab-i-Yazdi for the emperor's steps.

Bait (*verse*)

Because the way was ornamented by the royal feet on it, it made the envy of Chinese house.

The emperor passed through the bazars which were fully decorated with shops.

Bait (*verse*)

All sides were beautifully equipped and were laced with every necessary commodities (of life). The uncountable number of quantities of gold and gems were scattered from all sides to grace the occasion.

Bait (*verse*)

The planet felt helpless in counting the treasure, showered, and similarly Venus was also unable to calculate them.

From all sides, the edifice was canopied with brocade and velvet while silken-curtains and coloured pillars with the entire ground, covered with the golden cloth by the decorators (*farrashans*). (p. 139) A large tent, made of felt cloth outside and brocade and velvet inside, was fixed there. The floor of brocade, velvet and silk was further decorated with rugs from Khurasan and Iran, with incomparable refinement.[1] The rooms inside were decorated with paintings in blue-colours. The palace which had attractive chambers on all sides, its walls were polished white with lime so those were shining like mirror and one could see his reflection in them. The beauty, arranged there put to shame the Chinese art gallery and made the sky envy.[2]

The programme of the assembly of pleasure started. Male and female singers with their sweet and melodious voices started singing on the music of Sarod and other instruments which touched the height of the sky. Hearing the soul-stirring music of the party Venus itself came up to the roof of the sky and it observed this spectacular scene of the assembly in deep-wonderment. The music which was coming out of Barbad, made its face glean with delight and led to happiness and pleasure. It opened the Khurasani music in the Hindustani style which touched the height of skies.

Misraa (*a hemistich*)

The musicians played music like the songs of a nightingale.

Reputed poets and prose writers composed the choicest

poems and prose which they recited and presented there. The pleasing recitations, humours and elegant pleasantries made the convivial gathering unique among thousands. Wonderfully pleasing discussions like magic and chaste conversations wiped out sorrow and sadness from the hearts of the pessimistic persons. The only recitation was for the advancement of everlasting empire and the sun of the sky of the realm. (p. 140)

Beautiful rich women were burning with frankincense and aloe-wood in gold and silver fire-places and the fragrant vapours rising out of them, were giving eternal life to the souls. Whatever requisite provisions and equipments required for making the assembly delightful and enjoyable had all been collected and its host was also fully adorned with entertainment of the guests.

Misraa (*a hemistich*)

The assemblage of enjoyment was attractive like the faces of beauty. During the same time, reputed chefs prepared gourmet food, innumerable like stars in the sky. As a result of too many varieties of food and provision of all kinds of drinks, appetite had itself vanished from the world. So many varieties of delicious dry fruits and sweets were prepared to serve that the grandeur of the garden of paradise was astonished. (p. 141)

The perfect and amicable arrangements impressed the emperor and he cast his affectionate eye on the Khan, conferred a white khilat (robe of special quality) with other honours on him. The emperor sat on the throne and all kinds of presents such as swords, studded-daggers, belts, jewelled aloe-burners, bowls placed before him in boats (trays) of gold and silver. The breeze full of ambar and musk was refreshing the souls of the angels even in skies.

Many other golden and silver articles, besides chandeliers, plates and water-jugs of gold and silver were also presented. The finest pieces of cloth such as zarbaft of Rum, velvet of Europe, kamkhab-i-Yazdi, atlas-i-Khatai of Bukhara, studded dupatta and turbans, Deccani jewelled boxes, golden thread of Gujarat and the royal muslin of Sunargaon were also presented to him. (p. 142) A horde of twenty-five elephants, who could run in the battlefield like fire and wind with their controlling crooks (ankush), frightening the eyes and throwing their trunks in anger like a polo ball . . . and looking like pythons who could pull down the sky with their trunks were also presented. The mahavats had decorated the trappings of their mountain like elephants with velvet and brocade of Europe, which were glittering like thunder and lightning.

A special (khasa) elephant, whose tusks were covered with gold and decorated with precious rubies and gems, ornamented dressed with cornelian and precious pearls, was also presented. (p. 143)

Arabi horses, with lightning speed, Iraqi and Turkish horses, challenging the circling sky like clouds, in whose hoofs nails were fitted to walk slowly like the shadow of wall or to run fast to outrun their own shadow if they wish. The row of burden bearing camels with their high ridge like humps, with the speed of wind were also presented. For the blessed princes who are the pearls of crown and throne, beautiful, angel like maid servants, diamond, ruby and Firuza were presented. (p. 144) All the presents were appreciated by the princes. The Khan presented gifts to his near and dear ones along with his servants and attendants of the emperor.[3]

Duaa (prayer) for His Majesty

By the grace of the Almighty that this fortunate house is decorated like the palace of Nausherwan due to the blessed visit of the emperor. The world is being illumined by his justice. May God grant him more and more power of justice and may He grant everlasting life to the emperor! May God, who is great, make still stronger the true faith through Muzaffar Nishan, Wazir! We rely on it.

NOTES

1. *Bait* has been left. See pp. 138-39.
2. *Nazm, Masnavi* and *Bait* have been left. See p. 140.
3. Abul Fazl only mentions the emperor's visit there. *AN*, II, 365. Neither of the contemporary and near contemporary sources contain these details except Arif.

OCCURRENCE 25

Description of the Buildings of the Dar-ul-Khilafat, Agra with a Brief Illustration of its Lofty Fort, Built by the Grace of God

It should not remain unknown to the most skilful and expert engineers and artists that the name and fame of emperors rise high by their lofty edifices. Thus the saying has been well known that the names of kings remain alive for ages on account of their buildings. [When the Almighty, the Creator, brought into existence the contents of the world, created the distance of time, place, sky and earth, He did not issue any command to any until His creation work was over. Thereafter He addressed His creatures, "Look at My creation". "Do they not see sky over their head and now we have created it", He further said.]

These prefatory words signify that the purpose of construction of buildings cannot be described in words. According to elders, "The nobleness of a person is known by his buildings and his courage can be judged by visiting his abode." (p. 145)

Now if we deeply think over the above-mentioned introductory lines, we will realize that among the various monuments, which have been raised by the monarchs of the world, the edifices of the Darul-Khilafa, Agra can serve as a model for all others.

Bait (*verse*)

[He is the one who confers dignity on emperors of regions, it is the fruit of the blessed favour.]

In past those great emperors, who by taking advantage of the magnificence of their times, had constructed palaces or similar other edifices, so that their great splendour and grandeur be thereby exhibited. Praise be to God that in this last period, the creator of both the worlds has endowed emperor Jalal-ud-Din Muhammad Akbar, who is His shadow on earth and is the ruler of His land, with such capacity and all such materials that he might lay the foundations of a fort in the city of Agra, which is one of the great cities of Hindustan and is full of all sorts of precious things.[1]

Therefore, the reputed and expert architect laid the foundation at an auspicious hour on Sunday A.H. 981/1573 A.D. because Sunday is a good day for the construction of buildings.[2] Great experts of the art kept in view the finer aspects of fort in mind. Two thousand stone-cutters and the same number of sculptors and masons were engaged for the work. Besides them, eight thousand labourers were employed to bring stones for its construction in time. One thousand carts, loaded with stones, brought it daily from Fatehpur Sikri while granite pieces by hundred boats were brought on the bank of river Jamuna.[3]

Bait (*verse*)

Everywhere the sky began to run fast because it was not possible to drag the weight of those stones.

The fort was built of red sandstone on the bank of river Jamuna (p. 146) like the palace of the unlimited pleasures such as the palaces of Paradise where in canals flow under them. Its walls and boundaries were made very strong and durable.

Masnavi (*rhyme*)

May your palaces be inhabited always, and the eye of evil-mongers may remain far from it! This palace, which kisses the sky would have been better if it had been built on the ninth sky.

The city is so prosperous and well-populated that its opulence and prosperity are the insurance of happiness. Cheapness of commodities there and its profitable regions are flourishing meadows of plentiful gains. Its unparalleled edifices are the envy of the city of Iram. The city with its attractive buildings has nothing comparable to it. Dajla-i-Baghdad watching the flow of river Jamuna went into hiding (with shame) and has blushed. Its forehead has shrunk with dry lips and tearful eyes. Even the fountain of Elixir Vita looks small before it. Keeping in view the necessities of daily life of the people, the emperor has put countless boats and ships on the banks of river (for bringing necessary things). The tremendous crowd of merchants and traders of all races from the four corners of the *Orbit terra firma* with the object of trade started gathering in so that the capital city, Agra, had become the whole of Hindustan by itself, as it were. The growth of even the smallest town was amazing because it had grown bigger than Baghdad and Shiraz. Among the most notable were the cities of Delhi and Lahore. There was not even one karoh of land in the entire Hind which was left unfit either to be built upon or for cultivation.

Bait (*verse*)

It is such a blessed city and such a fortunate country that the sun during its life has never witnessed the likes of it. (p. 147)

In reality all its walls as well as its arches have been built in red-stone,[4] in such a wonderful way that not only imagination is amazed at it, but even the sky was feeling shy of its spectacle. The depth of its plinth is one cubit Akbar Shahi, the width of the wall fifteen yards and the height (of the wall) from the base to the top fifty-five yards.[5] The base is touching the level of water. In the width of the rampart, the palaces of queens have been built as also seats wherefrom to watch sights (in the distance), and the circular wall of every bastion is made strong by means of lime (cement). All round the walls a strong escarpment (stopping embankment) has been made of stone and lime, so that the water of the ditch may not be able to damage the walls of the fort, and the base of the fort also be viewed.

A moat twenty yards in width has been made round the wall. Within a short time owing to the huge crowd of visitors it is looking like Jama-i-Misri or the crown of Egypt. It was shining bright with its beauty and grandeur. The proof of claim of freshness of these monuments lies in the fact that the rays of its cast are based on justice and kindness, which is evident on its surface and by the details of the houses and shelters which are seen suitably built outside the fort.

Bait (*verse*)

There was no building, possessing of such grace and if there happens to be one, then it has no grace.

On one side of the fort high palaces have been built in red stone which seem to be the envy of paradise, and the upper chambers have been decorated with a variety of floral designs. Its floor is made of stone and its ceiling has been covered with such fine sculptural ornamentation, that even 'Mani' (a famous architect who was so vain about his knowledge that he had claimed prophethood), is lying prostrate with amazement. The scenes from the side windows are like those of paradise. Whoever enjoys or witnesses its extensive dimensions, arrangement and skill of constructions, considers it a symbol or model of the administration of the empire. (p. 148) By his organising ability the emperor has entrusted the charge of supervision and construction of it to the loyal servant of the state Muhammad Qasim Khan, Chief flotilla (Mir Bahar). In accordance with the imperial farman, the above-named Khan completed the construction of the grand edifice with red stone in three years time.[6] Four gates (portals) were opened on four sides. The work which others could not have finished in ten years, the superintendent and co-workers accomplished in such an excellent way that experts were amazed at it, and uttered words of wonderment at this surpassing achievement of the builders. No wonder therefore, the Mushtari from the height of sixth sky recited praises for the emperor.[7]

Duaa (*prayer*) *for His Majesty*

May God preserve this founder of Sultanate and give him power and stability!

Qita (hemistich)

Two monuments, which are like paradise on high, have been completed during the reign of Sahib-qiran (Akbar) of the seven zones; one at the capital city, Agra, and the other at Fatehpur Sikri at the residence of Shaikh Salim, the heaven has with its two ancient pens written the date of those two grand edifices in the following words.[8] (p. 149)

NOTES

1. See also *AN*,.II, 247, *MT*, II, 174 and *TA*, II, 179.
2. The construction work of the fort started in A.H. 972/1564 A.D. *TA*, II, 179, *MT*, II, 74, *Zubda*, fol. 117 and *AN*, II, 246.
3. Four thousand workers were deployed. See *ibid.*
4. This fort is built of red stone and its fencing is done with iron. *AN*, I, 247.
5. Abul Fazl says that its width is three yards while height is sixty yards Padshahi. *Ibid* while Badauni says its width is ten yards and height sixty yards. *MT*, II, 74 while Nizamuddin says that its width is ten yards. *TA*, II, 179.
6. Abul Fazl says that it was completed in six years. *AN*, II, 247, while Badauni says in five years. *MT*, II, 74 but Nizamuddin says in four years. *TA*, II, 179.
7. *Abiyat* (verses) has been left. See pp. 148-9.
8. Badauni says that both fort at Agra and Fatehpur were completed in A.H. 979/1571 A.D. The date as mentioned above also comes the same. While Abul Fazl and Nizamuddin say it was completed in A.H. 982/1574 A.D. *AN*, II, 247 and *TA*, II, 179. There is complete disagreement among the contemporary historians.

OCCURRENCE 26

Description of Laying Foundation of the City, Fatehabad Sikri by the Orders of His Majesty and its Process of Construction

Among those primary structures on which depends the administration of the world and evergrowing monuments whereupon the eyes of His Majesty's armies are illumined, are situated in the fort of Agra. As the city of Agra was the capital of the empire; its planning and construction, which have been discussed earlier, were kept in mind.[1] (p. 150)

When the emperor returned to Agra from Ajmer in the month of Rabi II, A.H. 979/August, 1571 A.D., he issued an order for laying the foundation of the city of Fatehpur Sikri.[2] When the architects and planners presented the map of the proposed construction to the emperor, he instructed that houses be built and gardens be planted within the compound and covering the neighbouring hills for about two to three karohs. It was further ordered that no one should interfere or obstruct the building of houses there, and land should also be freely allotted to those desirous of it. Moreover, the constructors of houses would be its owners and they shoud be encouraged to populate the barren land of the region around. Thereafter, sculptors and stone-cutters started their respective works. In short, the work started with good luck and kind blessings, which deserved all appreciation, was completed within a short span of time. The portions of land which were lying barren like the dry hearts of lovers and were yearning for a touch of an artist's hands, began to glow like the rosy cheeks of the beloved and thereby splendour and freshness were imparted to it. The wild land all around, which had been the hunt of foxes, groaned with flourishing plants, and the city soon became filled with mosques, bazars, baths, sarais (for merchants) and such other buildings for the good of the people.[3]

In A.H. 984/1576 A.D., an imperial order was issued that from the court up to the gate which faces the capital city beautiful shops of red stone with lime plaster may be built. Moreover, four bazars well designed and decorated were also built near it. (p. 151) Towards the bazars three arches of red stone were built of such beauty that even the imagination felt amazed at them and even the lofty dome of the sky began to feel ashamed before them. . . . Moreover, His Majesty ordered that when the season of Kharif was to commence, expert architects and hardworking masons should prepare the sketch of the city of which the walls be made i.e. its width thirty Akbari karohs from its base and gates should also be constructed on all sides. It was hoped that it would be completed in a very short time. Besides the said monuments which should be regarded as the model of exceptional engineering skill of the emperor, there is a blessed palace (like the one which Luqman s/o Mandaz had got built by the famous architect Samnar for the residence of Emperor Bahram Gaur) which is the guardian of the house of the state and its dignity, and on account of which nine skies seem to be ashamed and amazed and which has the height of the sky and its ornamentation.

In the courtyard of this high editice, which touches the sky, beginning from one side four chambers, four raised platforms and four halls have been made so skilfully that the watchmen of all the eight paradises feel staggered with wonderment. Royal houses and government offices have been built around it. In the centre of the courtyard a tank[4] is laid and its water is considered the blessing of the early dawn. The reflection of man's face can be seen very clearly in it which excels the mirror called *Jahan Numa*. One can see each particle of sand up to its depths, which can be counted and even the eggs of the fish can be seen.[5] (p. 152)

Bait (verse)

This pond is like a river, not that it is a river without head or tail.

In A.H. 986/1578 A.D. the pond was emptied of its water and in its place it was filled up with copper, silver and gold tankas in such a way that intelligence was helpless in sounding its depth, nor the imagination of travellers could see its banks.[6]

NOTES

1. *Qita* and *Bait* have been left. See pp. 149-50.
2. Badauni says that the emperor in A.H. 976/1569A.D. laid the foundation of great edifice on the mountain near the Khanqah of Shaikh (Salim Chishti). Mosques etc., were completed in five years time and it was named Fatehpur. *MT*, II, 109 and 225.
3. *Bait* has been left. See p. 150.
4. Anup Talau. Its length and width were twenty yards while its depth was of two men's height. *AN*, III, 246. But Badauni says that it was twenty yards long and three yards deep. *MT*, II, 339. For a full account of the tank see *Tuzuk* also.
5. While Nizamuddin says in A.H. 987/1579 A.D. See also *AN*, III, 246 and *MT*, II, 265 *TA*, II, 339. *Abiyat* have been left. See pp. 152-54. Irfan Habib, *The Economic & Social Settin, Fatehpur Sikri*, edited by Michael Brand and Gleen. D. Lawry, Mary Publications, 1987.
6. Description of the foundation of Fatehpur Sikri follows in the construction of Agra. As such Arif has not followed any chronological order.

OCCURRENCE 28

Description of His Majesty's March Towards Gujarat with Imperial Forces, His Conquest of That Dominion (Vilayat) by the Grace of God and Mentioning Some of Events Also

As the world conqueror and wise planner, the emperor had decided to pay a visit to the shrine of Khwaja Muin-ud-Din Chishti, (p. 156) he set out from the region Fatehabad Sikri by the end of Safar,[1] A.H. 981/June, 1573 A.D. On his way, he asked for a fast running horse at Sanganer and went off for hunting.

The Emperor issued a farman that everyone of the torch-bearers and gunmen should become attentive towards hunting of lions and tigers, resembling the speed of lightning. The attractive forest whose cool breeze due to the beginning of the monsoon, had removed the dust from the heart, and the hand of the Almighty had, in order to preserve the honour of gardens, produced green grass and flowers on the ground.[3]

The king did so much hunting that the hunting ground looked blood red like a ruby of Badakhshan. While returning, the emperor confronted a mighty lion before whom even the (Babar) lion of the jungle bends his head like a cat.[2] (p. 157) The lion-throwing emperor threw it down with the point of his lance. After thus killing it, he went to the tomb of . . . Saiyed Husain, rider of white horse, which was situated in the fort on the hill top at Ajmer.[3] There he placed his head on its threshold with due humility and reverence like a humble son.[4]

On the 10th of Rabi-ul-Awwal[5]/21st July of the said year, he obtained the grace of paying homage at the paradise like shrine. Along with him, the princes and some of the queens of his seraglio also performed perambulation there.

At the same time, the emperor decided to annex the dominion of Gujarat. Therefore, some of the senior Khans and amirs were ordered to join Mir Muhammad Khan, who was the subedar of Nagore, Ajmer and Jodhpur up to the frontiers of Gujarat. He himself went to Ajmer. An imperial farman was issued directing the above named Khans to appoint the right and left wings of the army. Thereafter the emperor, marching from Ajmer followed them.[6] (p. 158) During the same time, the happy news of the birth of Prince Muhammad Daniyal Mirza, who was born on the night of Friday, 4th Jamadi, II/12th October of the above-mentioned year was received.[7] God willing the child will be a source of prosperity and happiness of humanity till the Day of the Judgment, by the grace of the Prophet and his progeny.

On 8th Jamadi-us-Sani[8]/16th October the abovementioned Khan reached Sirohi. While he was sitting on his masnad, in his palace, he invited those messengers, who were deputed by Raja Man,[9] to meet and offer them betel as is the custom of the people of Hind.[10] One of the rebels out of that group, attacked the Khan with his Jamdhar (a small sword) and wounded him. He was killed on the spot[11] and the Khan recovered soon. The emperor was grieved to hear it and he reached there on[12] 10th of the same month/18th October. However, Dost Muhammad,[13] son of Tatar Khan, became martyr in that melee.

During the same time Yar Ali Beig Turkman with twenty Qazalbash came as the agent of Sultan Muhammad Mirza,[14] son of Nawab Shah Tahmasp and presented some fast running horses. (p. 159) Even before the imperial retinue could reach Pattan, which was one of the famous cities of Gujarat, Sher Khan Fauladi,[15] its ruler, leaving his son behind, marched to Ahmadabad and launched his attack against Atimad Khan[16] there. Ulughi Mirzas,[17] who were the sworn enemy of the emperor and had control over Baroach[18] and Baroda,[19] came out and expressed their determination to help the Khan. But no sooner did the news of the arrival of the

The enemy had come to fight the sun but his stars did not stand with him and his steady feet.

At last, Ibrahim Husain Mirza decided to run away and he escaped that very night from there. But the gallant soldiers followed him and they soon found their way, barred by a narrow and thorny passage, coupled with thorny bushes and inaccessible trees, which were spread over on both sides like the anxious heart of enemy. So it was found impossible to advance further.[44] Just at that juncture the emperor roared loudly like a lion and called his men. Hearing his voice, their courage returned and the enemy scattered in confusion like the 'seven stars' (p. 163) and threw dust of defeat on their faces.[45] The imperial forces marched out of Baroda the same night and the family of Ibrahim got separated and proceeded to the South.[46] On 25th Shaban/31st December His Majesty turned his attention to lay siege to the fort of Surat.[47] Being frustrated, Ibrahim Husain diverted his march towards Agra. He entered the environs of Delhi, through Nagore, and then crossing (the two) rivers, he repatriated towards Sambhal and finally fled to Punjab. Khan-i-Jahan and other nobles of Punjab chased him and defeated (him) near the village of Talanba.[48] His brother Masud Husain was arrested while escaping. Ibrahim Husain surrounded by the Balochis was struck by an arrow. At last he was captured by Saeed Khan. He died at Multan.[49] On 20th Safar A.H. 982/21st June, 1574 A.D. Saeed Khan[50] brought his head to Agra while Khan-i-Jahan presented his brother. It was ordered that he should be brought to court with eyes sown. Accordingly, he was presented. However, he was pardoned, his eyes were reopened and was imprisoned in the fort of Gwalior.[51]

Bait (verse)

If the enemy is captured, don't take him lightly, but if you don't want to dishonour or kill him, at least he should be put into prison.

The fort of Surat, which stands on the shore of the Arabian sea was one of the most famous forts of Gujarat and its strength could be easily estimated. Keeping it in mind, the emperor decided to conquer it. (p. 164) Meanwhile, Muhammad Husain Ulughi, leaving some persons, took to flight with a few foolish fellows. This troop, being proud of and relying on the strength of the fort, decided to fight. The emperor arrived on 6th Ramzan[52]/31st December there. The imperial army undertook the charge of laying siege to it. In the nick of time, news was received that Sher Khan Fauladi had joined hands with the Afghans of Pattan and Ulughi Mirzas, gathered outside Pattan. There they laid a siege to Pattan and besieged Saiyed Ahmad Khan Barha in the fort.[53] The news blazed the fire of his wrath. Immediately, an imperial order was issued that, "Mirza Koka entitled Khan-i-Azam, appointed the commander of the force, while Qutbuddin Muhammad Khan,[54] Shah Muhammad Khan,[55] Shah Badagh, Naurang Khan[56] and Muhammad Murad Khan[57] along with the contingent of Malwa, Rai Sain and Chanderi, besides a number of troops, should proceed for the help and assistance of Mirza Aziz Kokaltash and they should kill or expell them." Ahmadabad was assigned to Mirza Koka. Mir Ala-ud-Daula has given the date of this incident.[58]

The above-named Khans, starting from their respective jagirs, came and joined the army of Mirza Koka. On 10th Ramzan/4th January, 1574 A.D. the assemled forces, marched towards Pattan. (p. 165) On their arrival at Pattan, the army was first arranged into proper divisions and the stock of equipments required was taken. Various units were arranged like this: the centre under Aziz Koka, Shah Badagh Khan and their men; the right arm under Qutbuddin Khan and his followers while on the left wing Shah Muhammad Khan, Muhammad Murad Khan and some other Khans. Naurang Khan was appointed the Van of infantry. On the other side, Sher Khan Fauladi too with his sons and the Afghans arranged the battlefray. Taking the centre position, he appointed Ulughi Mirzas on the left and right. Thus the battle commenced on 19th Ramzan/13th January 1574 A.D. with great zeal and valour.[58]

Frankly speaking, it was the Day of Judgement. The imperial army was raising tremendous noise and the soldiers and horsemen had brought an earthquake over the plains and the hills. The noise of cry and piteous protestation of the Afghans were coming from the other side. Everybody had left his place and both the forces were engaged in hand to hand fight. Shouts heard engaged were, "catch him, kill him and take him." During the heat of action, Shah Muhammad Khan faced some angry soldiers. Though he fought bravely, he received some cuts on his hand and head and he ran away towards Ahmadabad. Some of the Khans also started fleeing. It seemed as if they were struck by an evil-eye. They floated the rumour that the imperial army had lost. Those who had escaped to Ahmadabad were told of it by those mischief-mongers and they created the impression all round that the imperial army had been defeated. It created fear and despair in the hearts of the supporters of Islam which overwhelmed them. They had become strangers to *Faith* also.[73] (p. 166)

Mirza Koka and Shah Badagh Khan, who held the centre, confounded and scattered the enemy in the very first onslaught. Advancing forward, they set aflame the fire of battle to such a degree that the cups of swords were full of the wine (blood) of slaughtering heads. "Allah will fully help you", was being heard all round.[74]

Qutb-ud-in Muhammad Khan, who was on the right side, was making targets of the enemy by his sword, arrow and lance while a section of the army was sacrificing their lives for the sake of the emperor. The arrows of the messengers of death had opened their mouths while the mastery of swords was using its tongues. Although lances were being hurled at the imperial army, the shield of courage was resisting them. When the clubs were raised with might, the shields received them well.[59] (p. 167)

When Sher Khan, the Afghans and the Mirzas saw the valour and courage of the royal forces, they realized that there was no chance of moving further. Having made a momentary movement of sacrifice, the air of royal good luck changed into the breeze of victory and the victorious banners began to show the light of triumph. Sher Khan and the Mirzas turned their backs and fled away. So one batallion was destroyed in the fire of plunder and loot and it was drowned in the river of torture.[60] Saiyed Ahmad Khan Barha[61] and the other Khans, who were imprisoned in the city of Pattan, came out and conveyed the happy news of victory to the emperor. Mirza Koka and Qutbuddin Muhammad Khan returned safely, loaded with a huge booty. Later Mirza Koka went to Surat and on 20th Shawwal/13th February, obtained the happiness by kissing the royal feet. Qutbuddin Muhammad Khan also along with other Khans crossed Gujarat and reached the town of Mahmudabad. (p. 168) Ikhtiyar-ul-Mulk, who had fled with some Abysinians was hiding in the forest where a battle ensued but the imperial forces captured them. In short, the authority of the imperial army was fully and firmly established there.

Qutbuddin Muhammad Khan and other Khans kissed the royal feet when the emperor returned to Mahmudabad after capturing the fort of Surat.

It has already been recorded in the preceding pages that the emperor himself laid the siege of the fort of Surat.[62] The foolish commandant of the fort Hamzeban,[63] being proud of the strength and equipments named it fire engine, got themselves busy in its defence. When the emperor sat on the throne (masnad), they started vomiting tons of fire from their guns which fell on the imperial army. The emperor visualised the existing situation with depth and ordered that deep trenches be dug on its left and right sides which made the army secure. The castle of the fort was visible by means of a microscope without any obstacle. It was the most massive and strong fort. It faced the Arabian Sea.[64]

(p. 169) Because the strength of the fort was inclined to submit before the good luck of His Majesty, and its impregnability was in despair before him, it was at once decided that mines should be constructed to serve as (Sabats), a covered passage connecting two houses without delay, the work started and in no time there were holes in its walls and passages opened to enter into it. With the help of supervisors, canons and instruments for hurling stones were installed and its towers were smashed like a bathive and demolished into dust. It frightened the garrison inside the fort and they were amazed by the bravery of the royal army. They did not understand (what they should do). The foolish Hamzeban was perturbed. Immediately, he sent a messenger to confess his guilt with a petition that "Muhammad Husain Mirza fled to the jungle while this miserable is out of his wits with fear at the attack of the imperial army. If the emperor was inclined to pardon them and treat this pathless company with mercy, he (messenger) will at once go running and it was granted." Hamzeban with the guilty party, came and stood under the shadow of the king's mercy.[65] On 23rd Shawwal, A.H. 982/26th February, 1574 A.D. Hamzeban and his party were beaten with fists and fully tormented so that all others would get a lesson.[66] (p. 170)

By the end of the above-mentioned month, Raja Bahara Jiu,[67] who was well-known among rulers of the frontiers of Gujarat and the Deccan, arrested Sharfuddin Husain and presented him in a wretched condition before the emperor. He had been a rebel for the last ten years.[68] His Majesty remarked, "We had opened for you the door of our liberality and kindness, and you in return for all those obligations and favours, became disobedient and disloyal and enlisted yourself among the gang of rebels, and you were creating all types of troubles and turbulence. You told your foster brother that you hurled arrows and wounded us. Your confession had made you worth of being killed according to the Shariat."[69] That ungrateful fellow had no answer except keeping his mouth shut. In brief, His Majesty ordered that the ungrateful fellow, whose actions were despicable and the list of his crimes too long, should be bullied with fists and fistcuffs, curses and abuses be heaped upon him and he be then thrown in front of elephants. Then a farman was issued that the corrupt and degraded fellow should finally be thrown into a prison and he be placed under the custody of the Bakhshis.[70]

At last, His Majesty was free from the affairs of Gujarat, he turned to relaxation and enjoyment.

When the precious country fell under the supreme command (of the emperor), the hands of rebels shrank too short to touch the skirt of his dignity, then the wine of his enjoyment demanded the power of the use of liquor. It was the same flavour, demanded by other countries also.[71] (p. 171)

By chance it so happened that the messengers of the Firangan (the Europeans) who were settled in the port of Daman on the coast of the Arabian Sea, came and brought some card loaded with the Portuguese wine with them. Its scent turned the lions of skies dead-drunk, and even the innocent denizens of earth thought of enjoying its effect. They were given fast running horses in return.[72]

The fact was that the collection of provisions of enjoyment induced the emperor to drink and for this purpose he adorned the throne in the Diwan-i-Khas. The wine served shone in the cups like the light in the eyes of noble man. (p. 172) The hiding screen was removed away from the face (cheeks) and the swab of forgetfulness had been taken away from the ears, and the senses had been plundered from the head. His face was shining like the sun by the effect of wine, as fire rising from the earth. The sparks of flames of wine had purified the wealth of life of the drinkers by burning it. That day Mirza Koka, Muzaffar Khan, Lashkar Khan and some persons of lower rank, who had joined the paradise like assembly had taken 'arq' and 'tari' and were behaving as if they had wine. The emperor enjoyed the assembly till the end. Let us hope that the emperor's mind would not be dim by the dust of intoxication, and the dust of the road would also not settle on the beautiful face of the favourites of the festivity. To sum up, the next day, which was the 1st of Ziqada/5th March of the above-said year,[73] the emperor started from the fort of Surat and decided to return from Gujarat. The fort of Surat was conferred as Jagir on Umdat-ul-Mulk Qilji Muhammad Khan.[74]

The emperor reached Baroach on his way. Jajjar Khan Habshi, who was one of the amirs of Gujarat, killed Changez

Khan, former administrator of Baroach and some provinces of Gujarat without any reason. The mother of the deceased came and complained against Jajjar Khan. On the basis of her complaint, the date of suit (complaint) was fixed for 8th of the current month/13th March which was the day of Naurauz. The emperor, after duly considering the case ordered that Jajjar Khan be punished under the feet of an elephant[75] and he was crushed to pieces. Thus his Id of Naurauz turned into the night of grief. (p173)

Marching stage by stage, the emperor encamped outside Ahmadabad. On 18th Ziqada/23rd March Atga Khan was appointed in charge of the Sarkar of Gujarat while Qutbuddin Muhammad Khan and Naurang Khan of Bharoach, Baroda and Champanir. Saropa, sword and horse were also given as presents to them and they were allowed to proceed to their respective assignments.

On the day of Id-ul-Zuha the emperor left Ahmadabad and reached on 8th Zi-hijja/9th January 1575 A.D. in the town of Setpur,[76] which was a dependency of Pattan, Ahmadabad, which had been the seat of the Sultans of Gujarat, was entrusted to Mirza Koka entitled Khan-i-Azam while the Sarkar of Pattan to Mir Muhammad Khan and his descendants. Having bestowed suitable robes, elephants and horses on them, they were allowed to go. Thus having taken into possession the territory up to the shores of the Arabian Sea, the emperor entrusted the management to the Khans.[77]

It had been mentioned that a farman was issued, summoning Jumdat-ul-Mulk Muzaffar Khan from Agra; so he came and kissed the royal feet in the fort of Surat. The emperor conferred on him numerous gifts, i.e. two crore and fifty lakh tanka-i-muradi[94] from the Sarkar of Sarangpur and Ujjain which were operating under Malwa, a fine robe and a studded horse. He was then permitted to leave for his jagir.[78] Covering stage by stage, the emperor reached Ajmer on 10th Muharram A.H. 983/11th May, 1575 A.D.[79] He visited the shrine of . . . . Muinuddin Chishti. Then he came to the town of Ambar.[80] The emperor took along with him Prince Mirza Muhammad Daniyal who was born there. (p. 174)

On 2nd Safar, A.H. 983/3rd June, 1575 A.D. the emperor reached Fatehabad Sikri. The nobles and the inhabitants of the city celebrated the return of the emperor with great ecstacy. All the places and bazars were decorated, while the houses and buildings were beautified like paradise. For a number of days the city of Agra continued to be a city of festivities while sorrow and grief vanished from it like an evil-eye. The city seemed like an abode of happiness and one where all sins were forgiven. The flowers of the gardens bloomed. Blessing descended on the royal mansion just as the moon in its celestial zone, pearl in its wrapper, soul in body, earth in garden, virgin in paradise and happiness in the world. The throne of the realm became more and more beautiful, bright and full of splendour by seeing the august face of the emperor.[81] In short, all the four sides of Hindustan were decorated by the king's order so that they excelled all the eight paradises. All worries from the intoxicated eyes of the Turks vanished, but the beauties of Hindustan remained worried.

Duaa (prayer) for His Majesty

May the Almighty make the curtains of unending wealth of the emperor, whose reign extends up to the seven skies, as strong and enduring as the stars and planets of sky, and make his banner big enough to serve as an umbrella for the sun by the grace of the Prophet and his progeny![82]

Notes

1. 20th Safar/2nd July, *Mirat-i-Ahmadi,* (hereafter *Mirat*), I, 114. See also *TA*, II, 236 and *MT*, II, 139.
2. *Bait* and *Nazm* have been left. See pp. 156-57.
3. After the killing of the lion, the emperor first paid visit to the tomb of Khwaja Muin-ud-Din Chishti and then to the tomb of Saiyed Husain Khang Sawar. See also *AN*, II. 371.
4. *Nazm* has been left. See p. 167.
5. Abul Fazl says on Friday, 15th/26th July. *AN*, II, 371 while Nizamuddin says on Thursday, 15th/26th July. *TA*, II, 236 and Badauni mentions only the date i.e. 15th. *MT*, II, 139.

6. On Sunday, 22nd Rabi-us-Sani/1st September, the emperor started from Ajmer. *AN*, II, 372, *TA*, II, 236 and *Mirat*, I, 114.
7. See also *NM* fol. 200, *AN*, II, 373. *MT*, II, 139 and *TA*, II, 236. The date 15th Jamadi-ul-Awwal, A.H. 979/6th October, 1571 A.D. given by Jahangir in his Tuzuk does not seem correct. *Bait, Masnavi* and *Bait* have been left. See p. 158.
8. On 15th/23rd October of the said month. *NM*, fol. 201. See also *TA*, II, 237. *MT*, II, 140 and *AN*, II, 4.
9. Raja Man Singh Dewra. See *AN*, III, 4 and *Mirat*, I, 114.
10. See also *Zubda*, fol. 137-a, *AN*, III, 4. *MT*, II, 140, *TA*, II, 237 and *MR*, I, 717.
11. Nizamuddin says Muhammad Sadiq Khan killed him. *TA*, II, 237. Muhammad Quli Khan. *NM*, fol. 201-a, while Bahadur Khan killed him. *AN*, III, 4 and *Mirat*, I, 114.
12. On 16th Jamadi II/24th October. *MR*, I, 777. On Monday in the month of Jamadi-us-Sani/October. *NM*, fol. 201 while Nizamuddin says on 20th/28th October which seems appropriate also because the emperor halted four days at Nagore when he received the wounding news at Meerta. *TA*, II, 238.
13. See also *TA*, II, 238 and *NM*, fol. 201-a.
14. Abul Fazl says Sultan Muhammad Khuda Banda, the ruler of Khurasan. *AN*, III, 5 while Hakim-i-Hirat. *NM*, fol. 201-a.
15. Sher Khan Fauladi, son of Ain-ul-Mulk, one of the amirs of Gujarat unleashed sedition and destruction after its conquest by the emperor. He however died early in the year, A.H. 998/1590 A.D. See also *AN*, and *TM*.
16. When the emperor reached Qasba Diha, Sher Khan sent his relations Muhammad Khan and Bahadur Khan for strengthening the fort. See also *AN*, III, 5. *TA*, II, 238 and *Mirat*, I, 115.
17. Abdul Karim entitled Itimad Khan Gujarati was one of the great nobles of Gujarat. He joined the imperial service after the conquest of Gujarat and the emperor conferred a high mansab on him. He died in A.H. 994/1586 A.D. at Agra. *ZK*, 349-50. See also *TM* and *TA*.
18. Ulugh Mirza and Shah Mirza, sons of Shan Mirza, who had animosity with the emperor. *AN*, II, 280 and 331, *MU*, III, 192 and *MR*, I, 207.
19. It implies Baroach.
20. Sher Khan Fauladi left Mandu via jungles, reached Surat. *Mirat-i-Sikandari* 367, while Junagarh, says *Tarikh-i-Gujarat*, 56.
21. Surat. *Mirat-i-Sikanderi*, 367 while Surath *Mirat*, I, 115. *Masnavi* has been left. See p. 159.
22. See also *AN*, III, 6. *NM*, fol. 201-b and *Mirat*, I, 115.

23. Saiyed Ahmad Khan was the brother of Saiyed Mahmud. *TA*, II, 438 and *MU*, II, 378.

24. It was done on 7th Rajab/13th November. *Zafar-ul-Wali*, II, 565. Ain-ul-Mulk Shirazi entitled Badauni was one of the nobles and court poets. He died in the night of 27th Zi-hijja, A.H. 1003/24th August 1594 A.D. at Handiya. His real name was Ali. See also *TA*, *MT*, *AN* and *SS*. *Bait* has been left. See p. 160.

25. On Saturday. *NM*, fol. 201-a. See also *TA*, II, 239 and *MT*, II, 141. Sultan Muzaffar Gujarati entitled Nanu was presented by Mir Khan Yasawal before the emporer who fixed three rupees salary per month for him. In A.H. 1001/1592 A.D. he cut his throat with a razor and died. For details see also *AN*, III, 6, *Mirat*, I, 115, *MT*, II, 141 and *MU*, I, 93.

26. See also *Zubda*, fol. 37-b, *NM*, fol. 201-b, *TA*, II, 239 and *MT*, II, 141.

27. Saiyed Hamid Khan, son of Saiyed Miran, son of Saiyed Mubarak Bukhari Gujarati was one of the nobles of Akbar. He died fighting against the Afghans in the early Ziqada, A.H. 994/November, 1586 A.D. *MU*, II, 394, *Zubda*, fol. 137-b.

28. Ulugh Khan Habshi was one of the slaves of Sultan Mahmud Gujarati. He later joined the imperial service and rose to a high position. He remained alive up to A.H. 1009/1600 A.D. *MU*, I, 87 and *AN*, II, 280.

29. Shah Abu-Turab was the first rank Saiyed of Shiraz. He came to the imperial court with some nobles of Gujarat and became one of the trusted nobles. He led the party of Hajis. He died in A.H. 1005/1596 A.D. at Ahmadabad. *MU*, III, 26 and *AN*, III, 217.

30. Jhajhar Khan was one of the nobles from Gujarat. He was crushed under the feet of an elephant for the killing of Changez Khan. See also *AN*, *MT*, *NM*, *TA*, *MR* and *SS*.

31. Ikhtiyar-ul-Mulk, Yar Hindi Sultani was one of the nobles from Gujarat who joined the imperial service. Later, on some pretext, he laid siege to Ahmadabad. He was killed by Suhrab Turkman. *AN*, III, 61, *TM*, 981, see also *MT*, *MR*, *NM* and *SS*.

32. He joined the imperial service in A.H. 983/1575 A.D. *AN*, III, 7, 142 and 208.

33. Malik-ul-Sharq, Muhammad Jiu, son of Babu, was one of the nobles, who joined the imperial service. He died on 3rd Rabi-ul-Awwal, A.H. 992/5th March, 1584 A.D. at Pattan. See *TM*.

34. *Rubai* has been left. See p. 160.

35. He was one of the nobles of Akbar. He died in A.H. 983/1575 A.D. *AN*, III, 140. See also *TM*, and *IJ*.

36. Ibrahim Husain Mirza, son of Muhammad Sultan Mirza was one of the grand sons of Umar Shaikh Mirza, son of Amir Timur. For details see also *MT*, *AN*, *MR*, *TA*, *NM* and *SS*.

37. See also *AN*, III, 8 and *Mirat*, I, 118. *Bait* has been left. See p. 160.
38. See also *NM*, fol. 201-b, *MT*, II, 141, *Zubda*, fol. 137-b, *TA*, II, 240 and *AN*, III, 9 while Sunday, 2nd Shaban/8th December. *Mirat*, I, 118.
39. This incident took place before the emperor's departure towards Khambat. Itimad Khan was imprisoned there. *AN*, III, 10, *Mirat*, I, 119, *MR*, I, 779 and *Tarikh-i-Gujarat*, 71. *Rubai* has been left. See p. 161.
40. In the month of Shaban/December. *Zafar*, II, 57.
41. *Bait* has been left. See p. 161.
42. While Nizamuddin says Rustam Khan Rumi. *TA*, II. 24. See *AN*, III, 11 and *MT*, II, 142.
43. Mir Muhammad Khan.
44. Not more than one hundred karohs. *NM*, fol. 202-b while forty karohs. *AN*, III, 13, *MT*, II, 142. *Mirat*, I, 120 and one hundred and fifteen. *MR*, I, 781 and II, 212. *Bait* has been left. See p. 162.
45. See also *AN*, III, 16, *TA*, II, 244, *NM*, fol. 203-b and 204-a and *MR*, I, 783.
46. *Bait* has been left. p. 162-63.
47. Wife, Gul Rukh Begum, daughter of Mirza Kamran, uncle of Akbar, son of Muzaffar Husain Mirza and these persons escaped to the Deccan. The Khans chased them up to fifteen karohs but they could not capture them. *AN*, III, 16, *Mirat*, I, 122, *MR*, I, 783 and *NM*, fol. 204-a.
48. For details see also *NM*, fol. 204-b, *TA*, II, 245 and *MR*, I, 783 and II, 213.
49. Palta. *AN*, III, 37 and Nanba. *MR*, II, 218.
50. Saeed Khan Chaghata was one of the great nobles. He held Multan Sarkar in fief. For details see also *ZK*, 292-96 and *MU*, II, 403.
51. Abul Fazl has not mentioned it while *MR*, *TA* and *NM* contain it.
52. See also *Ibid.*
53. See also *NM*, fol. 207-a, *Zubda* fol. 140-a, *AN*, II, 18 and *MR*, I, 785.
54. Qutb-ud-din Muhammad Khan, brother of Khan-i-Azam, held a mansab of 5000 and rose to the rank of Amir-ul-Umara. He received martyrdom at Baroda by the hand of Sultan Muzaffar Gujarati. *ZK*, 347 and *MU*, III, 56. See also *AN*, *TA*, *MT*, *MR* and *SS*.
55. Shah Muhammad Khan Atga, brother of Khan-i-Azam Shams-ud-Din Muhammad Atga was one the nobles and he held the mansab of 2000. He died in A.H. 997/1589 A.D. *MU*, II, 542 and *TA*, II, 251.
56. Naurang Khan Bahruz, son of Qutb-ud-din Muhammad Khan performed good services on behalf of Mirza Abdur Rahim at Gujarat. He held post at Malwa and later Gujarat. In the early days of Ramzan, A.H. 1002/May, 1594 A.D. he died at Junagarh. *MU*, III, 59. See also *AN*, *NM*, and *TM*.
57. Muhammad Murad Khan held a jagir at Ujjain first. He assisted Mirza

Aziz Koka against Mirzas. He died in A.H. 988/1580 A.D. *MU*, III, 219. See also *ibid.*

58. This incident has not been recorded in other contemporary and near contemporary sources.
Bait has been left. See p. 163. See also *NM*, fol. 202-a and *Zudba*, fol. 143-a.

59. *Qita, Masnavi* and *Bait* have been left. See pp. 164, 65, 66.

60. *Qita* has been left. See *ibid.*

61. Saiyed Ahmad Khan Barha, brother of Saiyed Mahmud Barha, held a mansab of 3000. His bravery was more manifest than the sun. *ZK*, 359. For details see also *NM*, fol. 206-a, *TA*, II, 438 and *AN*, III, 168.

62. Naharwala. *AN*, III, 24 and *TA*, II, 238.

63. He held the charge of Qurchiyan but due to ill-luck he joined the rebel and was alive till A.H. 988/1580 A.D. *AN*, III, 17 and 320.

64. See *AN*, III, 18 and *NM*, fols.205-a. Nizamuddin says that due to the intensity of firing, the cattles perished. The emperor shifted the encampment near the bank of the Gopi pond. *TA*, II, 246.

65. *Nazm* has been left. See p. 167. For details see also *Mirat, MT, MR, TA* and *Farishta.*

66. See also *NM*, fol. 206-a, *TA*, II, 247, *AN*, III, 28, *MT*, II, 144 and *Mirat*, I, 124.

67. Abul Fazl says that it took one month and seventeen days. *AN*, III, 28 while two months. *Zubda*, fol. 39-b and *TA*, II, 247. The Raja held a mansab of 5000. *ZK*, 152.

68. Abul Fazl says Bharji, the ruler of Baklana. *AN*, III, 29. See also *TA, Zubda* and *Farishta.*

69. Sharfuddin Husain escaped from Agra in A.H. 970/1562 A.D. He was with Changez Khan, one of the nobles of Gujarat. Thereafter, he joined the Mirzas and created sedition. At last he was arrested and presented before the emperor. *AN*, III, 30 and *TA*, II, 249.

70. He was imprisoned in the fort of Gwalior. *Farishta*, I, 260. See also *AN*, III, 40.

71. 72. *Bait* and *Abiyat* have been left. See pp. 170-71.

73. On Sunday, 4th Ziqada/8th March, *NM*, fol. 207. See also *Mirat, AN, MR* and *TA*.

74. Qilij Muhammad Khan, hailed from the vicinity of Kabul. He rose to higher position, held Jaunpur as his fief. He died on 21st Shaban, A.H. 1022/26th September, 1613 A.D. at Peshawar. For details see also *ZK*, 260-5, *TA, SS, NM, MT* and *MU*, III, 69. *Qita* has been left. See p. 172.

75. Nizamuddin says that the elephant's name was Man Mal. *TA*, II, 350.

76. Abul Fazl says Sadhpur. *AN*, III, 33, Sitapur, *TA*, II, 253 while Saiyedpur. *Mirat*, I, 127.

77. *Bait* has been left. See p. 173.
78. See also *AN*, III, 33, *MT*, II, 149 and *TA*, II, 203.
79. Abul Fazl says on 12th Muharram/13th May. *AN*, III, 38 and *NM*, fol. 207-b.
80. Abul Fazl says Anber, situated in Jaipur. *AN*, III, 39.
81. On Tuesday. *NM*, fol. 207.
82. *Masnavi* has been left. See p. 174.

OCCURRENCE 29

Description of the March of Hazrat Khaqan Akbar towards Ahmadabad, Gujarat, Assassination of Muhammad Husain Mirza and Ikhtiyar-ul-Mulk by the Blessings of God

(p. 175) Thereafter the emperor, the weilder of justice, illumined the face of valour by shining the sword and it heralded the banner of success. On his return from Gujarat, he went to Agra and then went to stay in Fatehabad Sikri. In the month of Rabi-ul-Akhir, A.H. 982/August, 1574 A.D. (Atga Khail) who had been entrusted the administration of the entire region of Gujarat sent a report, stating that "some mischief-mongers, including Muhammad Husain Mirza, Shah Mirza,[1] Ikhtiyar-ul-Mulk and sons of Sher Khan Fauladi, who had escaped after their defeat at Pattan and were hiding in the forest, have again emerged as sardars, raising the dust of hostility. Being intoxicated with their rebellious intention, they have come and laid siege to Ahmadabad while its administration was being run by Mirza Koka entitled Khan-i-Azam". He further submitted, "It would be better if His Majesty may come himself and arrest them before launching an attack on him. If even a single person out of the horde managed to escape death then surely others would also find a way of running away."[2]

The emperor decided to teach them a lesson immediately. He did not only resolve to punish them, but suppress their sedition, launched in Gujarat, and protect its inhabitants also. The royal command was promulgated that the imperial standards should be ready with two thousand brave warriors before sun rise and they should also leave in spite of the rainy season. (p. 176) The renowned warriors were also asked to join the expedition. Lashkar Khan, Shujaet Khan[3] and other amirs put into order their troops and they marched towards Gujarat without delay. The emperor himself marched off, accompanied by gallant warriors, numbering two thousand, reputed lion killers. Very soon the realm of Gujarat became the envy of the moon and the sky and from the dome of the lofty halls of state, and by the blows of world conquering sword, the ornament of the universe, all the signs of the existence of rebels were wiped out from the four corners of the world.

Bait (*verse*)

No estimate can be made of your army because each soldier of the troop is equal to a thousand in valour.

To be brief, on 24th Rabi-ul-Akhir[4]/23rd August of the aforesaid year everyone of the warriors, mounting either on fast running camels, capable of covering hills, dusty deserts and jungles or on Iraqi and Turkish horses who could overrun the world and by whose thunder like the lightning and by the anxiety created by whose speed the splendour of thousands of years was eclipsed and by whose fast speed during march their feet touched the rainbow and made it a mound and covered in one jump four or five stages.

(p. 177) In the holy Quran, it has been said about Hazrat Sulaiman that the wind of morning and evening was under his command which took him wherever he desired to reach. The same was true with the emperor's march that he was flying like the wind or the sun when it shines in the day, it overwhelms the whole world or like the sky which carries the stars in one night from east to west. In the same fashion he mounted on a dromedary and reached his destination (like an angel).[5]

The emperor covered the distance of nearly five hundred karohs[6] from Fatehabad Sikri to Ahmadabad within nine days.

The emperor like huma, when he marched, covered a distance of 140 (one hundred and forty) karohs within two and half days only[7] and reached Ajmer to pay homage at the shrine of Khwaja Muinuddin Chishti by whose reverence victories were being achieved, and prayed for the grant of success in this expedition also. (p. 178)

At the time of *Asr* (evening prayer)[8] the emperor came out of the shrine of blessings. Nawab Mirza Khan, Mirza Ghyasuddin Ali Akhuand,[9] Asaf Khan,[10] Abdullah Kejak Khwaja,[11] Saif Khan Koka,[12] Zain Khan,[13] Saiyed Abdullah Khan[14] and others with a force of twenty thousand warriors were ready to join him. Marching forward they reached the town Chitaran[15] and rested for a day. Next day, they reached the town Sojat by mid-night and marched away from there early morning, thinking that the imperial retinue, which had started earlier would have reached Jalor.[16] Some of the selected turned their reins towards it while the rest reached Bhagwanpur in the afternoon. The emperor also reached there with his retinue. It was reported that Jalor was very far. So they turned towards Sirohi, but having lost way, again turned towards Jalor and on Friday, 28th August of the said month in the afternoon they reached there. The entire army got together also. The emperor organised the army and distributed horses and presents among them. Later the emperor mounted a horse one pahar past at night to be there. On Saturday, he reached the town of Devsa,[17] which was twenty miles from Pattan and deputed Asaf Khan to bring its administrator Mir Muhammad Khan. In short, Mir Muhammad Khan was completely surprised and could not believe that the emperor himself had arrived and would also be coming up to the gate of Pattan. As soon as the emperor made his appearance, at once Mir Muhammad Khan fell at the royal feet and kissed them and made the dust (of his feet) the collyrium of his eyes. (p. 179)

While the imperial army was being camped within the boundaries[18] of the pargana of Ahmadabad and Gujarat, a band of miscreants tried to enter (the camp) with the intention of pilfering. But the watchman's eye fell on them and in a single attack most of them fled away like dust, while the rest were slaughtered. However, their chief[19] presented himself before the imperial throne.[20] The news bearers were bringing information continuously that Muhammad Husain Mirza, Faulad Khan and Ikhtiyar-ul-Mulk were unleashing tyranny and oppression upon the people and they had also besieged the city of Ahmadabad with a large army. It had put Khan-i-Azam, Qutbuddin Khan and other nobles in great distress and trouble. Immediately, mounting a fast running horse, the emperor left for Ahmadabad. The moon like march of the emperor's conveyance was covering with dust even the shining sun.

Bait (*verse*)

The messenger of your fame is travelling across the world, does not allow even suspicion to accompany you, i.e. to say he runs faster than even imagination.

When the eastern breeze was blowing in the forest and plain and the reputed brave and warriors who had fought battles gallantly, with their (sharp and strong) arrows were able to compete with the hawks in going up the skies, and at the thought of their python-bodied lances lions vacate their abodes (forests). The imperial army under the command of Shujaet Khan, reached the vicinity of the city of Ahmadabad. On Wednesday, 4th Jamadi-ul-Awwal/2nd September of the same year after performing the morning prayers, Ghyasuddin Ali Khan Akhund was summoned and was asked to say on which side were the army of invisible spirits (rijal-ul-ghaib) that day. He performed the requisite method and put the coat arms on him. Thereafter, he offered prayers to the Almighty for success. Then he, mounting his horse, entered two karohs inside Ahmadabad. Word was sent to Khan-i-Azam to get ready and go out. It was also reported that the rebels had been aware of all this and seemed well-prepared.[21] (p. 180)

The emperor then made a surprise attack on Muhammad Husain Mirza, Ikhtiyar-ul-Mulk and the garrison of Faulad Khan. The first named rebel who was fighting like a lion and was running on his horse here and there was captured. Ali Bakhshi tied his hands behind him and presented him before the emperor. In short, the emperor said, "First, you, turning the face of rebellion from the service of the lord of the world, and shed the blood of people in Malwa, devastated their property there, intended to cast away the covers or curtains of the Muslim families and finally you sought help of the Gujaratis and became their supporter (leader). And handing him over to one of the Rajas, he got engaged in the battle." That Raja, seeing the rule in the mirror of sword of anger, as the proverb says:

Misraa (*a hemistich*)

It is good that the head of the mischief-monger who unleashes trouble in the country, should hang in shame.

So in a stroke the boat of that vain fellow broke down by the wind of wrath and he began to buffet in the sea of trouble and hardship. (p. 181)

In this engagement Saif Khan Koka was killed. But the pen of destiny had drawn the line of fall on the sheet of his actions. While Ikhtiyar-ul-Mulk who had more life, sent his brave men to fight. The lion-hearted emperor himself fought so bravely in this terrible war that if Rustam and Isfandiyar were present there they would have hanged their heads in shame and would have uttered "bravo" a hundred thousand times. The emperor received a wound on his groin while the gallant warriors were colouring the sand with their blood but their firing swords were piling heaps of enemies on the battlefield.[22] Meanwhile Shah Mirza and the sons of Sher Khan Fauladi could not bear the brunt, though they raised disturbances and disturbed the sleep of peace. However in the midst of battle they fled away with a small band.[23] Being (p. 182) frightened by the wind like sword, a storm of dust rose up in the battlefield, and all at once throwing down at every two or three steps of it, from the four houses of the chess of misery lost all their five senses and they were overwhelmed with such terror that they could not distinguish between seven and eight. Such a glorious victory was gained so easily which brought fame and name also.

Bait (verse)

The stories of Kaus and Qaiqubad were thrown into oblivion, and the account of Dara and Ardwan became mere fancies.

The accomplishment of victory made it clear to the world how a kingdom be ruled and how the enemy be crushed. The kingly resolutions, which were made to solve the people's difficulties, became evident. Khan-i-Azam, Qutbuddin Muhammad Khan and the rest of the nobles of Atga, who were under siege, came out and raised the voice of prayer and praise for the emperor. They kissed the royal feet and received the shower of favours. They recited the following *Bait*:

Bait (verse)

Our king has again come to our quarter, as water has come again to our canal.

At an auspicious hour the emperor entered the city of Ahmadabad and the region of Gujarat was adorned by setting his blessed thereon. During his fifteen days[24] stay in Ahmadabad, he conferred infinite favours on Mirza Ghayasuddin Ali, Mir Bakhshi, with the title of Asaf Khan. He was also entrusted the charge of organising the forces at Gujarat. (p. 183)

Thereafter the imperial army left to return to the capital, Agra. Marching fast, it reached Fatehabad Sikri within ten days. With the return of the emperor, it seemed as if the environs luck and blessings returned. As Shah Mirza, who had fled from the battlefield and was passing his time in the jungles of Gujarat and by means of all manner of excuses, reached the night of his life, he too died.

Duaa (prayer) for His Majesty

May God preserve the sun of this king of the world by whose benevolence and justice he brightens the fate of unblessed creatures like us! The shadow of this just king may remain on the head of the unfortunate creature like us as long as the sun moves and sky goes round! May the glory and greatness of this price victory remain safe and sound from crumbling and decline!

NOTES

1. Shah Mirza was the grandson of Muhammad Sultan Mirza who was related to Umar Shaikh Mirza, son of Timur.
2. *Bait* has been left. See p. 175.
3. Shujaet Khan was the sister's son of Tardi Baig Khan. He held a mansab of 5000. He was killed by his servants in A.H. 988/1580 A.D. *ZK*, 332 and *MU*, II, 559. See also *AN*, *MT*, *TA* and *TM*.
4. On Saturday by fourth of the day. *Mirat*, I, 129. See also *AN*, III, 33, *TA*, II, 264, *MT*, II, 165 and *MR*, II, 220.
5. *Bait* has been left. See p. 176.
6. Badauni says, "Four hundred karohs." *MT*, II, 167 and *MR*, II, 221-22. Qita has been left. See p. 176.
7. Badauni says one hundred karohs which was covered in two days. *MT*, II, 165 and *NM*, fol. 208-b. *Nazm* has been left. p. 177.
8. On Tuesday, 26th Rabi-us-Sani/25th August. *MT*, II, 165 and *TA*, II, 265, while Tuesday, 26th Rabi-ul-Awwal/24th July. *Mirat*, I, 129.
9. According to Nizamuddin, "Khwaja Mir Ghyasuddin Ali Akhund entitled Naqib Khan, son of Mir Abdul Latif, was one of the great nobles of Akbar and Jahangir. He died at the age of 80 in the month of Rabi-ul-Akhir, A.H. 1023/May, 1614 A.D. at Ajmer". *TA*, II, 265. See also *MT*, *HI* and *Tuzuk*.
10. Mirza Asaf Khan, Mirza Ghyasuddin Ali, son of Aqa Mulla Qazvini was one of the nobles of Akbar. He died in A.H. 989/1581 A.D. *MU*, I, 90. He was one of the three Asaf Khan of Akbar's time.
11. Khwaja Abdullah Kejak was one of the nobles of Prince Daniyal. He died in Ziqada A.H. 1009/April, 1600 A.D. *MU*, III, 179. For details see also *AN*, *TA* and *TM*.
12. Saif Khan Koka was the elder brother of Zain Khan Koka. He held a mansab of 4000. He died fighting against Muhammad Husain Mirza on 5th Jamadi-ul-Awwal, A.H. 981/3rd September, 1573 A.D. *MU*, II, 373. See also *ibid*.
13. Zain Khan Koka was one of the great nobles of Akbar. He held a mansab of 5000 Zat and Sawars. He died on 20th Rabi-ul-Awwal, A.H. 1010/9th September, 1601 A.D. at Agra. For details see *ZK*, 184-90, *MU*, II, 462. *TA*, *AN*, *HI* and *MT*.
14. Saiyed Abdullah Khan, son of Mir Khwanda Chugan Beigi was one of the nobles of Akbar. He died in A.H. 997/1588 A.D. in Kashmir. *MU*, II, 400. See also *ibid*.
15. Jetaran. *AN*, III, 44 and *NM*. fol. 209-a.

16. Situated in Jodhpur.
17. Desa. *AN,* III, 46 and *NM.* fol. 209-a. Nizamuddin says that the emperor reached Desa on 2nd Jamadi-ul-Awwal, A.H. 981/31st August, 1573 A.D. *TA,* II, 265. *Bait* has been left. p. 179.
18. Boundaries imply Gadhi which is situated at a distance of 15 karohs from Ahmadabad. *NM,* fol. 209-b. See also *AN,* III, 47.. *Mirat,* II, 140. *MT,* II, 166 and *TA,* II, 267.
19. His name was Rawalya, servant of Sher Khan Fauladi. *Mirat,* I, 130 and *AN,* II, 64.
20. It is one of the numerous example of Arif leaving of a topic unfinished.
21. *Bait* has been left. p. 180.
22. *Bait* and *Masnavi* have been left. *Ibid.* pp. 180-81.
23. *Misraa* and *Bait* have been left. *ibid.* pp. 181-82.
24. Five days. *NM,* fol. 211. On Sunday, 16th Jamadi-ul-Awwal/15th July the emperor left Ahmadabad so it may be assumed that he stayed ten or twelve days. *AN,* III, 64. See also *MR,* II, 225. *MT,* II, 170 and *TA,* II, 273. *Bait* has been left. p. 183.

OCCURRENCE 30

Description of the Appointment of Muzaffar Nishan to the Wizarat, Assuming the Office of the Master of Pen, Noted for Thriftness and Mentioning Some Other Developments

The wise, kingdom adorning, of penetrating conscience and prudent vakils and wazirs are indispensable for opening the gates of the gifts of God, and for the firms foundation and consolidation of power. The matchless skill and prudence bring within a moment the length and breadth of the country under control. (p. 184) At the time of preserving the integrity of the country by throwing out the enemy, they deploy large armies with skilful counsel and arrange the battlefields, i.e. the centre, the rear, the right and the left wings of the army, with firm resolution, determination and experience.

Bait (verse)

By the wise-counsel of the enlightened and intelligent wazir, the affairs of the empire (government) are being performed with great economy.

As the scriber of destiny had assigned the offices of vakil and wazir to Muzaffar Nishan, the emperor, after the conquest of Gujarat, laying the foundation of palace at Fatehabad Sikri, thought deeply about the management of the affairs of government and the enforcement of revenue regulations. Therefore, he decided to summon Muzaffar Khan from Sarangpur (Malwa) where he held his Jagir. Accordingly an imperial order was issued. Muzaffar Khan who had great loyalty and obedience started accordingly. On 4th Rajab-ul-Murajjab, A.H. 981/31st October, 1573 A.D., he arrived at Fatehabad Sikri to kiss the royal stirrup.[1] Thus he became the recipient of the honour on 18th[2] of the said month/14th November, 1573 A.D. and was treated with great favour and kindness and was raised to the distinction of high position of the office, i.e. was honoured by being allowed to serve the carpet of His Majesty which was the object of being kissed the kings of Ajam[3] and was the place of worship for the kings of the world.[4] (p. 185)

On 24th Rajab, A.H. 981/20th November, 1573 A.D. Muzaffar Khan was appointed the vakil and wazir of the empire and was adorned with the robes of office. So the charge of revenue and vakalat was handed over to him, and thus he was the recipient of high honour and great fortune, besides authority. At once he assumed its charge. He began by reducing the expenses, i.e. extravagance of the Khans and wazirs in the affairs of general administration and revenue. He did decide matters relating to administration or affairs of the army and the subject, giving them proper thought and consideration.

Bait (*verse*)

Though the enemies hearts quailed by the wrath of the Khan, the legitimate works of friendly persons became easy by the grace of hopefulness.

The Khan discharged his duties with great civility, justice and grace, and carried out the administration of financial affairs with such dedication and efficiency that if king Soloman were alive he would have bowed in submission. The emperor promoted the Khan to higher and higher positions. The Khan too appointed honest, thrift and efficient officers as trustees (amin) throughout the empire for discharging the work. As a result of great kindness and efficiency of administrative machinery the unkind day with its pains, troubles and oppressions which the Mughals were suffering at the hands of disloyal and treacherous Hindustanis, was entirely wiped out.

Bait (*verse*)

The garden of the empire became happy and prosperous

and the thorn of tyranny was removed from head of the dedicated worker.

Regulations were imposed to tone up the administration of all sections of the government so that its work be done honestly and responsibly. (p. 186) In his own department, he impressed with his love of justice and fostered the welfare of the people with strict discipline. However the emperor decided to remain occupied himself in supervising the details of both the general and revenue affairs. On it the Khan made a humble protest and felt disappointed. Though farmans and parwanas were being issued under the royal seal, he became frightened by the wrath of the emperor. Becoming worried of his own safety, he became silent.

Misraa (*a hemistich*)

The wise man is never oblivious of the king's wrath.

On the 18th Shawwal, A.H. 981/11th February, 1574 A.D. His Majesty went on pilgrimage to the tomb of Khwaja Muinuddin Chishti of Ajmer.[5] In the same year the forces were collected from all quarters and it was despatched towards Gaur and Bengal.[6] The nobles and Khans, having assembled, crossed the river Ganga. In the month of Zi-hijja/March[7] of the said year, Mirza Aziz Koka entitled Khan-i-Azam came from Ahmadabad (Gujarat) and received the blessings by kissing the royal feet. The emperor returned to the capital city Agra from Ajmer in the said month and year.

Duaa (*prayer*) *for His Majesty*

May the sun of the kingdom of the ruler of the age which is the shadow of the benefaction of the Creator remain protected from the eclipse of the decline of the world!

Notes

1. See also *AN*, III, 67, *TA*, II, 286 and *MT*, II, 171.
2. Thursday, 17th Rajab/13th November. *NM*, fol. 213-b. See also *ibid.*
3. Countries outside Arabia particularly Iran, Turan and Turkey.
4. *Bait* has been left. See p. 185.
5. According to Nizamuddin, "On 17th Ziqaddah/10th March, the

emperor went to the tomb covering five karohs on foot." *TA*, II, 279 while Badauni says he went on 12th. *MT*, II, 171.

6. The capital of Bengal which had been in turmoil.
7. On 23rd Zi-hijja/16th April of the said month, the emperor left Ajmer for hunting. He reached Fatehpur Sikri on 7th Zi-hijja/31st March. *AN*, III, 82, *MT*, II, 172 and *TA*, II, 281 while Thursday, 6th Zi-hijja/30th March. *NM*, fol. 213.

OCCURRENCE 31

Description of the Circumcision Ceremony of the Exalted Princes

The knowledgeable guides of the law and the custodians of the rules of the *Shariat* are well aware that by the good luck of the people the emperor was fully equipped with the rules and of its ordinances also. Being full of firm resolve, he diverted his mind to the arrangements for the circumcision of the Princes in accordance with the *Sunnat* rules.[1] (p. 187) Accordingly, on Thursday, 25th Jamad-us-Sani, A.H. 982[2]/12th October, 1574 A.D. the Prince Salim, nicknamed Shaikhu, Mirza Sultan Muhammad, entitled Pahari Jiu and Mirza Daniyal were ceremonially circumcised. The ceremony was performed with great ecstasy and splendour. A poet recited on the said occasion:

Bait (*Verse*)

By the force of circumcision, the mud became full of blood, and the two leaves were destroyed.

When Prince Shaikhu attained the age for beginning his education by the benevolence of His Majesty Qadir-i-Alim, [3] who was adept in reciting the Holy Quran, was appointed to teach the prince. When he had attained enough proficiency by the learned Maulana Mir Kalan, the preceptor, made him recite the *Kalma* on Wednesday, the 22nd Rajab, A.H. 982/8th November, 1574 A.D.

NOTES

1. See also *NM*, fol. 210 a-b.
2. According to Abul Fazl, Badauni and Jahangir, "This ceremony was performed in A.H. 981/1573 A.D." *AN*, III, 74, *MT*, III, 170 and Preface of *Tuzuk*, 5.

3. According to Badauni and Nizamuddin, "Mir Khan Harvi was a pious man. He was one of the grand sons of Maulana Khwaja Kohi. He died in A.H. 981/1573 A.D. at the age of 80 in Agra." *MT*, II, 170 and *TA*, II, 276.

OCCURRENCE 32

Description of Laying Siege of Gaur and Bengal after the Rebellion of Wretched Daud, the Emperor's March, His Success and Some Other Events that Happened During the Same Year

Every good action which is recorded in eternity and in obedience to the power of God, it is mentioned in the Court of God's judgement where souls assemble; all that is (p. 188) acquired by good intentions and the believers obtain it and their spiritual faculty itself imparts courage to them to secure it and then it appears on the heights of blessedness.[1]

Surely the light of the fortune of the emperor was shining everyday on his face. And every hour was the proof of his benevolence which was becoming evident on the pages of creation. For this reason when the emperor, a patron of the darvesh, for the second time returned from the conquest of Gujarat, he on the way again paid homage at the shrine of Khwaja Muinuddin Chishti at Ajmer. Whenever he returned from any battle it was his resolute to go to Ajmer, the abode of Muinuddin Chishti.

At the same time, Khan Khanan on whom the title of Khan Babam[2] was bestowed and who held the charge from the frontier of Jaunpur to the vilayat of Gaur, submitted a petition that, "the ill-starred Daud,[3] wali of Gaur and Bengal, had turned away his face from obedience by throwing away the collar of loyalty, and rejecting the way of friendship and attitude of hospitality, in spite of the fact that the noble Khan had sent men of amity and had come to know of the disloyalty of that wretched Afghan, but owing to his innate civility had still treated him with kindness and affection but to no avail".[4] (p. 189)

Although his father and uncle had been loyal, paid tribute and had obediently carried out all the imperial orders, the ill-starred Daud threw away that tradition, and closed the ongoing door. He strengthened the forts of Patna and Hajipur which were situated on the frontier of Gaur and Bengala and raised the standard of rebellion. The report of the above-mentioned Khan broke the fire of royal dignity and blazed its prestige with such fury as if the flame of the emperor's wrath would consume the whole world. He began to plan how to suppress that turbulent.

Immediately a farman was issued requiring Khan Khanan to proceed in that direction while the commanders[5] of the army were also ordered to follow him. The Khans who held jagirs in the east such as Muhammad Quli Khan Barlas,[6] Muhammad Qiya Khan,[7] Khan-i-Alam,[8] Majnun Khan Qaqshal,[9] Baba Khan Qaqshal,[10] Wazir Khan[11] and Shaham Khan[12] Jalair should accompany the said Khan in the suppression of the hostile Afghans. And the other nobles and Khans of Malwa such as Muhammad Murad Khan Mirak,[13] Ahmad Khan Kolabi,[14] Khalideen Khan[15] and Atimad Khan[16] etc. should come to Agra and without delay start for the front. Lashkar Khan, Mir Bakshi and Raja of Rajas, Raja Todar Mal,[17] should also proceed and arrange the imperial forces there. The emperor at an auspicious hour by the end of Safar, A.H. 982/June, 1574 A.D. undertook his march for the destruction of the root and branch of the Afghans. At this time when the sun was entering into the zone of Surtan and the ground was burning owing to the scathing heat and the crocodiles owing to the sharp rays of sun were lying in the rivers of fire; just as the stars fell into the high zones. Rubies were melting from the heat of the air of mines, and even the granite (or diamonds) in the depth of water were like melted rubies, owing to the intensity of heat of the sun. (p. 190)

The emperor entrusted the charge of the protection of Darul Khilafa, Agra to Shahabuddin Ahmad Khan. Thereafter the emperor along with the princes and ladies of the harem boarded the boats and set sail as if a river within a river started flowing and as if the moon had made its dome in the water.[19]

After a few days when they reached near Manikpur, the rainy season began with great force and the thick black cloud overcast the sky and hid its blue roof and the lightning was shining like lamps of neon, and its thunder was making a rumbling noise in the dome of the sky. (To conclude) such a heavy downpour came as if all the seven seas had been poured out or Noah's flood had visited again.[19] (p. 191)

In short, when the emperor, reached Banaras[20], the princes and ladies were taken out of the boats and they were sent to Jaunpur by the end of Rabi-ul-Awwal[21]/July. The emperor himself started on 4th Rabi-us-Sani/24th July from Bibi Sarai,[22] which was near Jaunpur, with determination of going to Patna and Hajipur. When they reached Tirmuhani, which was the confluence of the river Sarvar and Ganga,[23] that day thirty boats[24] including some of the emperor and imperial army were drowned. Lot of goods and two tigers[25] of the emperor were washed away. The emperor had to pass a day in the town of Muner,[26] and deputed Mirza Ghyasuddin Ali Akhund to circumambulate the tomb of Shaikh Yahya Muneri,[27] the revered on his behalf and also sent some money to be distributed among the poor and needy. On 18th, Rabi II/11th August of the said month[28] the emperor reached the royal camp where Khan Khanan with other nobles and Khans achieved the grace by kissing his feet. The emperor's flag touched the sky and the rays of his affectionate light from the sun of his forehead, fell on the ground of hopes of Khans and amirs. When Daud, the ill-starred and shameless fellow, came to know about the march of the imperial standards, throwing away the reins of self-respect, restrain and patience, he became nervous. Khan-i-Alam together with a group of gallant soldiers swimming like crocodiles across the river entered Hajipur, and on 19th, Rabi II/12th August took possession of it. As soon as Daud, the ill-starred received the news of it, he shut himself up in Patna fort where he had sought shelters and placed his comfort also.[29] (p. 192) On 20th,[30] Rabi II/13th August of the said month when he was dead-drunk, some of his amirs, thinking it to be advisable, threw him into a boat in the same condition and they were saying:

You preferred to run away rather than fight.

He opened Gujer gate and taking a few noted elephants and some part of treasures, rubbing the dust of defeat on his head, he fled away. The Afghans who were in Patna escaped by way of river and land. A large crowd began to board boats while the stronger threw weaker into the river.

In this way those people were drowned. Those who could not run by land, met their end in wilderness or in rivers, from fright. The bridge, which was built across the river Pun Pun[31] collapsed too on account of the passing over it of elephants and big crowd of the Afghans and thus they were destroyed.[32] (p. 193) The news reporters of success submitted that "Yesterday on account of the devastating attack and the awe and fear of the king of land and sea, the enemy had simply taken to heel and was ruined." And the voice of the hidden world came that "help is from the side of God". The star of victory rose on the east when the fort of Patna was also captured. The emperor himself advanced as far as Daryapur.[33] Gujar Khan,[34] a famous chief, ran away with his followers after hearing it. Majnun Khan Qaqshal and some other warriors followed them. They found themselves at the crossroad of a river and brandishing swords, they jumped into the river. About three or four hundred persons were drowned. The Khans and the royal army captured three hundred[35] of Daud's finest elephants and despatched them for the inspection of the august eye. Lashkar Khan and Sadiq Khan[36] were sent to Patna to call the senior Khans and amirs. After four days they reached Ghyaspur[37] and offered the customary congratulations to the emperor. He conferred the vilayat of Patna and Bihar up to the frontier of Gaur-Bengal on Khan Khanan and he stayed in the fort of Tanda which was the capital of Bengal. The region of Hajipur was given in Jagir to Muhammad Quli Khan Barlas. As some parts of the said vilayat had come under the imperial charge, those were also distributed as jagirs among Khans and amirs. The annexed eastern land of Gaur-Bengal, was added to the imperial dominions.[38] (p. 194)

When the emperor was satisfied with the arrangements of land, which was suitably distributed, he diverted his attention to destroy the very existence of the wretched Daud and the Afghans. He exhorted Khan Khanan, Muhammad Quli Khan Barlas, Majnun Khan, Baba Khan, Ashraf Khan, Khan-i-Alam and other Khans and amirs to maintain proper and orderly administration in their respective jurisdictions and they should also make efforts to capture the wretched, Daud. Accordingly they left in right earnest for the assigned task.[39] While Muzaffar Khan with some other Khans was sent to take the charge of Rohtas fort and as per order he handed it over to Farhat Khan.[40] Sadiq Khan was entrusted with the duty of transporting the elephants though two of the famous elephants captured from Daud were drowned. The Khan was accused of carelessness and hence he could not go to perform *kurnish.* It was ordered that as long as the Khan would not capture ten elephants of the same quality, he should not come to the court. The entire region of Jaunpur was added to the Khalsa Sharif and Mirza Mirak entitled Rizvi Khan[41] was made its incharge. Mirzada Ali Khan[42] and Shah Ghazi Khan[43] with some other salatin (amirs) were appointed to assist in the affairs of Bihar. After making amicable settlement of the administrative problems of the province of Gaur-Bengal, as per designs of the emperor, he turned his attention towards Jaunpur.[44] On 5th Jamadi-ul-Awwal/24th August of the said year, he reached Jaunpur. When the Giver of kingdoms opened the gate of His empire and put into his possession the bridle of the government of the world and the sun of royal fortune attained its zenith, and the shadow of the power of God's shadow rose to the heaven. (p. 195)

Then whichever side you move, power and fortune will move with you side by side.[45]

The messengers of good news were sent in all directions of Hindustan to give news of success and good attainment (to the people). At the same time, Alama-tul-Ulema Qazi

Nizam Khan Badakhshi,[46] came from Kabul and was given imperial employment. The emperor granted unlimited favours to him such as Rs. 5000 (rupees five thousand) in cash, studded sword[47] and expressed his very concern for him. Moreover, he was given the charge of Parwanchigiri,[48] which was a high office of the empire.[49]

The emperor set out on 9th Jamadi-us-Sani[50]/16th September from Jaunpur via Lucknow and Qanauj. On 27th Rajab/13th November of the said year he reached Darul Mulk, Delhi. He desired to pay visit to the tombs of late saints and his father which he did with sincerity, he prayed for their souls peace and distributed alms among the poor and needy. (p. 196) During the same time Bakshi-ul-Mulk Mirza Ghyasuddin Ali entitled Asaf Khan with Mirza Koka and some Atgas, who had been appointed to organise the army at Gujarat, came and obtained the honour of kissing the royal feet. He was given the office of Mir Arze[51] besides Mir Bakshi. In this way he was honoured among his contemporaries. On this very occasion a special belt and ink-stand with golden pen were also bestowed on him. During the early days of Shaban/20th November, the emperor left Hazrat-i-Delhi for Ajmer. On the way the emperor spent few days in hunting. As he travelled, he got the way measured and at a distance of every three or four karohs towers were erected.[52]

Mirza Koka entitled Khan-i-Azam came from Gujarat[53] and he was honoured being allowed to kiss the royal hands. Some other Khans who were posted in Gujarat also came and had the honour of kissing the royal feet and received untold favours and riches. Husain Quli Khan entitled Khan-i-Jahan, who was the hakim of Lahore, too came and kissed the royal feet. It had been the habit of the emperor either to march on any expedition or after his return from it, he used to pay homage at the shrine of Khwaja Muinuddin Chishti for his blessings. This time, he remained occupied for several days there and revealed his cherished desires for blessings. In fact whenever he paid homage, he did it with dedication. Anyone who saw such deep-seated dedication and concentration on his part, was touched. Being satisfied, he decided to return to Darul Khilafa, Agra. (p. 197) In short, the lord of victory and triumph, having subjugated the world, wanded his way towards Agra. The imperial retinue reached its blessed destination by the end of the month of Ramzan A.H. 982/25th December 1574 A.D. and the sun of favours and kindness began to shine on the denizens of the world.[54]

Duaa (prayer) for His Majesty

May the expanse of the world be ever brightened by your light and may the courier of the hopes of persons be the envy of the garden by the fragrance of your breeze! May the sun of the Sultanate of Khaqan Akbar always rise from the horizon of honour and success, and the sun of majesty, good fortune and prosperity shine over your kingdom for ever and ever, by the grace of the Prophet and his progeny!

Notes

1. *Bait* has been left. See p. 188.
2. Arif has recorded the address of Akbar to him. Actually Khan Babam was not the title. Akbar used to address Bairam Khan as Khan Baba. He never conferred any such title on Munim Khan, Khan Khanan who is referred to here. *Tazkira,* 270.
3. Daud, son of Sulaiman Khan who was the permanent resident (Dara) of Bihar and Bengal, was however killed by the imperial army after four years. For details see also *MU,* I, 651, *AN, TA, MT, MR, SS* and *Farishta.*
4. *Nazm* and *Bait* have been left. See p. 188-89.
5. Tawachins i.e. Sardars.
6. Muhammad Quli Khan Barlas was a great noble. *ZK,* 326.
7. Qiya Khan held a mansab of 2000. *Ibid.,* 471.
8. Khan-i-Alam, Chalma Beig went with Mirza Kamran in A.H. 960/1552 A.D. to Mecca. He was granted a mansab of 3000 sawars with the title of Khan-i-Alam by Akbar. He fought against the Mirzas and captured Hajipur. He died fighting against Daud at Takraui in A.H. 982/1573 A.D. *ZK,* 346 and *MU,* I, 632. See also *AN, NM, HI, TA, MT* and *SS.*
9. Majnun Khan Qaqshal held a mansab of 5000. *ZK,* 370.
10. He belonged to the tribe of Qaqshal. He performed excellent services

in the conquest of Bengal and Gujarat. He died in A.H. 989/1581 A.D. *MU*, I, 391. See also *AN* and *MT*.

11. His real name was Sultan Ali and was a brother of Abdul Majid Asaf Khan. He received the title of Khan, rank of wazir and mansab of 5000. It is said that in the middle of Ramzan, A.H. 995/August, 1587 A.D. he died in Bengal. *ZK*, 337 and *MU*, III, 929. *Ibid.*, also.

12. Shaham Khan was a noble of old standing and he held a mansab of 3000. *ZK*, 334 and *MU*, *II*, 603. See *ibid.*, also.

13. He was a great noble. *ZK*, 338.

14. He was not in the campaign. *AN*, III, 67.

15. According to Abul Fazl, "He was alive up to Rabi-ul-Awwal, A.H. 992/March, 1584 A.D." *Ibid.*, 431. The rest about him could not be found.

16. He was one of the amirs of Salim Khan, son of Sher Khan Sur. Under his government, he rose to a mansab of 3000. The Bhakkar Sarkar was granted in his fief. He was killed by his servant, Maqsud Ali on 10th Rabi-ul-Awwal, A.H. 986/17th May, 1576 A.D. at Bhakkar. *ZK*, 355-56 and *MU*, I, 88. See also *AN*, *TA*, *MR* and *Tarikh-i-Sindh*.

17. Raja Todar Mal was a Khatri by caste and was a clerk. Through the intermediary of Muzaffar Khan, he rose to the rank of Wazir and remained with full authority for a period of seventeen years. He held a mansab of 4000. He died in Muharram, A.H. 998/November, 1589 A.D. near Lahore. *ZK*, 341 and *MU*, II, 123.

18. Badauni and Nizamuddin say on Sunday. *MT*, II, 173 and *TA*, II, 284. Abul Fazl only mentions month, Safar/June. *AN*, III, 87. *Bait* has been left. p. 190.

19. Badauni says only Prince Salim. *MT*, II, 175. See also *TA*, II, 284, *AN*, III, 87 and *NM*, fol. 214. *Nazm* has been left. p. 190.

19. It is not recorded in other contemporary and near contemporary sources. *Bait* has been left. See p. 191.

20. The princes and queens were sent from Yahyapur to Jaunpur. *AN*, III, 88, *TA*, II, 287 and *NM*, fol. 214-b.

21. On 2nd, Rabi-us-Sani/22nd July the emperor reached Yahyapur. *Ibid.*

22. It is situated seven karohs from Jaunpur. *NM*, fol. 214.

23. The rivers, Saruwar, Ganga and Khakhar.

24. Other sources except. *NM*, fol. 214-b are silent.

25. The owners were Daulat Khan and Dil Rang. *AN*, III, 94.

26. Muner is situated in Patna (Bihar).

27. Shaikh Yahya, Sharfuddin Muneri, a contemporary of Sultan Nizamuddin Auliya Dehlvi, is the reputed saint of Bihar. For details see also *Gulzar-i-Abrar*, *Mirat-i-Alam* and *Abrar-ul-Akhiyar*.

28. On Wednesday, 18th Rabi-us-Sani/8th August, he reached Patna. *TA*, II, 29 and *NM*, fol. 214-b. See also *MT*.

29. *Qita* has been left. p. 192.

30. Saturday, 20th Rabi-us-Sani/13th August, *NM*, fol. 215-b and 216-a. *AN*, III, 98, *MT*, II, 180 and *TA*, II, 292. *Bait* has been left. p. 192.

31. Great river which is situated in Bengal. *NM*, fol. 216-a.

32. *Bait* has been left. p. 192.

33. It is situated near the bank of river Ganga at a distance of 26 karohs from Patna. *TA*, II, 294.

34. Gujar Khan entitled Rukn-ud-daula was one of the great nobles of Daud. He was wounded by Khan Khanan. After the victory, he died in he month of Ziqadah, A.H. 982/February, 1575 A.D. For details see also *TM, MT, AN, TA* and *SS*.

35. Fifty or sixty elephants, belonging to Daud were captured. But after the chase of Gujar Khan about four hundred elephants fell into the emperor's hand. *NM*, fol. 216-b, *MT*, II, 182 and *TA*, II, 293.

36. Sadiq Khan i.e. Sadiq Muhammad Khan Duldai was one of the great nobles of Akbar. He held a mansab. He died on 10th Shaban, A.H. 1005/19th March, 1596 A.D. in Shahpur, Deccan. *MU*, III, 724. *Ibid.*, also.

37. According to Nizamuddin, "It is situated near the bank of river Ganga". *TA*, III, 295.

38. For details see also *NM*, fol. 217 and *TA*, II, 296. *Qita* has been left. p. 193.

39. On 2nd Jamadi-ul-Awwal, A.H. 982/20th August, 1574 A.D. the imperial order was issued for them. *AN*, III, 104, *MT*, II, 182. and *TA*, II, 295.

40. Farhat Khan, Khasa Khail was one of the servants of Humayun. He held a mansab. He died in the sedition of Raja Gajpati in A.H. 984/1576 A.D. *ZK, MU*, I, 13. See also *Ibid.*

41. Mirza Mirak entitled Rizvi Khan was from the Saiyed family of Mashhad. He had animosity with Khan-i-Zaman Quli Khan so the emperor ordered that he be crushed under the feet of an elephant. But he was saved on the submission of emperor's relations or near ones. Favours were conferred on him by appointing him diwan-i-Jaunpur and later Bakhshi of Bengal. *ZK, MU*, III, 218 and *TA*, II, 246.

42. Mirzada Ali Khan, son of Muhtaram Beig performed services in Gujarat, Bihar, Rajputana and Kashmir. He held a mansab. He died in the middle of A.H. 995/1586 A.D. fighting against the Kashmiris. *ZK* and *MU*, III, 257. See also *AN, MT, Tarikh-i-Kashmir* and Tazkira Gunahi.

43. Shah Ghazi Khan, son of Saifuddin Muhammad entitled Ghazi Khan,

was one of the nobles of Akbar. He held a mansab also. He died in A.H. 1001/1592 A.D. in Bengal. *ZK, NM,* fol. 217-b. See also *AN.*

44. Badauni and Nizamuddin say on Monday, 6th Jamadi-ul-Awwal/24th August. *MT,* II, 182 and *TA,* II, 296 while Monday, 7th Jamadi/25th August. *NM. Qita* has been left. pp. 194-95.
45. *Bait* has been left. p. 195. Tautology is quite funny.
46. Qazi Nizam entitled Qazi Khan belonged to Badakhshan. He was the pupil of Mulla Isamuddin Ibrahim, son of Muhammad Isfrani. He presented himself before the emperor at Khanpur. First, the title of Qazi Khan was conferred on him, followed by Ghazi Khan. He died at the age of 70 in Rajab, 992/July, 1584 A.D. *ZK, NM,* fol. 217-b and *MU,* II, 857. See also *AN, MT* and *MR.*
47. See also *TA,* II, 297.
48. According to Nizamuddin "Parwanchi implies the person who takes the noting of imperial farman." *TA,* II, 297. See also *NM.*
49. See also *MT,* II, 182.
50. The emperor reached Delhi in Rajab/November. *Ibid.,* II, 184 and *TA,* II, 298.
51. Mir-i-arz, superintendent of petition.
52. Arif seems unaware that those towers were made at regular intervals.
53. According to Abul Fazl, "Mirza Koka and Khan-i-Jahan Bahadur reached Narnaul from Patiala. They left for Gujarat in the middle of Ramzan/January." *AN,* III, 111 and *MT,* II, 299.
54. The emperor left Delhi in the early days of Shaban/November reached Ajmer in early days of Ramzan/January and in the middle of the said month reached Agra. *AN,* III, 110. See also *MT,* II, 185 and *TA,* II, 299.

OCCURRENCE 33

Description of Rampaging Plague and Famine in Gujarat in the Beginning of the Year and the Conquest of Baker Fort with Heroic Deeds

In the beginning of the year A.H. 982/1574 A.D. the rays of the justice of His Majesty began to rise out of the horizon of his mercy and graciousness. Thus he ordered that in every vilayat and pargana, which were under the imperial domain, the whole land should be divided into zones, yielding the revenue of one crore tankas and each of them be entrusted to an experienced officer, assisted by *Karkuns* and *Fotedars*[1] (clerks and treasurers). It was further ordered that reports about all villages, whether under cultivation or not, should be prepared and sent to the imperial officers. The area of all those land should be measured and their boundaries be fixed. Records should be maintained of all the land fit for cultivation, and the same be brought under plough within three years and every possible effort should also be made to gear up and increase the production. The account of *Rabi* and *Kharif* harvests should be maintained separately, but it must be maintained honestly and faithfully even of the barren land also. (p. 198) The *aima* land[2] was to be recorded on the names of beneficiaries so that it be known how much land in a province was under (*aima*) grants and how much under regular revenue administration so that the real position of a vilayat or pargana might be understood.[3] The motive was that the weak should not be afraid of the tyranny and oppression of the powerful. The land records were prepared and completed and the estimate of revenue was settled. It helped to understand how much was due from Khalsa lands.[4] The *amils* and *karoris*[5] were to submit to the state exchequer accordingly. The emperor was of the view that the said rules, regulations and orders should be promulgated in such a perfect manner that the vicissitudes of the time and the other incidents might not have any effect on them in any way and nothing might be done in violation of them. He therefore declared the entire land from Jaunpur and Banaras up to the Indus with Multan and Lahore as Khalsa land. Land grants and jagirs were abolished within it. For everybody, i.e. the Khans, amirs, soldiers, higher or lower, salaries were fixed on monthly basis. They were required to present their horses, properly branded[6] and their armours for the inspection of bakhshis. On the basis of inspection of weapons, their salaries were to be fixed which were to be paid every month from the imperial treasury. Once in a year or after every campaign, the horses and armaments were to be checked according to the entries made in the state records. It was obligatory that horses and arms be neither sold nor presented to anyone after the imperial inspection. Moreover, the bakhshis must every year report that everything was in order or not.[7]

Plague and famine in Gujarat

During the said year plague and famine visited Gujarat. The rulers considered it the spoils of battles, caused by filth and rotten stench, while men of piety believed that the calamity was the result of immoral deeds of persons.[8] Maulana Rum in his *masnavi* has said the following:

Bait (*verse*)

Pestilence spreads in the country owing to adultery and famine comes when persons fail to pay zakat. (p. 199)

The real fact was that everywhere, owing to the growth of population and enormous increase of persons, all sorts of evil deeds began to be committed. Due to it, the believers in God and righteous persons cited evidence that under such condition the fire of poverty and sufferings grew big, followed by all sorts of misfortunes and sufferings. Accidents uproot and destroy both young and old. As a result of such happenings, in the hearts of the dark-eyed women of Gujarat, whose eyes were like the deer of the forest of Tibet, blood was always running owing to their being sorrowful. The pestilence continued for five or six months.[9] The people had not witnessed such aweful disaster for a long time, they felt utterly helpless and dreadful. Many people went out of the province and became exiles. The intensity of pestilence reached to the extent that everyday hundred cart-loads of dead bodies were taken out of Ahmadabad, which were thrown into ponds and covered with mud. Those were in addition to the dead who were carried on biers and bed steads and were properly burried. The commodities became so severely dear that man had to content with a single loaf of bread per day, and even that had to be eaten secretly to avoid being noticed by those who were starving and as soon as the sun rose they had it secretly. Everywhere a man was being sold for a single loaf but no buyer was to be had. Except hunger no other winding sheet was available for the dead. Owing to want of both space and money, graves could not be dug up for burial. Ultimately, the deadly pestilence spread over the Sarkars of Pattan, Baroach, Baroda and indeed engulfed entire Gujarat. The famine was so severe that the price of one maund of grain shot up to one hundred and twenty copper tankas, equal to six rupees.[10] Provision and fodder for horses and camels was nowhere to be had. So they scraped the bark of trees, crushed it and made it soft by soaking it in water and fed their cattle on it. Its after effects were numerous. (p. 200)

In the year when the imperial standards were being directed towards the east, Gaur and Bengal to uproot and destroy the Afghans, information was received that Sultan Mahmud,[11] the ruler of Bakar fort and certain other parts of Sindh died on 2nd Safar, A.H. 982/24th May, 1574 A.D. Muhib Ali Khan,[12] son of late Mir Khalifa, who had his connection with that family as a vakil and was appointed the incharge of Sindh two years before, was present on the outskirts of the fort, sent the golden keys of it to the imperial court. Thereupon, Gesu Khan Bakaval Beigi was appointed the Kotwal and administrator of the fort of Bakar. But Gesu Khan was barred by Muhib Ali Khan and a clash ensued there. Gesu Khan however boarded a boat. On 8th Jamadi-us-Sani/25th September of the said year, he entered into the fort with the help of its inmates and held its charge. The petition of Gesu Khan was received which contained that "by the grace of God and the kind attention of the emperor such a fort which was very difficult to conquer has come into possession". The news-bearer broke the happy news of success and the deer of victory was let loose.

In the palace of Jaunpur where the emperor was encamping, Khwaja Jahan who was one of the great Khans of the state, started after the victorious army came and kissed the royal feet. (p. 201) Suddenly by the decree of fate, he developed a serious disease in his foot and he had to separate himself from the imperial troops at Lucknow[13] for treatment. But his ailment aggravated daily and in the beginning of the month of Shaban/November (of the said year) he passed away and his dead body was brought to Agra.[14]

Duaa (prayer) for His Majesty

May victories and succours of His grace remain with the emperor throughout his reign and may the court of the existence of the emperor remain far away from fear and misfortune!

NOTES

1. The word Fotedar is used for the official who measures land. For details see M.A. Ansari, *Administrative Documents of Mughal India,* (ed.) with English Translation, Delhi, 1984, P. Saran, *The Provincial Government of the Mughals,* Bombay, 1973, I.H. Qureshi, *The Administration of the Mughal Empire;* Karachi, 1966. H.H. Wilson, *A Glossary of Judicial and Revenue Terms,* London, 1885.
2. Land granted free to men of learning or religious men. See *ibid.*
3. Arif uses uncommon and inapropriate terms.
4. See also *AN,* III, 117 and *MT,* III, 190.
5. According to Abul Fazl, "One hundred and eighty two amils were deputed to take into possession the Khalsa land. Every amil, who was incharge of a crore tankas worth of land, by profession was called a

Karori." *AN,* III, 117 and *NM,* fol. 204-b. See also *Ain,* 156 and *TA.* II, 30.

6. During the reign of Ala-ud-din Khalji, it was the rule, Sher Shah followed it with certain modifications and Akbar adopted it in his 20th regnal year. *MT,* III, 190. For details see K.S. Lal, *Alauddin Khilji,* (Revised ed.) 1980, I. H. Siddiqui, *Some Aspects of Afghan Despotism in India,* 1979, Qanungo, *Sher Shah And His Times,* Bombay, 2nd edition, 1956, M.A. Faruqi, *Economic Policy of Delhi Sultans,* 1991.
7. This experiment was tried in 1575-76 A.D. not in A.H. 982/1574 A.D.
8. See also *MT,* II, 186 and *TA,* II, 301.
9. According to Nizamuddin, "It continued about six months." *TA,* II, 301.
10. See also *ibid* and *MT,* II, 186. It must be the double tanka.
11. Sultan Mahmud Khan, son of Mir Fazil Kokaltash, son of Adil Khwaja Isfahani, Wali-i-Bhakkar was from the Arghunia nobility. He died on 8th Safar, A.H. 982/30th May, 1574 A.D. at the age of 84. The emperor sent Muhib Ali Khan, Mir Khalifa for the conquest of Bhakkar fort. For details see also *AN, MT, IJ, TM, SS, TA* and *Tarikh-i-Sindh.*
12. Muhib Ali Khan, son of Mir Nizamuddin Ali Khalifa, was one of the great nobles of Akbar. He died in A.H. 989/1581 A.D. *MU,* III, 238 and *TA,* II, 435. See also *TM* and *IJ. Qita* has been left. p. 200.
13. See also *AN,* III, 109.
14. See also *TA,* II, 302.

OCCURRENCE 34

Description of the Expedition of Khan-i-Khanan Against Daud, the Contemptible Fellow, His Defeat and Submission for Peace and Certain Other Events Happened Aftermath

When Daud ran away from Patna, passing through Bengal, he reached Cuttack-Banaras[1] and strengthened its fort. Khan Khanan remained occupied in the expedition against him. The Khans and (salatin) amirs with the troop were appointed to pay full attention towards him. Daud made the said fort his abode and the Khan also moved towards it with his force which was reciting the following:

Bait (*verse*)

(We) bring out by our sword the lion from the forest and by means of our arrow shoot the moon from the sky.

When the army proceeded against him, it was instructed that they should go on clearing up the passage of the movement (of army). All the thorny hedges and rubbish heaps, and crossing the difficult routes through the thick forest be cleared. Daud came out to door die and on 20th Ziqada, A.H. 982/4th March, 1574 A.D. the Khan placed in full battle array several thousand brave and noted soldiers at a distance of about two karohs;[2] and the enemy on the other side assigned force on right and left wings and placed elephants each of whom was equal in size to a ponderous mountain.[3] (p. 202)

The soldiers had become crazy like elephants and everyone of them had lance, sword and dagger in his hand. Both the armies came face to face and stood firm like steel. Just as the ocean begins by the blow of wind to rise into waves, the armies started moving in the same manner. Soon the intensity of fighting became hot and by the dazzle of swords and lances the weather of the battlefield started raining fire and the death-dealing armies started clashing against each other in hand to hand fight. Lances and swords were hurled. The soldiers exhibited such bravery that the soul of Rustam was also saying 'bravo'. Some of the Khans lost reins:

Bait (*Verse*)

With the point of lance and sharp arrow, they scraped off colour from the face of the sun.

In the thick of battle Khan-i-Alam was killed while Lashkar Khan got wounded and he too died after ten or twelve days. On the enemy's side, Gujar Khan, the most famous warrior, was killed. But the force of their attack was so powerful that it appeared as if they (the Afghans) might send the ball of success in the pole of victory to the destined end, having supressed one troop, they thought that they had achieved success. (p. 203) In this critical position Khan Khanan, who was holding the command in the centre, was left alone, even then he acted with usual courage and manliness. He received five or six wounds on his head, face and hand which shook him completely. However, in the midst of the reckless killing and capturing, a voice of happiness was heard. The troop which had become confounded and terrified, suddenly came to the centre and started shouting victory which marked the flow of blood on both sides like the Euphrates and the Tigris. Daud Afghan was proud of his having a large number of elephants, and was vain enough to think that he was very brave, but when he saw the terrific onslaught of the imperial army, his hope changed into despair so the eyes of the Afghans became dimmed. No doubt, Daud struggled in every possible way to save the Afghans, but all in vain. He realized that defeat was inevitable and ran away from the claws of calamity. A large number of persons were killed on both sides and finally the sun of victory arose from its place of good luck. Daud shut himself in the fort of Cuttak-Banaras while Khan Khanan along with other Khans stayed and laid a siege to it. Though

Daud felt ashamed of his behaviour, he was afraid to negotiate peace, on the other hand he was also feeling uncertain about the renewed hostility.[4]

Khan Khanan deputed a messenger to Daud, reminding him of the favours conferred on his father and uncle by the emperor, advised him to use good sense in this affair, and that he ought to realize what would be the consequences of opposing (the emperor). It was also impressed upon him that if he were to behave in a friendly manner, he would be treated with honour and a part of the imperial domain would be bestowed on him to govern. Daud, now, realized that the cure for his grief and pain was nowhere else to be found except in the kindness and nobleness of the Khan. Removing from his mind all fear and suspicion, he used his good sense and conveyed the message that "I am a humble slave.[5] As the emperor had by his kindness and mercy honoured my father, I too lay my head on the foot-sill of submission". In reply the Khan sent a message of good advice and said, "Whatever has happened, it was hidden behind the curtain of destiny and has also become known. (p. 204) Now, I forgive all your past faults; pray whatever has happened, may God forgive it. If you come like a son, you will receive even more love and kindness than your father. You may come without any fear or anxiety so that the dust of confusion and conflict may be washed away from your mind and heart". The messenger[6] was asked to return. Daud now began to behave as one who had been at fault. The Khan treated him with special consideration. Khilat and a studded-sword with belt were bestowed on him.[7]

The charge of Orissa and Cuttak-Banaras was given to him and after accepting due presents, from him, he was permitted to leave.

When Khan Khanan was paying his attention towards Daud, sons of Jalal-ud-Din Sur[8] with some other Afghans and the Raja of Gorgat[9] (*sic*) assembled at one place. When Majnun Khan Qaqshal, who was in Gorgat, came to Gaur and Tanda, they captured the fort. Some of them devastated that area around and they waited the arrival of the Khan. But

Muin Khan,[10] Majnun Khan and their brothers defended the city. As soon as the rebels received the news of the approach of Khan Khanan, they took to their heels and found shelter in the hills and forest of Gaur-Bengal. On 10th Safar, A.H. 983/22nd May, 1575 A.D. Khan Khanan reached the environs of Tanda. At the same time Junaid[11] Afghan, son of Daud's uncle, entered Bihar with a numerous force and took it into his possession. The Khan, however, rested a few days in Tanda and he chalked out a plan with his companions that the city of Gaur, which was situated on the bank of river Ganga and had many high mansions, should be preserved and inhabited. Accordingly, all the inhabitants of Tanda were transferred to Gaur and it was declared the capital of Bengal. But owing to its bad climate, the (p. 205) men in command became indisposed as "Whatever God wishes He does". A company of the Khans including Ashraf Khan, Muin Khan and Haji Khan Sistani perished. The Khan himself fell seriously ill and he too died on 19th Rajab/25th October, of the said year.

Towards the close of the year Mirza (Aziz) Koka was subjected to demotion, his estate was forfeited and the province of Ahmadabad (his jagir) was also included in the Khalsa land. A brief description would be like this. As it has been written earlier that after the conquest of Gujarat the emperor granted it in jagir to Atka family and its capital Ahmadabad was also added to it. Mirza Koka also wished to take it. Although the city had lost much charm due to incessant battles, it was still attractive like the worried locks of the beloved. In short, when Mirza Koka succeeded to establish his power in the centre of the province and the *huma* of the kindness of the emperor cast the shadow of mercy and favours on the inhabitants of the province which established the rule of justice also and it began to make progress everyday and it became a source of jealousy for those foolish people. So when the emperor decided that all the Khans and amirs, senior or junior, should put on their dresses and arms and get their horses branded. On the basis of inspection, their monthly pay would be fixed, Mirza Koka refused to abide by the order. His refusal hurt the emperor greatly, and he dismissed him at once in the beginning of Zi-hijja/March of the same year and sent him behind bars like Yusuf. (p. 206) Shaikh Ibrahim[12] was appointed to guard him. Afterwards he was set free and he lived peacefully.[13] In the month of Shaban, A.H. 986/14th October, 1578 A.D. when the emperor returned from Punjab to Fatehabad Sikri, Mirza Koka being ashamed of his action, presented himself and kissed the royal feet. Thus he became enriched with countless royal favours. The same year (A.H. 986/1578 A.D.) Mir Muhammad Khan, the Khan's uncle who was the administrator of Pattan (Gujarat) died.[15]

Duaa (prayer) for His Majesty

May the threshold of the king remain safe ever by the blessings of the favours and kindness of God! May the evil-eye never disturb the glory and magnificence of the king by the help of the Exalted God!

Notes

1. Cuttak-Banaras, the capital of Orissa.
2. The battle took place at Jatura. *TA*, II, 304; Bajhura, *MT*, II, 194 and Abul Fazl says at Nakruhi or Takruhi. *AN*, III, 122.
3. *Bait* has been left. p. 202.
4. See also *TA*, II, 306 and *MT*, II, 195.
5. According to Nizamuddin, "Daud sent the message of peace to Khan Khanan". *TA*, II, 308 and *MR*, I, 831. See also *ibid.*
6. His name was Fátu or (Qatlu) and Shaikh Nizam was sent from Khan's side. *AN*, III, 130.
7. The celebration of peace took place in the month of Muharram, A.H. 983/April, 1575 A.D. *ibid. Bait* has been left. See p. 204.
8. Jalal Khan Sur died in A.H. 983/1575 A.D. *AN*, 135. See also *TR* and *MR*.
9. Ghurah Ghat. *AN*, III, 131. See also *ibid.*
10. According to Badauni, "Muinuddin Ahmad Khan Farkhandi and Ansari Harvi came with Humayun from Kabul. Akbar appointed him haris of Agra and he was honoured with the title of Khan in the 7th regnal year. He died in A.H. 983/1575 A.D. in the encampment at Gaur." *MT*, II, 192 and *MU*, III, 216. See also *AN*, *TM* and *IJ*.
11. Junaid Afghan, son of Daud's uncle, had joined the imperial service

but he escaped from Agra. First he reached Bihar and later Bengal. He got injured near Ak Mahal in A.H. 984/1576 A.D. *AN*, III, 181, *MT*, II, 192. See also *TM* and *SS*.

12. Shaikh Ibrahim, son of Shaikh Musa, son-in-law and sister's son of Shaikh Salim Chishti of Sikri. He rose to the mansab of 1000, was given the charge of Fatehpur Sikri in the 23rd regnal year. He died in the early days of Ziqad, A.H. 999/August, 1591 A.D. *ZK*, 372 and *MU*, II, 570.
13. Khan-i-Azam confined himself in his garden which was built by him at Agra and stopped coming and going out. *MR*, I, 838.
14. See also *AN*, III, 261 and *TA*, II, 353.
15. Mirza paid his respects on 4th Rajab/6th September. *MR*, I, 837.

OCCURRENCE 35

Description of the Visit of Nawab Sulaiman Shah Mirza from the Vilayat (Dominion) of Badakhshan and His Reception by the Emperor

Nawab Sulaiman Mirza[1] had ruled the country of Badakhshan up to the frontiers of Hissar Shadman, Qanduz and Baghlan according to the Chaghtai and the Turkish laws. When differences cropped up between him and his grandson, Mirza Shah Rukh, he expected help from the emperor because of his relations with him. When he realized that the people and army of Badakhshan had become hostile to him and it was not possible to stay there, he decided to take shelter at the imperial court. Sulaiman Mirza reached the bank of Nilab (Indus) which was the frontier of Hindustan and sent his humble petition to the imperial court which was accepted. The emperor sent Khwaja Agha Jan,[2] Khazanchi of the Peshkash and Raja Bhagwan Das[3] parwanchi for his reception and it was ordered that due respects should be given throughout his journey. (p. 207)

Further account of this incident is that Sulaiman Shah Mirza had grown old but was still ruling Badakhshan. His wife,[4] a very sagacious old lady, was managing the affairs but she too had died. After her death Shah Rukh Mirza, either at the instigation of the army or on his own made a resolve to stand against his grandfather. He came out of the fort Qanduz and reached Kolab. With the help of a company of soldiers and tribal leaders, he collected an army and marched to the capital of the kingdom, Badakhshan. He brought under his command all the brave warriors from Hissar Shadman up to the frontier of Kabul and held it under his possession. Mirza Sulaiman got terribly worried and non-plussed.

He had no way out except to say good-bye to the country. Shah Rukh Mirza himself bade him good-bye and turned him out from there. He therefore, came to Hindustan via Kabul which was the shelter of the learned and the place of hope for honoured kings.[5]

Thereafter Shah Rukh Mirza occupied the throne of Badakhshan without any hitch and the entire hilly region fell into his hands. Nawab Sulaiman Mirza arrived at the court of the king of kings on 12th[6] Rajab, A.H. 983/17th December, 1575 A.D. On his arrival at Mathura,[7] which was at a distance of fifteen karohs from Fatehabad Sikri,[8] the emperor despatched some Khans and amirs to receive him suitably. On both sides of the route elephants clad in full armament[9] and tigers wearing velvet and zarbaft (of Europe) dresses were standing in line at a distance of three to four karohs.[10] (p. 208)

The emperor embraced Nawab Sulaiman Mirza and inquired his well-being. When the Princes came to the assembly, Nawab Mirza greeted them with much affection and love. He made them sit in his lap and kissed their cheeks and heads. The emperor looked after him and always enquired with a lot of affection and respect about him. A festive assembly was hosted in his honour which astonished the chief of heaven also. The bejewelled and golden plates, big bowls, made of Chinaware sugar pots and countless other delicious dishes were served. Due respect was extended to the Mirza after the assembly was over. He used to visit the court once or twice a week. Then after some time, some Khan conveyed the desire and request of Mirza to the emperor to go on a pilgrimage to Mecca as well as Medina. His Majesty granted it. Therefore, he went through Gujarat and by the end of Zi-hijja/March, boarding a ship, left for his destination.[11] (p. 209)

Duaa (prayer) for His Majesty

The fortunate shadow of the empire and the blessing of everyday increasing justice may remain forever on the forehead of the greatest man of the world and the most superior man among the progeny of Adam! And may the sun of the king's greatness and brilliance continue to shine over these slaves for ever and ever!

NOTES

1. Mirza Sulaiman was the ruler of Badakhshan. He was turned out of Badakhshan at the instigation of the people of that land. Having fled in utter helplessness and compulsion, he came to Mirza Muhammad Hakim in Kabul and sought his help. But the latter did not help him. While coming to Hindustan, he faced much hardship created by the Afghans, he, however, succeed in reaching the bank of the Indus and sought refuge which was accepted by the emperor. So a sum of Rs. 50,000 with government regalia and some Iraqi horses, as a token of welcome were sent for him with Aqa Khan Khazanchi and Raja Bhagwandas. *ZK,* 47-48.
2. Aqa Jan Khazanchi, *Ibid.* See also *AN,* III, 156 and *MR,* I, 837. While Nizamuddin and Badauni say Aqa Ḳhan. *TA,* II, 214 and *MT,* II, 214.
3. Raja Bhagwandas, son of Raja Bahar Mal, was among the great nobles of Akbar and had attained the mansab of 5000. He died in Muharram, A.H. 998/November, 1589 A.D. at Lahore. *ZK,* 152 and *MU,* II, 129. See also *Ibid.* Actually his name was Bhagwant Das. But he never held any such office as Parwanchi, i.e. a secretary for writing out royal orders in Punjab at this time. *MR.* I, 837.
4. Her name was Harem Begum, daughter of Sultan Avais Kolabi from Qabach tribe. She died in the beginning of A.H. 983/1575 A.D. *AN,* III, 154. In the translation of Blocman of Ain-i-Akbari, her name is given as Khurram Begum, vol. I, 312.
5. *Bait* has been left. p. 207.
6. On 15th Rajab/20th October. *MT,* II, 215, *TA,* II, 315 and *MR,* I, 838.
7. According to Badauni, "Mathra." *MT,* II, 215 and *MR,* I, 838 while Nizamuddin says Mathurah, which was situated at a distance of 20 karohs from Fatehpur. *TA,* II, 315.
8. Abul Fazl says three karohs. *AN,* III, 156 while Badauni and Nizamuddin say five karohs. *MT,* II, 215 and *TA,* II, 315. *Nazm* has been left. See p. 208.
9. The word Chokandidar is not found anywhere. Abul Fazl has also not mentioned it in the long list of the accoutrements of the elephants given by him.
10. The emperor granted him Rs. 50,000 in addition to commodities. He was also given Rs. 20,000 more from the treasury of Gujarat and Qilij Khan was asked to accompany him. *ZK,* 51. See also *AN,* III, 161-3, TA, II, 319, *MT.* II, 218 and *MR,* I, 842. Abdur Rahim, *Mughal Relations with Persia and Central Asia,* Islami Culture, vols. VIII & IX, 1934-35,

N.R. Faruqi, *Mughal Ottoman Relations: A Study of Political and Diplomatic Relations Between Mughal India and the Ottoman Empire.* Delhi, 1989.

11. Other sources are silent about it.

OCCURRENCE 36

Description of Some Affairs of Hajipur, Tirhut and Bihar and the Escape of Junaid and other Afghans out of Fright

The emperor started for the capital after the conquest of Bihar and Bengal. He, however, sent Muzaffar Khan to take possession of the fort of Rohtas with some other Khans. The Khans sat around it and decided to send a messenger through Bahadur[1] to its commander, appointed by Daud, for submission. He replied that "this fort has been entrusted to me by my lord and chief. Unless and until he does not order me to surrender, it is impossible for me to incur violation of trust." Therefore, they discussed the existing situation and decided that it was difficult to capture it as per the declaration of its commandant while the emperor was also far off. Unless the hand of conquest did not come, it would be useless to lay siege to it because it was very massive and strong. It competed with the blue sky in height while in loftiness was equal to two bastions. There were enough number of forms within it which could supply food to the garrison and other necessary equipments were also beyond count.

(p. 210) Muzaffar Khan and other Khans lifted its siege and everyone returned to their respective places. The above-mentioned Khan diverted his attention towards Chaund and Sahasram[2] which were under the control of the Shaligh[3] of Rohtas fort. He however captured those two mahals (parganas) and stayed[4] there for some days. In the meanwhile, Junaid came to the vilayat of Bihar frustrated, entered into an alliance with the Afghans and they captured it. At the same time Muzaffar Khan was favoured with the royal blessings. An imperial farman was issued conferring on him the charge of the Sarkar of Hajipur. From the above-mentioned parganas, the Khan came to Patna. When the report of turbulence and sedition created by Junaid and his companions[5] (Afghans) reached the court, a farman was issued, appointing Muzaffar Khan, the commander of the imperial army with other Khans for its suppression. It was also advised that a bridge be constructed across Pun Pun river for crossing the army. But Wazir Khan and some other Khans opposed it and they refused to cross the river. The Khan was aghast to know their unfriendliness. Meanwhile, a group of the Afghans took possession of Hajipur, which was his jagir, by killing the agent, shiqdar and a number of other persons. Immediately, he left for Hajipur by boat, and after killing the Afghans and conspirators, he entered into it. Thereafter, he went in their pursuit and resolved to reach and cover that mountainous and forest area in the vicinity of Hajipur wherein were a large number of fortresses which were very safe hide-out for them. He, therefore started in that direction. During his march several skirmishes took place but he fought very bravely. It so happened that on one occasion he rode on his horse, arrows and bow in hand and sword hanging from his neck, and went for the enemy while fighting vigorously, he sat in his place to rest. (p. 211)

Misraa (a hemistich)

If the approval of God was not there, how could it all happen?

Meanwhile Muhib Ali Khan[6] and Rumi Khan[7] with two thousand sawars, who were sent to assist the Bihar troops, came to Patna. A group of Khans comprising . . . Mir Muiz-ul-Mulk, his brother,[8] Shujaet Khan and Mirza Abdullah Khan[9] whose horses were not branded were thrown into a boat and sent to Khan Khanan. Before they could reach, Khan Khanan died.[10] The imperial farman was issued, posting them in Bihar for the assistance of the imperial army. Muzaffar Khan at last succeeded in expelling all rebels and returned to Hajipur. Then taking Arab Bahadur[11] and two thousand strong contingent, he crossed the river Ganga. His march created panic and Junaid became despondent while the Afghans fled away i.e. scattered like wary stars. No one could have imagined that Junaid and the Afghans would exhibit such cowardice.[12]

On 8th Ziqada, A.H. 983/7th February, 1576 A.D.[13] the Khan crossed the river Ganga with his companions in further pursuit of the Afghans. On their arrival at Ibrahimpur, the camping place of the Afghans, they found no trace of their being there. At the same time information was received that Khan-i-Jahan, Saeed Khan and Raja Todar Mal who had been sent for assistance, were waiting there on 24th, Ziqada/23rd February of the same month Khan-i-Jahan and Saeed Khan met Muzaffar Khan. On 1st of Zi-hijja of the same year after giving leave to the said Khans, he started for Bengal. Though he covered the jungle and hills, could not find the hideouts. So he returned. (p. 212) On his arrival in the region of Khalil, a pargana of Ghayaspur, he received an imperial farman dated 1st Safar, A.H. 984/30th April, 1576 A.D., requiring him to proceed to Bengal for the assistance of the imperial army there. In its obedience, the kettledrums for march were sounded and he moved with his troops in that direction. It was believed that the result would be good and success would also be achieved.

On 8th Ziqada, A.H. 983/7th February, 1576 A.D. the emperor had left Fatehabad Sikri for Ajmer for the pilgrimage of the shrine of the Khwaja and left Mirza Aziz Koka at Agra in the custody of Shaikh Ibrahim.

Duaa (prayer) for His Majesty

May the grand tree of the garden of this great emperor, conqueror of countries, by the water of the clouds of justice, remain fresh till eternity, and may God protect the blessed king from all afflictions!

Notes

1. Bahadur, son of Haibat Khan, was among the relations of the last ruler of Bengal. *AN*, III, 104 and 132. *Masnavi* has been left. See p. 209.
2. Chaundah and Shahsram. *AN, III*, 132.
3. Shaligh means Sardar.

4. It was his Jagir earlier. *AN*, III, 131.
5. Staying with his relations and Khans.
6. Muhib Ali Khạn Rohtasi was an amir, who held a mansab of 5000. He was well known in the world for (his) bravery, courage, generosity and consideration for others. He died in A.H. 996/1588 A.D. *ZK*, 354, Nizamuddin says that he held a mansab of 4000. *TA*, II, 437. See also *AN*, *MU*, *TM* and *IJ*.
7. Rumi Khan performed Haj in A.H. 983/1575 A.D. on behalf of the ladies. *AN*, III, 146.
8. His name was Mir Ali Akbar, the younger brother of the Mir. *AN*, III, 309.
9. Abul Fazl says Mirza Abdullah. *Ibid.*
10. He died in A.H. 983/1575 A.D.
11. Arab Bahadur was one of the nobles of Akbar. He joined the rebels and remained wandering for long. At last, he was killed in A.H. 994/May, 1586 A.D. in Bahraich. *ibid.* See also *MT*, *TA*, and *IJ*.
12. In the month of Safar, A.H. 984/April, 1576 A.D. *AN*, II, 160 to 168.
13. Badauni says 17th Ziqada/16th February. *MT*, II, 227 while Nizamuddin says 7th Ziqada/6th February. *TA*, II, 319.

OCCURRENCE 37

Description of Gaur and Bengal after the Death of Khan-i-Khanan and the Deputation of Khan-i-Jahan for the Administration of that Province

At the time of his death,[1] Khan-i-Khanan had instructed Shaham Khan Jalair that his treasure, stable of elephants and other personal possessions be impounded while Majnun Khan Qaqshal and Muhammad Murad Khan with other Khans and (salatins) amirs, should maintain defence of the parganas and vilayat, remaining in their respective positions. Its information be despatched to the imperial court and they should act according to the emperor's instructions. His will was not respected. However, its news was sent by the Khans to the imperial court. That very day an imperial farman[2] was issued that Husain Quli Khan entitled Khan-i-Jahan should proceed to Gaur and Bengal and assume the charge of administration there. Raja Todar Mal was also asked to accompany him and organise the revenue affairs of that Sarkar. On the basis of the farman in the beginning of Ramzan, A.H. 983/December, 1575 A.D. Khan-i-Jahan with his brother[3] and some of the Khans and amirs left for Bengal and decided that (p. 213) Muzaffar Khan be assisted in expelling Junaid and the Afghans from their hide-outs in the hills of Bengal and only then proceed towards it. They reached Jaunpur. On the same day Muzaffar Khan and Arab Bahadur with their troop crossed the river Ganga and advanced further. On receipt of information, Junaid took to heel. The said happenings have already been recorded earlier also. Khan-i-Jahan, Muzaffar Khan, other Khans and amirs, however, met at Ibrahimpur. On 1st Zi-hijja[4]/2nd March Khan-i-Jahan left for

Bengal with Todar Mal. On the way information was received that Shaham Khan Jalair, Qiya Khan, Majnun Khan Qaqshal and Muhammad Murad Khan, who were appointed to manage the affairs of the Sarkar of Gaur and Bengal with other Khans and amirs, agreed to leave their places without any ostensible reason. They reached Hajipur and Patna and a numerous bands of young men and soldiers had spread all around. As Daud, the accursed-fellow and other sardars of the Afghans found the vilayat empty, they captured it. The Afghans from the neighbouring areas came and joined him. Khan-i-Jahan, Raja Todar Mal and other Khans received this information at Tanda and they rushed immediately. Joining with the Khans and amirs of Gaur, Mungir and Bhagalpur, they marched to Tanda. On 23rd Zi-hijja,[5] A.H. 983/16th April, 1574 A.D. they reached Garhi which was supposed to be the gate of Tanda. Boats, which were a part of the navy were strengthened[6] and the brave warriors exhibited such admirable courage which frightened the rebels completely. After capturing Garhi,[7] they went in their pursuit which resulted in either their killings or arrests.[8] Those who managed to escape, went and joined Daud, the accursed. Ak Mahal[9] (Raj Mahal) which was situated in the narrow passage between Garhi and Tanda, became the refuge of the Afghans and they strengthened it for their safety as it contained the form of the hill on one side as a wall of safety. (p. 214) On the other side there was the river Ganga while on the third side a deep lake of black water.[10] It was so high that even the wind could not reach it, and even the foot of lighting once it got stuck in its marsh, becomes helpless to pull itself out. The Khans however, reached near it.

The distance between the opposing forces gradually narrowed down. Then a series of farmans[11] were issued requiring Muzaffar Khan and other Khans of Bihar and jagirdars of Tirhut[12] to proceed for the help of the army of Bengal. Therefore, the said Khans got ready but awaited the joining of other Khans near Bhagalpur for a few days.

When the Khans and jagirdars joined the army of Muzaffar Khan, he started on the 1st Rabi-ul-Akhir/10th June of the said year to join the army of Bengal. On Sunday 3rd Rabi I/12th June of the said month, Khan Jahan with other Khans and amirs who were present in the army, advanced to meet him and they handshook each other and returned to their camp next day.[13] (p. 215)

Bait (verse)

The sun, rising in the east, drove away the owls from the sky.

Muzaffar Khan along with a few other Khans came upon the embankment of a high mound to inspect and consider carefully the pros and cons of that battlefield and he then chose the spot of battle. On 14th of the month of Rabi/23rd June, Wednesday,[14] he discussed the plan of action with the Khans and amirs and it was decided that next day i.e. Thursday 15th Rabi-ul Akhir/24th July early morning, which was considered to be the most auspicious day of the week, the battlefield would be arranged. But the troops seemed to be delaying the plan by putting swords into sheaths and arrows into the bows. Muzaffar Khan objected to it and exhorted them to be quick as the wise have said.

On the Afghans side, Daud, the condemned, was making brisk preparations to start the battle of which the image was printed on the board of their minds. But some Khans on the imperial side were worried, and in their hearts they were full of fear, as they were not sure of success. In short, everyone was in a state of consternation because all those Afghans who were spread in Bengal, Bihar, Hajipur and Tirhut, had gathered with full preparations even deploying their navy there. The imperial army faced the scarcity of food grains. (p. 216) Its price shot up and they became weak.[15] Moreover, the rainy season set in. Soon the arrows of rain were falling from the clouds and swords of destructive lightning were piercing into the earth, making it a deep dense slush. Success seemed to be a stranger. But Muzaffar Khan, who had witnessed the succour and support of God to the imperial forces on several occasions was confident that His Majesty had always been the recipient of Divine Support. So his mind was at peace and he nurtured no fear. He was offering humble prayers to the Almighty saying, "If the mercy and help will not be granted to this humble then the whole preparations will go waste, and if thy guidance will not be with us at this juncture, then the course of success will become extremely difficult."

Abiyat (*verses*)

God knows that we are all worried, though we are master of the whole world (country); but we are utterly helpless from head to foot and are entangled in all sorts of difficulties.

After the prayer, he begged for victory. In short, on the morning of 15th (Rabi II/24th July) when the sun rose and daylight started spraying everywhere, then the red flag rose in the east and the brave warriors with grim determination advanced into the battlefield.[16]

Right and left wings were arranged suitably and the army was pushed forward opposite the enemy. Both the opposing armies approached Ak Mahal (Raj Mahal). Suddenly, Kalapahad, one of the famous chiefs of Afghans, well equipped with every weapon, emerged from the middle of the opposing force. (p. 217)

Then the fighters were organised and arranged after the manner of the pieces of chess which made the atmosphere sick and disgusted. Both armies began to move like a tempest of rivers of Akhzar and to attack each other like two mountains, made of steel, colliding by the face of wind.

Then from the right wing which was held by Muzaffar Khan, he came out on a mountain like elephant and coming to an elevated spot, surveyed the camp. He marked that the left wing, held by the Raja and Qaqshal was being pushed by the enemies. Immediately, he descended from it and like a flood, attacking the enemy pushed forward on the middle and left. As the driver of the elephant showed cowardice hence he cut his head with his sword, and advanced forward attacking and shouting down the opponents so that there seemed no difference between the killer and the killed. Owing to the heaps of wounded and killed the air of the plains became the air of mountains and the blood of the killed made the water of Ganga red.[17] (p. 218)

The breeze of victory began to blow on the imperial flags while the enemy's turned like their fate. The enemy retreated and about two thousand persons were slain. A graceful face appeared in the mirror of imagination and drums of success started sounding. A noise rose that Daud, the accursed was also slain.[18]

All the Mughals came forward from behind the Afghans and their leader Daud, the wretched, was captured and killed. The head of that unreliable person, who deserved to be impaled and who was the honour and mainstream of the Afghan army, was sent to the imperial court to set an example for the witnesses thereof. Many of his nobles were slain and Junaid, being wounded fled away but he too died after a few days.[19] Some of the amirs were sent in pursuit of the escaping Afghans. The victorious army started devastating and ruining the land and they succeeded in aquiring much booty and pushed forward. At this time, the Mughal army behaved like a hungry hawk, falling on a pack of pigeons or like a wild wolf finding himself in the midst of a horde of goats. About three hundred[20] elephants were captured and the grand victory was proclaimed in all the neighbouring countries, Khan-i-Jahan from the pursuit of the enemy, turned towards Tanda, the capital of Bengal. (p. 219) On Saturday Muzaffar Khan accompanied by the Khans, raising the standards marched towards Bihar. The common people thanked him and they began to live in their homes in peace and happiness.

Undotted (ain)

The heart of pride was broken and the victorious returned.

Draft of the Farman, Worth of Obedience

When such a splendid victory was achieved and the honourable Muzaffar Khan of good luck, turned back, he arrived in Patna, the seat of the administrator of Bihar. A grand imperial farman, containing infinite benevolence and favours was received. Its text as follows:

"Umdat-ul-Mulk Rukn-us-Sultanate Muzaffar Khan, who hopes for the imperial favour, may know that on 20th Rabi-us-Sani (A.H. 984/17th July, 1576 A.D.) Saiyed Abdullah[21] came and brought the news of the victory over Daud and presented his head there. It is a matter of profound sense of gratitude and regard for the Almighty.[22] He narrated the story of devotion and courage of (yours) and the nobles of Bihar. We did not expect such devotion and sacrifice from you. But you have performed your duty on battle-front a hundred times more efficiently as you used to do in the management of the household in accordance to our wish. May God shower His mercy on you! The good wishes for the empire consist in reality in the manner you have exhibited. Though the news was received late, it may be a blessing for you. Very soon, God willing, unbound favours will be bestowed on you and those who were associated with you, they will be summoned and will be rewarded duly. We wish that a detailed report of the performances and achievements of the nobles and amirs be submitted to us so that suitable rewards for everyone's services be also conferred on them. Whatever has been jotted down it should not be overlooked. (p. 220) It is settled that when your mind is free from all distractions and affairs, then you ought to convey to us that your heart is now fully pacified. Then we will summon you alone to the imperial court." The reason of issuing the said farman in regard to those events was that it might be known that the status and rank of the wazir, Muzaffar Nishan was made so high that very few wazirs had ever obtained such a position.

Duaa (prayer) for His Majesty

May the shadow of the kindness of this king i.e., Hazrat Khaqan Akbar's remain till the last Day on the forehead and head of all persons, and from his banners unlimited victories and countless benevolence be obtained!

Notes

1. See *MU*, I, 649.
2. See *TA*, II, 321.
3. His name was Ismail Quli Khan. He rose to the mansab of 3000. He had 1200 wives. While going to the court, he used to put a seal on their waistband. Ultimately, all the women joined hands and put poison in his food. He died during Akbar's time. *ZK*, 348. See also *MU*, and *TA*.
4. This date has not been recorded by other contemporary and near contemporary sources.
5. Other sources do not contain any date.
6. Boats (Niwara) used for the defence of the banks of the rivers.
7. Teliagarhi is situated near the river Ganga which protects like a sentry the narrow pass leading to Bengal.
8. Nizamuddin and Badauni say that one thousand and five hundred Afghans were killed and most of their sardars were arrested. *TA*, II, 321 and *MT*, II, 227. While all the sardars were killed. *MR*, I, 843.
9. Ak Mahal. *AN*, II, 162.
10. Daldal. *Bait* has been left. p. 214.
11. See also *AN*, III, 168, *TA*, II, 322 and *MR*, I, 844.
12. Mauza, situated in Bihar. *Bait* has been left. See p. 214.
13. It is not found in other sources.
14. 12th Rabi-ul-Akhir/21st July. *MR*, I, 847. *Bait* has been left. p. 215.
15. See *AN*, III, 178.
16. *Abiyat* have been left. See p. 216.
17. *Abiyat* have been left. See pp. 217-18.
18. See also *AN*, III, 182, *TA*, 325, *MR*, I, 848 and *MT*, II, 238.
19. *Ibid.*
20. Countless elephants were captured. *TA*, II, 325 and *MT*, II, 238.
21. Abul Fazl says, "As Saiyed Abdullah had brought the good news of the success of Man Singh over Rana Pratap. Akbar sent him to the house of Khan-i-Jahan and remarked that God willing, he will bring the news of Daud's defeat also. *AN*, II, 178.
22. *Bait* has been left. See p. 219.

OCCURRENCE 38

Description of the Conquest of Some Forts and Certain Other Happennings, Occurred During the Same Year (In Brief)

In the beginning of the year A.H. 984/1576 A.D.[1] the fort of Sewana[2] was captured by Shahbaz Khan, which was under the possession of Raja Chander Sen,[3] the accursed, son of Raja Mal Deo. Shahbaz Khan, the Mir Bakshi, was appointed its commandant. After taking it into the possession, the above-named Khan was sent to assist the army of Bengal. When he reached Jaunpur, news came that Raja Gajpati[4] had killed Farhat Khan, his father[5] and Qarataq Khan,[6] who were the imperial servants. He had also captured Saeed Khan and Bahadur Khan[7] who were deputed to assist the army of Bengal. (p. 221) Meanwhile, information was also received that Daud, the condemned, had been slain and victory over Bengal had also been achieved. As Gajpati was on the way to Bihar and Bengal, it was considered necessary to go to uproot that accursed infidel. They marched in his pursuit, who went deep into a forest and strengthened his defences. Shahbaz Khan was fully determined to besiege and fight with him. By the beginning of Jamadi-ul-Awwal, 984/ August, 1576 A.D. he posted his troops around Jagdishpur which was his hide-out, blocked the route to its fortress and laid a siege to the whole forest. Muzaffar Khan was resting after the victory of Bengal at Patna that time. Shahbaz Khan sent despatches repeatedly, stating that "he has laid siege to Gajpati, the accursed, his supply line has been blocked and he is in much trouble". He further appealed, "To send force for his help so that the siege may not have to be prolonged". Muzaffar Khan deputed Muhib Ali Khan and Arab Bahadur with a battalion of about six or seven hundred men and also a troop of amirs, numbering five to six hundred to the help of Shahbaz Khan. The moment reinforcements reached, he was defeated and fled away. Consequently, by the end of Jamadi-ul-Akhir/August all the estates and parganas which were under his possession, fell into the hands of the imperial servants. That accursed ran into the hills and forests and became a homeless wanderer. Hence his name or existence vanished completely and he was burnt in the fires of hell in that jungle.

Conquest of Sher Garh Fort

The fort of Sher Garh which was under the occupation of Gajpati was very massive and strong which he had given to his son. He came and supplicated for peace.[8]

Conquest of Rohtas Fort

When Shahbaz Khan was relieved of the affairs of Gajpati, he cast his hand on the fort of Rohtas[9] after a few days. The band of Afghans, who were in the fort, came out after obtaining certain promises and pledges and thus secured peace and safety. Thus within a short period several victories were achieved. Shahbaz Khan, taking the fort into possession, handed it over to his brothers.[10] On Shawal[11]/December of the said year he left for the imperial court.[12] (p. 222)

At last an imperial farman was issued that the brothers of Shahbaz Khan should hand over the fort of Rohtas to Muhib Ali Khan and they should proceed to the imperial court. Thus Muhib Ali Khan took into possession the said fort, its administration and other forts and dominion within its jurisdiction.

Duaa (prayer) for His Majesty

May the banners of the king of the world and flags of his splendour fly over all the corners of the world!

NOTES

1. See also *AN*, III, 168, *MU*, II, 180 and *Karnama-i-Rajputana*, p. 390. The date given by Badauni and Nizamuddin is not correct.

2. Abul Fazl and Nizamuddin say Sawana which was one of the famous forts of Ajmer. *AN*, III, 168 and *TA*, II, 301 while Badauni and Farishta say Sewana. *MT*, III, 186 and *Farishta*, II, 263.
3. Raja Chander Sen was the younger son and heir-apparent of Raja Mal Deo. He died in A.H. 989/1581 A.D. *MU*, II, 180.
4. He was one of the renowned zamindars of Bihar. Earlier he had performed excellent services with Munam Khan but after the latter's death he had started indulging in sedition and destruction of Bihar. *AN*, III, 169, *MU*, II, 591 and *TA*, II, 324.
5. The name of his father was Farhang Khan. *AN*, III, 169. See *ibid* also.
6. Qarataq Khan was with Muzaffar Khan Turbati at Jharkhan. He held a mansab. He died in A.H. 984/1576 A.D. See also *TM*, *AN* and *IJ*.
7. Abul Fazl says that he was Makhsus Khan. *AN*, III, 169 while younger brother of Saeed Khan Chaghta. *MU*, III, 324.
8. His name was Sri Ram. *AN*, III, 168 and 189. *MU*, II, 592.
9. First it was under the charge of Junaid, who handed it over to Saiyed Muhammad. *AN*, II, 189.
10. One of his brothers was Karamullah, who died in A.H. 1002/1593 A.D. *MU*, II, 601 and see also *ibid* and *TM*.
11. Month is given but date is not found.
12. *Abiyat* have been left. p. 222.

OCCURRENCE 39

Description of the Conquest of Rohtas Fort by the Imperial Forces, the March of Muzaffar Khan to Drive Out the Remaining Afghans, Their Execution and Imprisonment

It had already been recorded in the preceding pages that Jamdat-ul-Mulk Saif-ud-Din Muzaffar Khan was resting at Patna after his heroic performance against Daud and the Afghans for the last two months. During the same time an imperial farman was issued that he should march to conquer Rohtas fort. Respecting it, he started in the middle of Rajab, A.H. 984/October, 1576 A.D. for it. Muhammad Masum Kabli,[1] the jagirdar of the area, was despatched as advance guard. In the course of the journey, Muhammad Masum Kabli was informed that Husain Khan Afghan and some of his (Afghan) nobles were living unawares nearby. (p. 223) He rushed and attacked them with his force on that spot and killed a good many of them. Husain Khan was also slain. Muhammad Masum Khan informed Muzaffar Khan accordingly and he felt relieved.

Muzaffar Khan was determined to suppress the menace of Kala Pahad, who belonged to the force of Daud and Junaid. During the course of fighting in Bengal, he escaped and strengthened himself in the environs of Rohtas by unleashing panic and sedition there. After the success, Muhammad Masum Khan stayed in the village of Ashhar,[2] which was the part of his jagir. Kala Pahad bounced on him with a force of seven or eight hundred ferocious horseman and laid siege there. The Khan cut it like a furious lion and he himself surrounded them. The famous Abar[3] elephant, known among the Mughals and the Afghans, a frightful and destructive creature was pushed towards the horse of Muhammad Masum Kabli. It lifted and threw him on the ground. When he was on foot, the elephant driver also fell on the ground. Kala Pahad and other Afghans considered it a great achievement, they attacked the Khan and wounded him. Though he was on foot, he received injuries on his head and hand, but he earned a name among the brave soldiers.[4]

Bait (*verse*)

His head was separated by a sharp stroke of hand, has hand full of dust and face full of blood.

The elephant without its driver saw a great crowd of the Afghans shouting near the head of Muhammad Masum Kabli. It lost balance of mind and started to run amock. It turned against the Afghans and lifting them by its trunk, hurled them on the ground. They started running for life. (p. 224) It caused the reason of the Afghans defeat. One of the servants of the said Khan attacked Kala Pahad and inflicted a severe wound on him, resulting in his capture. When he was brought before Muhammad Masum, he was put to sword.[5]

The Afghans were either killed or taken as prisoners or they ran away. It happened by the end of Rajab, A.H. 984/December, 1576 A.D. Thereafter, the captured Abar (elephant) and the head of Kala Pahad were despatched to be presented before Muzaffar Khan. When this happy tidings was received by him, he thanked and offered prayers to the Almighty. He reached on the spot and sent Abar with other captured elephants to the imperial court. The Jumdat-ul-Mulk (Muzaffar Khan), marching stage by stage reached near the Rohtas fort. The inmates and guards of the fort submitted a petition containing — "We the slaves have been waiting to join your service and we will hand over the fort to you as soon as we receive your orders". As it had been mentioned Shahbaz Khan who was besieging Sher Garh fort of Gajpati and was about to complete his work, sent a petition to the emperor that he be granted the charge of Rohtas fort. It was granted. So an imperial farman was issued containing that those who were in its occupation, should hand it over to Shahbaz Khan without any hitch. Muzaffar Khan marched away in the direction of the mountainous region for the suppression of the escaped Afghans.[6] (p. 225)

Muzaffar Khan, covering the hills, appeared in the village of Kokra, where the Afghans had taken refuge. Being fed up, three to four thousand families of the Afghans were forced to vacate the place and a few of them were slain. The victorious army went to distant places and scaled the mountains there.[7]

During the course of march, they searched that route which was very deep, surrounded with numerous trees but could not find traces of the Afghans. During the search, the abode of the Afghans[8] of Yusuf, Sati, Adam[9] and Jauna[10] were found. Besides the booty, one hundred and sixty elephants were also captured from the Rajas of the hills which were sent to Patna to be despatched to the Darul Khilafat, Agra. Numerous Afghans were either killed or captured during the expedition and at last their very existence was wiped out from the province.

Bait (verse)

Whoever opposed you, was either killed or captured.

Pilgrimage to Ajmer

During the same year[11] the emperor decided to visit the tomb of. . . . Khwaja Muin-ud-Din Chishti at Ajmer. In the thick of expedition Shahbaz Khan, Mir Bakshi was appointed to capture the fort of Kamal Mir[12] (Kumbhar Mir). He laid a siege to it and wrested it easily.[13] Asaf Khan was appointed to capture the Idar[14] fort. The details of happenings of success of each fort would be given later. (p. 226)

The emperor decided to visit Hindawar, Gujarat and the Sarkar of Mandu. Hunting in the mountains and deserts of Banswara[15] and Mandu, he reached the border of the Deccan on 22nd Safar, A.H. 984/11th May, 1576 A.D.[16] Later he returned to Fatehpur Sikri with full grandeur and glory.

The wazir who was the root of the victories, played a very important role in annexing such victories. On the 1st of

Zia-hijja, A.H. 985/19th February, 1577 A.D. he stopped at Seur, which was under the Sarkar of Bihar. In the middle of Safar, A.H. 985/April, 1577 A.D. the Raja of Seur submitted himself before him and presented thirty thousand rupees with twenty elephants as peshkash. Keeping in mind the principle that the real pardon was to be granted by the person who possesses the power of punishment, he ordered the Raja to go the imperial court. While he himself passing through the hilly region on 24th/14th May of the said month, reached Suraj Garh.[17] Later he crossed the river Ganga and came to Hajipur. During the expedition countless wealth and treasure fell into the hands of the imperial servants. By the beginning of Rabi-ul-Akhir, A.H. 985/June, 1577 A.D. travelling by the side of the river (Ganga), they reached the village Sawaej[18] which was the dependency of Saran Basai.[19]

By the end of Jamadi-ul-Awwal/June of the said year, an imperial farman was issued containing: "The emperor was much pleased with the deeds of Muzaffar Khan and he has summoned him to the imperial court." Accordingly, he abided by it. When Muzaffar Khan reached Agra, he found that the emperor was preparing to pay a visit to the shrine of (p. 227) Khwaja Muinuddin Chishti at Ajmer. He rushed quickly and kissed the royal feet. At the same time a notable incident that occurred was that Muzaffar Khan was entrusted the charge of the central revenues and the office of vakil was also conferred on him.[20] He had brought with him eight lakh rupees and thirty elephants from the Khalsa land and his own jagir (Bihar and Hajipur) which were presented to the emperor who was pleased to accept the graceful offering and conferred favours on him. By the middle of Shaban/30th October, the emperor started from Ajmer. Hunting on the way, he reached Merta which was in the pargana of Nagore. Thereafter he started for Darul Mulk, Hazrat-i-Delhi. There he offered *Id* prayer at Idgah which was built by late Tatar Khan. Those events which occurred after the departure of the emperor would be narrated hereafter.

Duaa (Prayer) for His Majesty

May your high court and splendid throne remain full of friendship and love by the arrival of messengers! The perfection of your greatness and the spectacle of God's grace and brilliance may remain free from decline and evil eye for ever!

NOTES

1. Muhammad Masum Kabuli, belonged to the Saiyed family of Khurasan, was foster brother of Mirza Muhammad Hakim. He joined the emperor's service in 20th year, received the mansab of 500. In his success against Kala Pahad Afghan, he received an increase of 500 i.e. became the mansabdar of 1000. He died in the month of Shawwal, A.H. 1007/April, 1599 A.D. *MU*, III, 292. See also *TM, AN, IJ, SS* and *Tazkira.*
2. Its reference is not found in other sources.
3. Farishta says that the elephant bears the name Ayaz. II, 263.
4. See also *AN, SS, TM* and *IJ.*
5. *Bait* has been left. See p. 224.
6. *Bait* has been left. See *ibid.*
7. *Bait* has been left. See p. 225.
8. According to Abul Fazl, "Yusuf Patani, son of Fateh Khan, was present in A.H. 983/1575 A.D. in the battle of Jhar Khand. *AN*, III, 135.
9. Adam Patni, son of Fateh Khan was also present in the above-mentioned battle. *Ibid.*
10. Not traceable.
11. See also *MT*, 238 and *TA*, II, 326.
12. Abul Fazl says Kohal Mir (Kothal Mir) and dates it in A.H. 986/1578 A.D. *AN*, III, 328 and *Farishta,* II, 263. Kunblhmir, situated in Udaipur. *MU*, II, 263.
13. Farishta has followed Arif. See *Farishta,* II, 263.
14. Badauni says that it was situated in Gujarat. *MT*, II, 244.
15. Abul Fazl says Banswala. *AN*, III, 194. See also *Farishta* and *MT*.
16. Sunday, 23rd Safar/12th May. *MR*, I, 852.
17. Situated in Mungair, Bihar. *MT*, II, 242.
18. It is not mentioned in other sources.
19. The word Basai could not be traced.
20. See also *AN.* III, 238.

OCCURRENCE 40

Description of the Summoning of Asaf Khan to the Capital, Conferring on Him the Office of *Vikalat* According to the Recommendation of the Matchless Wazir (Muzaffar Nishan) and Some Other Happenings, Occurred During the Year

The causes of the opening of the gates of the gifts of the Almighty and the marks of the imperial succour and the evidence of the government of the world and the goodness of the state are the wise and sagacious vakils and wazirs who with their tactful handling grasp the secrets of various parts of the country (p. 228) in no time and apply the ointment of mercy and benevolence on the affairs of the time and at the time of defending the frontiers and expelling the enemies, collect armies of brave warriors and place them in proper array, the centre, rear, right and left wings of the army wisely and carefully.

On the basis of the above-mentioned facts it could be said that the emperor early in the year A.H. 985/1577, A.D. showed exceptional favours and kindness to the wazir, Muzaffar Nishan. An imperial farman was issued summoning him to the imperial court, saying that after settling the affairs of Sarkar of Bihar, Hajipur and Tirhut and finished whatever is needful in regard to those areas, then he should come towards the capital. Thus on the basis of the farman, Muzaffar Khan, having been fully satisfied with the management of them, granting jagirs to all Khans and amirs, who were sent there for his assistance and getting their horses branded and having inspected their arms — finally left for the capital. By the end of Jamadi-ul-Akhir/September, covering stages swiftly, he reached Agra.

During the same time the emperor having decided to go on pilgrimage to the tomb of . . . Khwaja Muin-ud-Din Chishti had already reached the district (territory) of Ajmer. Muzaffar Khan followed him fast and joined him on the way itself. The emperor, the world conqueror and pure-hearted, was extremely delighted to see the said wazir, the sagacious and refuge of the Khilafat. One of the favours granted to Muzaffar Khan was "When the emperor reached within one karoh of Ajmer, he got down from his horse as a mark of respect and submission to the saint and began to walk to his shrine. Muzaffar Khan also got down and began to walk towards the shrine. But the emperor out of infinite affection and kindness ordered him to select any special horse and accompany the party on horse back, although all other companions were walking on foot." (p. 229) In short, no other vakil or wazir, till the last, ever attained the rank and status which Muzaffar Khan obtained nor was it found in any book of history. The office of vakil was conferred on him, whose exterior is free from crookedness and whose views are clear and whose tact and understanding is full of experience and whose luck is youthful (promising) and whose guidance or reason is responsible, and is an assurance of economy and a matchless courage, and give sobriety and thought, and a part of the great revered by elders, organiser and counsel the sky of victorious splendour, the liberal giver of justice, destroyer of tyranny and oppression, the counsel of the shadow of God on earth the emperor, the sword of the world — and the faith, Jumdat-ul-Mulk Muzaffar Khan, may God grant him honour in his work! In one stroke, he obtained such a high office as a special case and a variety of other favours which are the outcome of the habit and practice of the emperor, were also granted, which became a part of the status of such an able and farsighted wazir. Khilat of golden embroidery was bestowed on him with a saddle and (rein). A special place was made to keep his seals so that it be kept at the right side and dictate what is to be written.

The affairs of the country and its administration became glorious and infinite freshness grew on the face of kindness and sympathy. The officials of government became happy. The world echoed courtesy and civility, so colourful as the faces of the beloved.[1] (p. 230)

Owing to the mercy and benevolence of the emperor, Muzaffar Khan adorned the seat of vakil with his noble personality and he, by the grace of his charm, humility and courtesy opened the doors of justice and fair play over the people of Hindustan and organised the working of the offices of vakil and wazir. In spite of his covetous position and awe, he showed such exaggerated respect and honour to the men of learning that the garden of their hopes blossomed forth, and by the words of his expression the plant of their desires flourished so much so that it began to cast its shadow. He was an expert in the art of writing secretly and fine in composition and regarding the policies of the state, he possessed a mysterious sense.

When the emperor began his return journey from Ajmer, he issued a farman containing that "a few writers should accompany Muzaffar Nishan and he should keep along with himself his officials and prepare the account to find out how much revenue has been acquired from Gujarat and Mandu and out of it the share of remuneration of all officers be fixed according to their respective ability and deed, and after showing his weapons and getting his horse branded, everyone should only receive his Jagir". Muzaffar Nishan distributed jagirs in right earnest. Thereafter, he followed the emperor. (p. 231)

On Thursday, the 25th Shaban, A.H. 985/November 19, 1577 A.D. a bright star sighted in the sky in the west, inclining towards the south and was surrounded by small stars like hyacinth. It remained visible for four gharis. The people of Delhi, Lahore and Agra went up to their roofs to watch it. "O men, you who have eyes, take lesson". It continued to appear up to the end of Shawwal/December 1577 of that year, and then it vanished. It is known as tail-star (comet).

On 14th Ramzan/15th November of the said year, Shah Ismail,[2] son of Shah Tahmasp, king of Khurasan and Iraq, was poisoned by his sister in collusion with some nobles. It is obvious that he was a victim of the comet.[3]

(p. 233) In the said year the administration of various places was entrusted to nobles. The administration of Gujarat was entrusted to Qutbuddin Muhammad Khan Atga,[4] Shahab Khan of Saranpur,[5] Shujaet Khan[6] of Malwa while Shah Fakhruddin Khan[7] and Shah Badagh Khan of Ujjain and the fort of Mandu. On 22nd Ramzan/4th December, 1577 A.D.[8] The emperor reached Delhi while hunting on his way.

"This poor, pitiable, heart-broken fellow i.e. the compiler of these pages had arrived in Delhi from Bihar as I was in the service of that Khan (Muzaffar Khan). When they reached the capital, Agra, I was dismissed and for some time I remained deprived of the pleasure of attending him, so much so that I became despaired. Later the Khan extended his kindness by sending a letter and summoned me back. Therefore, this slave obeyed it which was incumbent upon me, when I reached Delhi, I was favoured by being reemployed."[9]

His Majesty offered Id prayers in Delhi.[10] Then he left Delhi on 4th Shawwal/15th December, 1577 A.D. and travelling through hunting expedition passed certain towns such as Rohtak, Mahim,[11] Sanam[12] and Firozepur with the imperial army which marched slowly camping enroute, went on a pilgrimage to the tomb of (p. 234) . . . Hazrat Shaikh Farid Ganj-i-Shakar. On 12th of Zi-hijja/27th February[13] he reached Ajodhan which was known as Pak-Patan. On that day which was Friday, a group of learned persons, who were in the imperial retinue, kept vigil with him the whole night. The emperor stayed there for two days. Thereafter, he marched slowly, taking rest on the way and hunting, passing at a distance of ten karohs from the river Ravi. On the 1st of Muharram, A.H. 986/10th March, 1578 A.D. the compiler of these pages was moving with the victorious army and he received the honour of kissing the royal feet before his visit to the Shaikh's tomb.[14] On this occasion the mansab of the diwan of Sarkar of Punjab was assigned (to me) with the recommendation of the honourable Shaikh-ul-Islam, the refuge of Sadarat, Makhdum-ul-Mulk Maulana Abdullah. But I resigned the post without any reason. Then adopting the way of contentment, I chose the life of a dervish and faqir. I believe that the result will be good.[15]

Duaa (prayer) for His Majesty

May the shadow of the benevolence, grace and affection of the emperor and his care for his slaves which is the source of faith, devotion, peace and happiness, for a long time continue to cast its shadow on all men, etc., etc.!

NOTES

1. *Bait* and *Abiyat* have been left. See pp. 229-30.
2. Shah Ismail, son of Shah Tahmasp Safvi in collaboration with his sister, Pari Khanam ascended the throne in A.H. 984/1576 A.D. His son, Abbas ordered his assassination on 13th Ramzan, A.H. 985/24th November, 1577 A.D. at the age of forty-two for his elder brother's killing. *Tarikh-i-Iran,* 549. For details see also *AN, SS, MT,* etc.
3. Maulana Sheri has given in his ode (Qasida) a brief history of the comet. In his narration he says that when it rose, i.e., on what date, a description of it, and some examples, then he says that due to the liberal and human treatment of Akbar the people were happy and that the emperor is a most revered and fortunate person, etc., etc., . . . For details see pp. 231-33.
4. Qutbuddin Muhammad Khan Atga, brother of Khan-i-Azam held a mansab of 5000 and rose to the rank of Amir-ul-Umara. He held Bharoach in his jagir. He received martyrdom in Baroda at the hand of Sultan Muzaffar Gujarati. *ZK,* 347 and *MU,* III, 57.
5. Shahab Khan Shihabu-din Ahmad Khan Nishapuri was the retainer of Bairam Khan. He parted company with him and rose to the mansab of 5000. He rendered excellent services as vakil and subedar of Gujarat. He died in Malwa. *ZK,* 148, *AN,* III, 217 and *MU,* II, 569.
6. Shujaet Khan was the sister's son of Tardi Beig Khan. He held a mansab of 5000. He obtained martyrdom at the hands of his servant. *ZK,* 332, and *MU,* II, 557.
7. Shah Fakhruddin, son of Mir Qasim was from the family of Moosvi Saiyed of Mashhad. He came with Humayun in A.H. 961/1553 A.D. He held a mansab of 3000. He died in A.H. 986/1578 A.D. at Gujarat. *MU,* II, 556 and *AN,* III, 263.
8. Other sources do not contain it.
9. The reason seems that Muzaffar Khan did not show any favour to

Arif as he would have expected. On the contrary, he had displeased his master who dismissed him. But he was later retained.

10. Other sources are silent about it.
11. An old qasba, situated at a distance of five or six karohs from Rohtak in east Punjab.
12. It is also adjacent to Patiala, in east Punjab.
13. According to Nizamuddin, "On 2nd Zi-hijja / 9th February, His Majesty visited the tomb of the Shaikh." *TA*, II, 337.
14. Arif has not mentioned in what capacity he was there.
15. According to Abul Fazl, "The emperor appointed Makhdumul-Mulk, Abdullah Sultanpuri in A.H. 985/1577 A.D. for the administration of Sayur Garh, situated in the Punjab." *AN*, III, 234.

OCCURRENCE 41

Description of His Majesty's Excursion Trip to the Land of Punjab (For Enjoyment and Hunting), the Conquest of Kamal Mir (Kumbhal Mir) and Idar Forts During the Same Year by the Grace of God

(p. 235) It has already been stated that the emperor went first from Ajmer to Delhi and from there in between the vilayat of Punjab which was covered by slow marches. He, however, reached the border of Lahore.[1] Whenever he went out hunting with his hunters, it not only created hysteria in the hearts and minds of his companions, but unleashed a wave of terror among all beasts and birds of that region. So much so if birds had heard the news of his approach, they would have drowned themselves like ducks with sheer fright if they had had the power. If the ducks had known how to escape by flight from the bloody wildness of the enemy, they would have flown away. The dog would have barked at deer out of sheer fright. While the lion would have escaped from the hunters.[2] In short, the emperor continued it for some months. Though his intention was to play game, the real objects were; first, he wanted to keep himself aware of the condition of his subjects. If anyone throws the arrow of tyranny from his bow of oppression on the bird of others heart, then he was duly punished.[3] Second, the camps of the soldiers were to be inspected. If time permitted, he desired to go to Kabul, but he abandoned his plan due to its non-feasibility. The sister[4] of Nawab Mirza Muhammad Hakim was sent to give counsel and discuss some important matters with him.[5] Some employees of the imperial threshold were sent to escort the exalted lady to Kabul. (p. 236)

Third, a mysterious 'Divine Call' had descended on the emperor which tranced him completely.[6] The Divine call revealed a message to him regarding certain affairs while he was going towards the hunting ring.[7] It happened in the month of Rabi-ul-Awwal/May. As a result of this he got a lock of his hair cut there and most of his companions also did the same. The emperor gave up some of his engagements and turned his attention in the direction of the real purpose, and he named that spot as "mini-mecca".[8]

During the same time, the emperor ordered that one of the Rajputs who had committed a sin be flogged. After receiving two or three lashes, he lost all power to receive any more. He was a compound of ignorance so he thrust dagger into his stomach and died.[9]

During the same time i.e. by the end of Safar, A.H. 986/May, 1578 A.D. petitions of Shahbaz Khan and some other Khans were received which contained that the fort of Kamal Mir, which was under the siege of imperial forces for long, had ultimately fallen to them by the grace of God.[10] The reason of God's kindness was that he made the emperor the cause of prosperity of His creatures, and had imparted to his temperament the support of the Shariat. His heart too was actuated only by the object or raising aloft the banner of Islam and uprooting the foundations of infidelity. The fort of Kamal Mir was situated in the centre of the state, perched on the top of a hill, so that if any one had to see the sky from its top, he would have to look down into the sea (because the fort was higher than the sky). Imagination locked the power to witness its eminence; what strength the fancy would be able to measure the limits of its dimensions.[11] (p. 237)

The Rana Raja[12] of this place was very proud of (up to the limit of vanity) on account of its height and narrowness of its passages and among his contemporaries no one could match him and he did not submit to any emperor earlier. Many emperors tried to conquer it but they all failed. The emperor intended to subjugate it with 'Divine Power' so that it be a part of the state. Shahbaz Khan, who had been appointed last time for its conquest, captured it by resorting to fraud and deceit, and all the garrison, posted to defend, was so confounded that with all its arms, it could not move and remained standing in amazement. The imperial army entered the fort while the Rana fled into the forests and hills.[13]

A period of two years had passed when Asaf Khan[14] was appointed along with the other nobles commander of an army for the capture of the fort of Idar which was situated on the border of Gujarat. Because the time had come for the burning away (destruction) of the stars of the fate of its commandant, unfortunate and misguided one, he was overtaken by an unexpected evil condition for five days, and the sun of his life had also come near its fall. (p. 238) During the whole time a force of brave soldiers remained posted all around so that they would go on penetrating deep into the wretched land, and would rush over it by riding Arab horses and devastate it so as to wipe it out of existence. While the said state of affairs was going on, Asaf Khan was summoned to the court for some urgent administrative and revenue matters and Wazir Khan was sent to take charge of it. However, information was received in that year from Wazir Khan that by the grace of God and the blessings and good luck of the emperor the army entered into the fort and took it into possession. The fort which was proclaimed to be in full strength, proved hollow and it too fell to the soldiers of Islam. The Rai, unfortunate,[15] if he had not fallen into the net of misery and villainy and if he had behaved with humility before the world conquering emperor then his fate would not have blackened as now.[16]

Unfortunately the prudence of the ruler left the Rai into a lurch and his fort was also added to the list of the forts of the empire.[17]

Then the emperor by the middle of Jamadi-ul-Akhir/August of the said year, started from the Sarkar of Punjab and passing through Sahrand (*sic*) and Khizrabad, boarded a boat at river Jamuna and marched fast to Ajmer to pay homage at the shrine.[18] Muzaffar Khan and Khwaja Shah Mansur, who had been appointed wazirs, were left in

Delhi while the imperial army was ordered to accompany them so that they would be able to prepare quickly the army and the Karoris. (p. 239) After performing homage at the shrine, the emperor, reached by the middle of Ra-jjab/September at Fatehabad Sikri. The nobles and the victorious army, however reached by the end of the said month.[19]

Duaa (prayer) for His Majesty

May His Majesty by the Grace of God rule us![20]

NOTES

1. According to Badauni, "The emperor reached Delhi via Narnol. There he got engaged in hunting nearby Palam. In the later part of Ramzan, he reached Rewari. From there, he marched to Punjab through Hansi". *MT*, II, 252.
2. The gist is given out of long narration.
3. *Abiyat* have been left. See p. 235.
4. Her name was Sakeena Banu Begum, wife of Khwaja Hasan Khaldar and mother of Mirza Badi-u-Zaman and Mirza Wali. She died on 12th Rabi-us-Saani, A.H. 1014/17th August, 1605 A.D. at Agra. For details see *AN*, *IJ*, and *TM*. While she is said wife of Shah Ghazi Khan, son of Qazi Isa. *MU*, III, 815.
5. Abul Fazl says that Muhammad Hakim Mirza had created some disturbance but the emperor as mark of wisdom, sent her to counsel him. *AN*, III, 244.
6. Badauni says that this condition happened adjacent to Nandna. *MT*, II, 253.
7. Abul Fazl says that four days at Bhira. *AN*, III, 241, While in Rohtas *MR*, I, 859.
8. It is not mentioned by others. See also *AN*, III, 242 and *MR*, I, 859 and 860.
9. Badauni says that two years earlier a strong force under the command of Man Singh, son of Bhagwan Das was sent towards Gau Ganda and Konbhal Mir. *MT*, III, 228. See also *MU*, II, 160.
10. Jahil-i-murakkab signifies the state of ignorance in which a person deludes himself by believing a thing to be what it is not, i.e. to take a piece of rope to be a snake. What is the propriety of this term in this context, Arif alone could perhaps understand.
11. *Bait* has been left. See p. 237.
12. Rana i.e., Pratap Singh, ruler of Udaipur, son of Udai Singh and grandson of Rana Sanga. Abul Fazl, Badauni and Nizamuddin say

that his name was Rana Kaika. *AN*, III, 237, *MT*, II, 230 and *TA*, II, 326 and 340. Rana died in Jamadi-ul-Akhir, A.H. 1005/January, 1597. Karnama 107-9. See also *AN* and *IJ*.

13. The Rana aghast dressed shabbily, escaped towards mountains and the fort was captured. Next day the boundaries of Gokunda and the fort of Udaipur were captured. *MU*, II, 593. See also *AN*, III, 238 and 246, *MT*, II, 230-36 and 286 and *TA*, II, 332 and 340.
14. In the 21st year (A.H. 984/1576 A.D.) army was sent to capture Idar fort, followed by Asaf Khan and Khwaja Ghyas-ud-din Ali Qazvini also *MU*, I, 91.
15. Rai Naraindas Rothore, Zamindar of Idar. *MT*, II, 241.
16. *Bait* has been left. See p. 238.
17. On 3rd Jamadi-us-Sani/7th August the emperor reached Sadhura which was near Khizerabad. He boarded a boat and on 29th/2nd September of the said month and reached Delhi. He started on 1st Rajab/September (from Delhi) and reached Ajmer on 6th of the said month (8th September). *AN*, III, 254 and *TA*, II, 338.
18. Sahrand, known as Sarhind is situated in Punjab. As the sultans of Ghazni were confined from Ghazni to Sarhind, it became known as Sarhind.
19. Badauni says that on 29th/2nd Rajab/3rd September of the said month, he visited the shrine at Delhi . . . and in Rajab/end of September, he came back. He covered thirty karohs everyday and at last on 6th Rajab/7th September he reached Ajmer and next day left for Darul Khilafa, Fatehpur.
20. *Duaa* (prayer) for His Majesty contains nothing new.

OCCURRENCE 42

Description of the Construction of Jama Masjid at Fatehpur Sikri under the Glorious Regime of the Emperor

When His Majesty out of the light of his wisdom and courage laid the foundation of the city of Fatehpur, he also laid the foundation of the Jama Masjid in A.H. 986/1578 A.D. on the hill inside the vicinity of the palace. Reputed architects and experienced workers spread out sketches of its foundation and veteran craftsmen under the supervision of a head drew sketches of ornamentation. It was completed under the supervision of the descendants and relatives of late Shaikh Salim Chishti.[1] By means of extremely fine ornamentation, it became a very beautiful edifice. It had also been planned to build a mosque the like of which would rarely be found anywhere in the world and under the regime of the emperor it was completed in a short time. All its walls and chambers were made of polished red stone . . . while its tank was made of stone and lime. (p. 240) Its roof was made levelled up and hidden from the view. There were grills at intervals so as to allow the rainy water to flow through them to its tank, which could be used by the people. Indeed its tank is like the bride which had niches for her eye-brows and would provide comfort in it.

Turrets were made from which the voices of cocks and pigeons could be heard. Those who saw its fineness and strength were struck dumb with amazement. Its columns and storeys were so high that they need no elaboration. The building is so grand that it cannot be described in words. So it seemed to be futile to try and describe it in detail. Hence, a short description has been provided only.[2]

In short, the emperor offers prayers in the said attractive and refreshing building. Its pulpit is very high from which the Khatibs read Khutba in the emperor's name, in a very melodious and loud voice.

Undotted (E)

May not the Khutba in the name of anyone else be read in the seven climes except yours! (p. 241)

It be a matter of thanks giving to God that in the sacred building both the obligatory and non-obligatory prayers (namaz) were being performed. Proper provision is made for the Friday prayer of congregation from morning till late night.[3]

Duaa (prayer) for His Majesty

It is believed that for each one of the chambers a palace will be rewarded in Paradise and each brick which has been put by the emperor will be a source of reward (in paradise). A better life can surely be expected from Allah for the honour of the Prophet and his companions.

NOTES

1. It was constructed under the supervision of Shah Mansur. He was a man of reason, matter and economy so all the nobles were unhappy with him. They complained against him to Mirza Hakim and that unfortunate man was killed in the last days of Muharram, A.H. 989/February, 1581 A.D. *MU*, I, 653. See also *AN*, *MT*, *IJ*, *SS* and *HI*.
2. *Bait* and *Abiyat* have been left. See p. 240.
3. Badauni says that it was completed roughly in five years. *MT*, II, 109. See also *TA*, II, 225.

OCCURRENCE 43

Description of Sending Gifts and Presents by the Emperor to Bait-ul-Haram and Medina Through Sultan Khwaja

The caravan of Praise for the Almighty whose first stage "enter the heaven peacefully and happily", can be Kaaba, the blessed. The thankful travellers who in the evening of want and the wilderness of fatigue pray: "O! my God take me to blissful plane. Thou alone is the best guide, the leader, that Thou should show the way of benevolence to the walkers in the valley of Thy Grace, and give to the travellers in the ocean of Thy kindness the drink of Thy guidance. Thou lead on the right path whom thou like." (p. 242)

Hereafter, it may not be unknown to the circumambulators of the Kaaba of hopes, and those who pray in a corner of the Mosque of good luck that an imperial farman was issued in A.H. 985/1577 A.D. that "a messenger be sent to the nobles of Mecca and the elders of Medina and its attendants, in whose honour that house was built for the people in Mecca, is full of blessings and is a way for all the worlds and in it there are open marks which establish that it is the place of Hazrat Ibrahim. And an adequate amount be sent for the proper and stable administration of the holy places. In fact, no monetary assistance had been sent there from Hindustan."

Accordingly, Sultan Khwaja,[1] a reputed saint and known recluse, was chosen as the Amir to perform it. Under his command a group of people and a few lakh rupees,[2] collected from Zakat, were given to him to be distributed among the Saiyeds, the nobles and elders there. The rest of money was to be spent on the construction and repair works of the passage.

The boat carrying the pilgrims set sail in all peace and safety in the Arabian Sea destined for the holy city, and it is an obligatory duty for those who have the power or capacity. As the reward of Haj is (paradise) and nothing else. (p. 243) All this is exhibited. Every year when the month of Haj falls, the people like messengers come in groups or batches from distant places, i.e. far off, emaciate she camels for Haj and obtain their objects and face towards the mountains of Arafat go and cry loudly, "I am present", and during the performance of the commands of the Haj, prayers are observed in places of blessings. When you have finished your Haj, then remember your Allah that you have performed it. They recite the prayer according to the shariat, "O God forgive the Hajis and those for whom they pray. When you become deserving of this prayer, then only".

Bait (verse)

The inhabitants of sky call . . . and on behalf of the creatures of God. . . . and for Emperor Akbar offer prayers which match his charities.[3] (p. 244)

Finally, Sultan Khwaja performed the pilgrimage with his companions and also completed the assigned work. Thereafter he set to return to Hindustan. The emperor had just then made inquiries of his well-being. He, however, on 21st Shawwal,[4] A.H. 986/20th December, 1578 A.D. reached Darul Khilafat, Fatehpur and obtained the honour of kissing the emperor's hand. He appraised the emperor with all details. His companions were also honoured and were granted presents of horses and cash. Khwaja Sultan, who happened to be the descendant of Khwaja Ahrar,[5] was appointed to the mansab of Sadr.[6]

And this year in all the mosques of the empire, the title Amir-ul-Mumanin was added with the name of the emperor in Khutba.[7]

Duaa (prayer) for His Majesty

May the Almighty grant special favour to His Majesty! (p. 245)

Notes

1. Sultan Khwaja, Abdul Azim, son of Khwaja Dost Khawand Naqshbandi, Sadr-us-Sudur, did not come into contact with the emperor earlier. However in A.H. 984/1576 A.D. he was appointed leader of the delegation of Hajis. He died in A.H. 992/1584 A.D. *MU*, II, 379. See also *AN*, *MT*, *TA* and *IJ*.
2. Abul Fazl says that Khwaja was given six lakh and twelve thousand khilats to be distributed among the people of Mecca. *AN*, III, 193.
3. *Abiyat* have been left. See p. 243.
4. See also *MR*, I, 862.
5. Khawaja Ahrar, Khwaja Nasiruddin Ubaidullah, son of Khwaja Mahmud al-Shashi al-Takshandi ul-Naqshbandi from Samarqand was from Khurasan. He died in Rabi-ul-Awwal, A.H. 895/January, 1490 A.D. For details see *Gulzar-i-Abrar, HI* and *Silsila Nama of Safinat-ul-Auliya*, etc.
6. See also *MR*, I, 862.
7. For details see also *AN*, III, 270, *MT*, II, 270 and *TA*, II, 343. *Abiyat* have been left. See p. 244.

OCCURRENCE 44

Description of the Return of Mehdi Aliya (Revered Lady) and the Presentation of Mirza Muzaffar Husain by Maqsud Jauhari[1]

His Majesty visited the environs of Bahra[2] and the Sarkar of Punjab. At this time the patron of his slaves counselled and decided that the sister of Mirza Muhammad Hakim be requested to go to Kabul on a secret mission,[3] escorted by Saiyed Abu Ishaq[4] and Mehr Ali Saldoz.[5] Accordingly she reached Kabul and discussed certain matters with her brother (Mirza Hakim). It was also suggested that Mirza Hakim should marry his daughter with Prince Salim. Mirza Hakim gladly accepted her suggestion and sent his daughter with his sister to Hindustan. On 5th Zi-hijja, A.H. 986/3rd February, 1579 A.D. they reached Fatehpur Sikri and got themselves blessed.[6]

This year on 10th Shawwal/9th December, Maqsud Juhari[7] was deputed to Asir(garh) and Burhanpur to bring Mirza Muzaffar Husain, son of Mirza Ulughi. In accordance with the imperial order, the hakim[8] of Asir and Burhanpur got him arrested and despatched (him) to Agra. On his arrival at Agra he was sent behind bars. Later the emperor, who is the embodiment of kindness, granted him pardon by forgiving all his faults and misdeeds committed by his father and uncle earlier. In the month of Safar, A.H. 987/April, 1579 A.D.[9] he was released from prison and was given employment also. His mother,[10] who is the daughter of the deceased Mirza Kamran, came behind her son and kissed the feet of His Majesty.[11] (p. 246)

In the middle of the month of Ramzan,[12] A.H. 987/15th November, 1579 A.D. Husain Quli entitled Khan-i-Jahan, the subedar of Bengal died. On his expiry the emperor appointed Muzaffar Khan, the subedar of Bengal on 17th Muharram,[13] A.H. 987/15th March, 1579 A.D. while Hakim Abul Fateh,[14] Mirza Mirak[15] and Mir Adham[16] were posted as Amin, Bakhshi and diwan of the Sarkar respectively. At the same time Maulana Tayab[17] and Parkotam[18] (Purshotam) were also appointed the diwan and bakhshi of the Sarkars of Bihar, Hajipur and Tirhut and they left for their respective assignments. Soon a detailed account of these affairs as also of those mischiefs of miscreants, who had raised turmoil in that vilayat (dominion) shall be jotted down properly.[19]

In the first part of Rabi-ul-Akhir, A.H. 987 (by the end of May, 1579 A.D.) a terrible fire broke out in the premises of Farrashkhana at Fatehpur Sikri. It engulfed the imperial Shamiana (imperial canopies), Khargah (large and small tents), brocade and velvet curtains, atlas, silk, satin, and colourful embroidered cloth and varieties of carpets. The estimated loss was up to the tune of one crore rupees. The emperor however, did not notice it.[20] (p. 247)

By the middle of Rajab (1st week of September 1579 A.D.) the emperor again left for Ajmer. He visited the dargah of Khwaja Muinuddin Chishti and performed circumambulation there.[21] On his way back torrential rain lashed out and it continued for three days and nights. Soon it resulted in flood which washed out a large number of men, cattle and goods.[22] After the return of His Majesty from Ajmer, a hunting expedition and excursion feast were arranged in the beginning of Shawwal (4th week of November, 1579 A.D.) also.[23]

During the same time, it was brought to the notice of the emperor that Mirza Sulaiman Shah, who had gone to Mecca for pilgrimage as per imperial permission travelled through Iraq and Khorasan and performed the pilgrimage at holy Mashed. Thereafter, he returned to Qandhar and met Mirza Hakim in Kabul. Together in the month of Shawwal, they went to Badakhshan where reconciliation took place between Mirza Sulaiman and his grandson, Shah Rukh Mirza. Later on Mirza Muhammad Hakim returned to Kabul in the month of Safar, A.H. 988/March, 1580 A.D.[24]

Duaa (prayer) for His Majesty

May the greatest ambition of the great emperor of the east and the west be to bow at the threshold of His Majesty (Khaqan Akbar) and may the lintel of your door become the Kaaba (the holy centre) of the needs and desires of all men by the grace of the Prophet and his progeny!

NOTES

1. Arif gives no date and no sequence of events.
2. Probably Bhera.
3. See also *TA*, II, 340 and *MT*, II, 253 and 266.
4. Saiyed Abu Ishaq, son of Saiyed Rafi-ud-din, son of Saiyed Murshid-ud-din Safvi died before Ramzan, A.H. 1009/February, 1600 A.D. while besieging Asir (garh). *AN*, III, 782.
5. Mahar Ali Saldoz was earlier the retainer of Bairam Khan. Later he joined the imperial service and rose to the mansab of 2000. He died in A.H. 995/1587 A.D. *ZK*, 302 and *MU*, III, 217. See also *TA*.
6. Other sources do not contain the said suggestion.
7. Badauni says in Zi-hijja, A.H. 985/February, 1578 A.D. a firman was sent in the name of Raja Ali Khan by Maqsud Juhari to depute Mirza Muzaffar Husain to the imperial court. *MT*, II, 253. He was brought in Shawwal/December. *MR*, I, 861.
8. Raja Ali Khan Faruqi, son of Mubarak Shah, son of Adil Khan Faruqi, ascended the throne of Khandesh in A.H. 984/1576 A.D. and he died on 18th Jamadi-ul-Akhir, A.H. 1005/January, 1597 A.D. fighting against Khan-i-Khanan, Abdur Rahim. For details see also *AN*, *Farishta*, *SS*, *MR* and *IJ*.
9. See also *AN*, III, 266. *Bait* has been left. p. 246.
10. His mother's name was Gul Rukh Sultan Begum. *AN*, III, 206. While Gul Rukh Begum. See *TA*, *MT* and *MR*.
11. Mirza Muzaffar Husain, son of Mirza Ibrahim Husain, son of Muhammad Sultan Mirza Taimuri, was the grand maternal son of Mirza Kamran and he became the son-in-law of Akbar. He was alive up to Ramzan, A.H. 1009/February, 1601 A.D. *AN*, III, 787.
12. 19th Shawwal/18th December. *MU*, I, 645. See also *TA* and *TM*.
13. Abul Fazl says 3rd Farwardin, lunar month, the emperor started towards it. *AN*, III, 265.
14. Hakim Abul Fateh, son of Hakim Abdur Razaq Gilani paid his respects

to the emperor in the 20th regnal year. In the 24th year he was appointed the Sadar and Amin of Bengal, though he did not hold a mansab higher than 1000, however he reached the post of Vakil. He was distinguished for excellent intelligence, sublime nature, quick temperament and perfect learning among his fellow-beings and courtiers. He undertook his final journey in the course of Kashmir trip at the stage called Dhamtur and was buried at Hasan Abdal. *ZK*, 302. He died in Shawwal, A.H. 991/October, 1583 A.D. *MU*. I. 558. See also *AN, IJ, TA, SS* and *HI*.

15. Mirza Mirak i.e. Rizvi Khan.
16. Mir Adham, son of Arab entitled Niyabat Khan, son of Mir Hashim Khan Nishapuri was one of the servants of Akbar. He died on 8th Zi-hijja, A.H. 1001/26th August, 1593 A.D. *MU*, III, 809. *AN*, III, 160, 337 and 633. *MT*, II, 289.
17. Maulana Tayyab was summoned from Kaithal. He was appointed diwan of Bihar and Hajipur. *MT*, II, 266.
18. Parkotam stands for Par Khotam. He was bakhshi of Bihar and Hajipur and was one of the nobles of Akbar. He got wounded fighting against Arab Bahadur. After two days in A.H. 987/1579 A.D., he died. See also *AN, IJ, TA* and *SS*.
19. The promised account was not jotted down by Arif due to the reasons best known to him. Muzaffar Khan was besieged in Zand by the Afghan rebels, who killed him. Though Arif's account covers up to March, 1580 A.D., surprisingly he has not recorded it.
20. The other contemporary and near contemporary sources except *Farishta* have not mentioned the described holocast. *Farishta*, II, 264.
21. Badauni says that on 16th Rajab/9th September, of the said year, the emperor left for Ajmer. He did not go thereafter. *MT*, II, 272. On 16th Rajab/9th September, the emperor reached Darul Khilafa, Fatehpur. On 16th Shaban/9th October he reached adjacent to Khwas Khan's pond, situated at a distance of five karohs from Ajmer. *MR*, I, 867.
22. This important event is not mentioned by other contemporary and near-contemporary sources.
23. The emperor reached Dar-ul-Surur palace of Fatehpur on 21st Shawwal A.H. 988 (11th December, 1579 A.D.) *MR*, I, 868.
24. After performing Haj, Mirza Sulaiman reached Iran but he could get the help of Shah Ismail. Later, he visited Muzaffar Husain Mirza, the ruler of Qandhar and failed in his mission. Thereafter he went to Mirza Muhammad Hakim who too did not help him against his grand son. He at last made a compromise with his grand son and accordingly he got Hindukush and Taliqan, a city situated between Balkh and Marv. *AN*, II, 287.

BIBLIOGRAPHY

Only works relevant for a study of *Tarikh-i-Akbari*, have been listed. The bibliography is divided into four major sections: Sources, Dictionaries, Modern Works and Periodical Literature. It is arranged alphabetically on the basis of surname of authors. Collective works or Compilations or works which are better known by their titles are assigned places in accordance with the alphabetical order of their titles.

The following are the abbreviations used:

BM	British Museum
BIB. IND.	Bibliotheca Indica, Calcutta
BORS	Bihar and Orissa Research Society
GOS	Gaekwad Oriental Society, Baroda
IOLR	India Office Library & Records
IHR	Indian Historical Review, New Delhi
ICHR	Indian Council of Historical Research, New Delhi
IESHR	Indian Economic and Social History Review, New Delhi
JAHRI	Journal of Aligarh Historical Research Institute, Aligarh
JABS	Journal of Asiatic Society of Bengal, Calcutta
JAS	Journal of Asian Studies
JBBRAS	Journal of Bombay Branch of Royal Asiatic Society, Bombay
JPHS	Journal of the Pakistan Historical Society
JPHS	Journal of Punjab Historical Society
JSUR	Journal of Sindh University Research
JUPHS	Journal of Uttar Pradesh Historical Society
PIHC	Proceedings of Indian History Congress
PHC	Proceedings of Punjab History Congress
PPHC	Proceedings of Pakistan History Congress

PICO Proceeding of International Congress of Orientalists.

Persian Works

Abul Fazl, *Ain-i-Akbari*

Text ed. by Sir Sayed Ahmad Khan, Munshi Nawal Kishore, Lucknow, 1882.

English Translations of Vol. I., by H. Blochmann, Vol. II and III by H.S. Jarret, Bib. Ind. Calcutta, 1873, 1891 and 1894. Second edition of the respective volumes with revision, 1927, 1948 and 1949. Third edition/reprint, New Delhi, 1977-78.

Akbar Nama

Text ed. by Maulvi Agha Ahmad Ali and Maulvi Abdur Rahim, Bib. Ind. Calcutta, 1876-86. (Reprint) Delhi, Kitab Publishing House, 1977.

English Tr. H. Beveridge, 3 Vols., Bib. Ind. Calcutta, 1897-1921, (reprint) Delhi, ESS ESS Publications, 1973.

Abdullah, *Tarikh-i-Daudi*

Text ed. by S.A. Rashid, Department of History, A.M.U., Aligarh, 1969.

Aftabchi, Jauhar, *Tazkirat-ul-Waqiat*

Text ed. by Hidayat Husain, Bib. Ind. Calcutta, 1941.

Ahmad, Nizamuddin, *Tabqat-i-Akbari*

Text ed. by B. De and Muhammad Hidayat Husain, Bib. Ind., Calcutta, 1935.

English Tr. by B. De, Bib. Ind., Calcutta 1939.

Ahmad Yadgar, *Tarikh-i-Shahi*

Text ed. by M. Hidayat Husain, Bib. Ind., Calcutta, 1939.

Babur, Zahiruddin Muhammad, *Babur Nama*

Persian Tr. by Abdur Rahim Khan Khanan, Bombay, A.H. 1308/1890 A.D.

English Translation by Mrs A.S. Beveridge, London, 1821 (Reprint) Delhi, Oriental Books Corporation, 1979.

Badauni, Abdul Qadir, *Muntakhab-ut-Tawarikh*

Text ed. by Maulvi Ahmad Ali, Kabir-ud-din Ahmad and W.N. Lees, Bib. Ind., Calcutta, 1868.

English Translation of Vol. I by E.S.A. Ranking; Vol. II., W.H. Lowe and Vol. III., T.W. Haig, Bib. Ind., Calcutta, 1895-99, 1888-98 and 1899-1925. (Reprint) Delhi, Idarah-i-Adabiyat-i-Dilli, 1973.

Baruni, Ziauddin, *Fatawa-i-Jahandari*
Text ed. by Mrs. A.S. Khan, Lahore, 1972.
English Tr. by M. Habib and Mrs. A.S. Khan as *The Political Theory of the Delhi Sultanate*, Kitab Mahal, Allahabad. 1961.

Tarikh-i-Firozeshahi
Text ed. by Sir Sayed Ahmad Khan, W.N. Less and Kabiruddin Ahmad, Bib. Ind., Calcutta, 1860-62.

Bayazid Bayat, *Tazkira-i-Humayun Wa Akbar*
Text ed. by Hidayat Husain, Bib. Ind., Calcutta, 1941.

Daughlat, Mirza Muhammad Haider, *Tarikh-i-Rashidi*
English Tr. by E.D. Ross, London, 1898 (Reprint), Delhi, Sagar B.K. House, 1974.

Fani, Mohsin, *Dabistan-i-Mazahib*
Text lithographed, Nawal Kishore Press, Lucknow, 1904.
English Tr. by David Shea and Anthony Troyer, Bombay, 1862-63.

Farid Bhakkari, *Zakhirat-ul-Khwanin*
Text ed. by Saiyed Moin-ul-Haq, 3 Vols., Karachi, 1961-74. English Tr. by Z.A. Desai, 3 Vols., (Underprint), Idarahi-Adabiyat-i-Dilli, Delhi.

Farishta, Muhammad Qasim Hindu Shah, *Tarikh-i-Farishta* or *Gulshan-i-Ibrahimi*
Text ed. by J. Briggs, 2. Vols., Bombay, 1832.
English Tr. by J. Briggs as *History of the Rise of Mohammadan Power In India*, 4 Vols., London, 1829, (Reprint), Bib. Ind., Calcutta, 1908.

Gulbadan Begum, *Humayun Nama*
Text ed. & English Tr. by Mrs. A.S. Beveridge, Royal Asiatic Society, London, 1902.

Husaini, Kamgar, *Maasir-i-Jahangiri*
Text ed. by Azra Alvi, Asia Publishing House, Bombay, 1978.

Jahangir (Emperor), *Tuzuk-i-Jahangiri*
Text ed. by Sir Sayed Ahmad Khan, Ghazipur and Aligarh, 1864.
English Tr. A. Rogers and edited by H. Beveridge and published under the title *The Memoirs of Jahangir*, London, 1909-14.

Khan, Ali Muhammad, *Mirat-i-Ahmadi*
Text ed. by Saiyed Nawab Ali, Baptist Missions Press, Calcutta, 1928.

Khafi Khan, *Muntakhab-ul-Lubab*
Text ed. by Maulvi Kabiruddin Ahmad, Ghulam Qadir and T.W. Haig, 3. Vols., Bib. Ind., Calcutta, 1868.

Khan, Motamid, *Iqbal Nama-i-Jahangiri*
Text ed. by Abdul Hai and Ahmad Ali, (MS. Khuda Bakhsh Library, Patna).

Khan, Shah Nawaz and Abdul Hai, *Maasir-ul-Umara*
Text ed. by Maulvi Abdur Rahim and Ashraf Ali, 3 Vols., Bib. Ind., Calcutta, 1880-90.
English Tr. by H. Beveridge, completed by Beni Prasad, 3 vols., Patna, 1979 (Reprint).

Khani, Muhammad Bihamad, *Tarikh-i-Muhammadi*
English Tr. by M. Zaki, Bombay, Asia Publishing House, 1972.

Nihawandi, Abdul Baqi, *Maasir-i-Rahimi*
Text ed. by M. Hidayat Husain, 3 vols., Bib. Ind., Calcutta, 1940.

Nizami, Hasan, *Taj-ul-Maasir*
MS. Asafiya Library, Hyderabad.
English Tr. Elliot & Dowson, *The History of India As Told By Its Own Historians*, Vol. II, pp. 204-43

Nurul Haq Dehlvi, *Zubdat-ul-Tawarikh*
MS. India Office Library & Records, London.

Qandhari, Muhammad Arif, *Tarikh-i-Akbari*
Text ed. by Sayed Moinuddin Nadwi, Saiyeed Azhar Ali and Imtiaz Ali Arshi, Raza Library, Rampur, 1962.

Qaran, Mulla Abdul, *Tarikh-i-Mahmud Shahi*
English Tr. by S.C. Misra, GOS, Baroda, 1987.

Qazwini, Ala-ud-Daula, *Nafais-ul-Maasir*
MS. Subhanullah Collection, Maulana Azad Library, A.M.U., Aligarh.

Razi, Amin Ahmad, *Haft Iqlim*
Text ed. by Abdul Maqtadir, E. Denison Ross, A.H. Harley and Mahfuzul Haq (in complete) B 1-215-1918-38.

Sarwani, Abbas Khan, *Tuhfa-i-Akbar Shahi* or *Tarikh-i-Sher Shah*
MSS. Ethe 219.

Shahidi, Sadiq, *Subah Sadiq*
BM. MS. Edgerton, 1906.

Sikandar Bin Minhaj Gujrati, *Mirat-i-Sikandari*
Text ed. by S.C. Misra and Muhammad Lutfur Rehman, GOS, Baroda, 1961.

Sirhindi, Faizi, *Akbar Nama*
MS. B.M. Rieu 253 a., 10. Ethe 289.
English Tr. Elliot & Dowson, Vol. VI, pp. 116-146, London, 1867-77.
First Indian Edition, Kitab Mahal, Allahabad, 1964.

Shaikh Abdul Haq Dehlvi, *Tarikh-i-Haqqi* or *Zikr-ul-Mulk*
MS. Bodleian, Ousley 59.
(Transcribed in A.H. 1030/1620 A.D.) Maulana Azad Library, A.M.U., Aligarh.

Thattawi, Mulla Ahmad, *Tarikh-i-Alfi*
MS. Maulana Azad Library, A.M.U., Aligarh.

Wali, Mir Abu Turab, *Tarikh-i-Gujarat*
Text ed. with introduction and notes by Sir E. Denison Ross, Bib. Ind., Calcutta, 1909.

Dictionaries

Abdur Rashid Thattawi, *Farang-i-Rashidi*, 1653-54
ed. Abu Tahir Zulfiqar Ali Murshidabadi, Bib. Ind., Calcutta, 1857.

Munshi Tekchand, 'Bahar', *Bahar-i-Ajam*
1739-40 A.D., Lithographed, Nawal Kishore Press, Lucknow, 1916.

Anand Ram Mukhlis, *Mirat-ul-Istilah*
Translated under the title: *Encyclopaedic Dictionary of Medieval India* by Tasneem Ahmad, Delhi, Sandeep Publications, 1993.

Steingass, *Persian-English Dictionary.*
(Reprint) Munshiram Manoharlal Publishers Pvt. Ltd., 1973.

Fakhruddin Mubarak Shah Qawas, *Farhang-i-Qawas*
ed. Nazir Ahmad, Tehran, A.H. 1353/Dastur-ul-Afazil fi Lughat-il-Fazail of Rafi ed. Nazir Ahmad, Bunyad-i-Farhang, Iran, A.H. 1352.

Modern Works

Agrawal, C.M., *Akbar and His Hindu Officer, A Critical Study*, Jalandhar, ABS Publication, 1986.

Ahmad, Aziz, *Studies in Islamic Culture in the Indian Environment*, Edinburgh, 1964.

———, *An Intellectual History of Islam in India*, Edinburgh, 1967.

Ahmad, Tariq, *Religio-Political Ferment in the North West-Frontier During the Mughal Period — The Raushaniya Movement*, Delhi, Idarah-i-Adabiyat-i-Dilli, 1975.

Akbar, Muhammad, *The Punjab Under the Mughals*, Lahore, 1948.

Ali, M. Athar, *The Apparatus of Empire, Awards of the Ranks, Offices and Titles to the Mughal Nobility (1574-1658)*, Delhi, Oxford University Press, 1985.

Alvi, Azra, *Socio-Religious Outlook of Abul Fazl*, Delhi, Idarah-i-Adabiyat-i-Dilli, 1983.

Ambasathya, B.P., *Some Non-Persian Sources of Medieval India*, Delhi, Idarah-i-Adabiyat-i-Dilli, 1979.

———, (ed.) *Contributions on Akbar and the Parsees*, (Reprint of Articles by B.P. Karkaria and J.J. Modi, Published in J.B.R.A.S. 1896-1903, Patna, 1976.

Ansari, M.A., Jaweed Ashraf, Tasneem Ahmad, *Geographical Glimpses of Medieval India*, 3 Vols., Delhi, Idarah-i-Adabiyat-i-Dilli, 1989.

Ansari, M.A., *European Travellers Under the Mughals*, Delhi, Idarah-i-Adabiyat-i-Dilli, 1975.

Arnold, T.W., *Bihzad and His Paintings in the Zafar Nama*, London, 1930.

———, *Chronicle of Akbar, The Great, A Description of a Manuscript of the Akbar Nama*, Illustrated by the Court Painters, Oxford, 1937.

Ashraf, K.M., *Life and Conditions of the People of Hindustan (1200-1550)*, Delhi, (Reprint) Munshiram Manoharlal, 1970.

Askari, S.H., *Tabaqat-i-Baburi* (English translation), Delhi, Idarah-i-Adabiyat-i-Dilli, 1982.

Aziz, Abdul, *The Mansabdari System and the Mughal Army*, Lahore, 1945.

Band, Erster, *Hamza Nama*, Akademische Druck-U-Verlag Sanstalt, GRAZ, 1927.

Banerji, S.K., *Humayun Badshah*, Vols. I, II, 1941, Calcutta, OUP, 1936.

Barnes, H.E., *A History of Historical Writings*, 2nd revised edition, 1963.

Beale, Thomas William, *Oriental Biographical Dictionary*, Delhi, (reprint) 1971, Manohar, 1971.

Bedi, P.S., *Mughal Nobility Under Akbar*, Jalandhar, ABS Publication, 1985.

Bhargava, V.S., *Marwar and the Mughal Emperors (1526-1748)*, Delhi, Munshiram Manoharlal, 1966.

Bhatia, M.L., *Administrative History of Medieval India*, Delhi, Radha Publication, 1992.

Bilgrami, R.M., *Religious and Quasi-Religious Departments of Mughal Period*, Delhi, Munshiram Manoharlal, 1984.

Binyon, L., *Akbar*, London, 1932.

Brand, Michel and G.D. Lowry, *Akbar and Fatehpur Sikri*, Bombay, Marg Publication, 1987.

Briggs, John, *History of the Rise of the Mohammadan Power in India, till the year 1612 A.D., Tr. Gulshan-i-Ibrahimi or Tarikh-i-Farishta' of Muhammad Qasim*, Calcutta, Mukhopadhyay, 1966.

Brown, Percy, *Indian Architecture (Islamic Period)*, Bombay, 1968.

Burckheadt, J., *Judgement on History and Historians*, London, 1959.

Burke, S.H., *Akbar the Great Mughal*, New Delhi, Munshiram Manoharlal, 1989.

Butterfield, H., *Man on His Past: A Study of the History of Historical Scholarship*, Cambridge, 1955.

Burn, Richard, (ed.), *The Cambridge History of India*, Vol. IV, Cambridge, 1937.

Chitnis, K.N., *Socio-Economic History of Medieval India*, Delhi, Atlantic Publishers and Distributors, 1990.

Chopra, P.N., *Society and Culture During the Mughal Age*, Delhi, Agam Publications, 1988.

Collingwood, R.G., *The Ideas of History*, Oxford, 1946.

Commissariat, M.S., *History of Gujarat*, 2 Vols., Bombay, 1938, 1957.

Day, U.N., *Mughal Government 1556-1707*, Delhi, Munshiram Manoharlal, 1971.

Diez, E., *Akbar, Gottsucher and Kaiser*, 1961.

Elliot and Dowson, *The History of India as Told by its Historians*, Vol. VI, London, 1867, Allahabad, 1964 (reprint).

Elliot, Sir H.M., *Biographical Index to the Historians of Mohammadan India*, Calcutta, 1849.

Erskine, W., *A History of India Under the First Sovereign of the House of Timur*, London, 1854.

Farooqi, M.A., *The Mujaddid's Conception of Tauhid*, Lahore, 1940.

Farooqi, N.R., *Mughal Ottoman Relations*, Delhi, Idarah-i-Adabiyat-i-Dilli, 1989.

Ferguson, J., *History of Indian and Eastern Architecture*, London, 1910.

Finberg, H.P.R., (ed.), *Approach to History*, London, 1962.

Friedmann, Y., *Shaikh Ahmad Sirhindi: An Outline of His Thought and a Study of his Image in the Eyes of Prosperity*, Montreal, 1971.

Gahni, M.A., *Pre-Mughal Persian in Hindustan*, Allahabad, 1941.

Gardener, Patrick, *The Nature of Historical Explanation*, London, 1952.

Ghoshal, U.N., *A History of Indian Political Ideas*, Bombay, 1959.

Grousset, R., *Figure de Prone*, Paris, 1948.

Habib, Muhammad, *Sultan Mahmud of Ghaznin*, Delhi, 1962 (reprint), Delhi, S. Chand & Co., 1967.

Habib-ullah, A.B.M., *The Foundation of Muslim Rule in India*, Lahore, 1945.

Hasan, Ibne, *The Central Structure of the Mughal Empire in Northern India*, Delhi, Idarah-i-Adabiyat-i-Dilli (reprint), 1970.

Hasan, Mohibbul, (ed.), *Historians of Medieval India*, Jamia Millia Islamia, New Delhi, 1968.

Hasan, S. Nurul, *Thoughts on Agrarian Relations in Mughal India*, New Delhi, P.P.H., 1973.

Haq, S.M., *Islamic Thought and Movement in the Sub-Continent (711-1947)*, Karachi, 1979.

Hardy, Peter, *Historians of Medieval India, Studies in Indo-Muslims Historical Writing*, London, 1960.

Hodivala, S.H., *Studies in Indo-Muslim History: And Dowson's History of India as Told by its Own Historians*, Poona, 1957.

Husain, Yusuf, *Glimpses of Medieval Indian Culture*, ed. 2 Vols, Bombay, Asia Publishing House, 1959.

Irfan Habib, *Agrarian System of Mughal India, 1556-1707*, Bombay, Asia Publishing House, 1963.

———, *An Atlas of the Mughal Empire*, Delhi, Oxford University Press, 1982.

Irfan Habib and Tapan Ray Choudhuri, (eds.), *The Cambridge Economic History of India*, Vol. I, 1200-1750, Cambridge, 1982.

Ikram, S.M., *Muslim Civilization in India*, (ed), A.T. Embee, New York, 1964.

Iqbal, Muhammad, *The Re-construction of Religious Thought in Islam*, Lahore, 1944.

Irvine, W., *The Army of Indian Moghuls*, London, 1903.

Islam, Riaz-ul, *A Calender of Documents on Indo-Persian Relations 1500-1750*, Karachi, 1979.

Keene, H.G., *An Oriental Biographical Dictionary*, Delhi (reprint), Manohar, 1971.

Khan, A.R., *Chieftains in the Mughal Empire, During the Reign of Akbar*, IIAS, Shimla, 1977.

Khan, Iqtidar Alam, *The Political Biography of a Mughal Noble Munim Khan—Khan-i-Khanan*, New Delhi, Oriental Pubs., 1973.

———, *Mirza Kamran, Biographical Study*, Bombay, 1964.

Khan, M.A., *The Court of the Great Mughals*, Bachum, 1976.

Khosla, R.P., *The Mughal Kingship and the Nobility*, Allahabad, 1934.

———, *Administrative Structure of the Great Mughals*, Delhi, Manohar Publications, 1990.

Krishnamurti, R., *Akbar — The Religious Aspect*, Baroda, 1961.

Karkaria, R.P., *Akbar and the Parsees*, Calcutta, 1897.

Lal, K.S., *The Mughal Harem*, Delhi, Aditya Prakashan, 1988.

Lal, Muni, *Akbar*, Delhi, Vikas Publication, 1980.

Law, N.N., *Promotion of Learning in India During Muhammadan Rule*, London, 1916.

Malleson, G.B., *Akbar*, London, 1890.

———, *Akbar and the Rise of Mughal Empire*, Ambala (reprint), Bhagi Publication, 1972.

Marshall, D.N. and D.N. Tara, *Porevalle — Mughal Bibliography: Select Persian Sources for the Study of Mughals in India*, New Delhi (reprint), Munshiram Manoharlal, 1991.

Mehta, J.L, *Advanced Study in the History of Medieval India*, Vol. II, Delhi, Sterling Pubs. 1981.

Mishra, H.K., *Bureaucracy Under the Mughals (from 1556 to 1707)*. Delhi, Amar Prakashan, 1989.

Moosvi, Shireen, *The Economy of Mughal Empire C. 1595 — A Statical Study*, New Delhi, Oxford University Press, 1987.

Moreland, W.H., *The Agrarian System of Moslem India: A Historical Essays with Appendices* (Delhi), Oriental Books Reprint Corporation, 1968 (reprint).

———, *From Akbar to Aurangzeb — A Study in Economic History*, Delhi, Oriental Books Reprint Corporation, 1972 (reprint).

———, *India at the Death of Akbar: An Economic Study*, Delhi, Oriental Books Reprint Corporation, 1972 (reprint).

Mukherjee, R.K., *Economic History of India 1600-1800*, Allahabad, 2nd ed., 1967.

Mukhia, Harbans, *Historians and Historiography During the Reign of Akbar*, Delhi, Vikas, 1977.

Munilal, *Akbar*, 2 Vols., New Delhi, Vikas, 1980.

Naqvi, H.K., *History of Mughal Government and Administration*, Delhi, Kanishka Publishing, House, 1990.

———, *Urban Centres and Industries in Upper India, 1556-1803*, Bombay, 1968.

———, *Urbanisation and Urban Centres Under the Great Mughals 1556-1707*, Shimla, 1972.

Nath, Ram, *History of Decorative Art in Mughal Art Architecture*, Delhi, Motilal Banarsidass, 1976.

Nizami, K.A., *Akbar and Religion*, Delhi, Idarah-i-Adabiyat-i-Dilli, 1989.

———, *State and Culture in Medieval India*, Delhi, Adam Publishers and Distributors, 1985.

———, *Studies in Medieval Indian History and Culture*, Allahabad, 1966.

Ojha, G.H., *Rajputana Ka Itihas* in 3 vols. (Hindi), Ajmer, 1928.

Ojha, P.N., *Some Aspects of North Indian Social Life, 1556-1707*, Patna, 1961.

Pant, D., *Economic History of India Under the Mughals*, New Delhi, Kanishka Publication, 1990.

Pandey, A.B., *The First Afghan Empire in India*, Calcutta, 1956.

Prasad, Ishweri, *The Life and Times of Humayun*, Longman, 1955.

———, *Mughal Empire*, Allahabad, Chugh Prakashan, 1974.

Prawdin, Michael, *The Builders of the Mogul Empire*, London, 1963.

Philip, C.H., *Some Historians of India, Pakistan and Ceylone*, Oxford, London, 1961-62.

Qanungo, K.R., *Sher Shah and His Times*, 2nd edition, Bombay, 1956.

Qaisar, A.J., *Building Construction in Mughal India: The Evidence from Painting*, Delhi, OUP, 1988.

Qureshi, I.H., *The Administration of the Mughal Empire*, Karachi, 1966.

———, *Akbar*, Delhi, Idarah-i-Adabiyat-i-Dilli, 1987.

———, *Akbar, The Founder of the Mughal Empire*, Karachi, 1979.

Ray, Niharranjan, *Mughal Court Painting*, Calcutta, Indian Museum, 1952.

Ray Chaudhuri, Tapan, *History of India*, Vol. I, (1200-1750 A.D.), Cambridge, 1982.

Roychoudhury, M.L., *The Din-i-Illahi or the Religion of Akbar*, 2nd ed., Calcutta, 1952.

Rizvi, S.A.A., *Religious and Intellectual History of the Muslims in Akbar's Reign with Special Reference to Abul Fazl*, New Delhi, Munshiram Manoharlal, 1975.

———, *Muslim Revivalist Movements in Northern India in the 16th and 17th Centuries*, Agra University, 1965.

Saran, Parmatma, *The Provincial Government of the Mughals*, Bombay, 1973.

———, *Studies in Medieval Indian History*, Delhi, 2nd eds., Delhi, 1952, Motilal Banarsidass, 1964.

Sarkar, Jadu Nath, *Mughal Administration*, Calcutta, 1952.

———, *Studies in Mughal India*, Calcutta, 1919.

———, *India Through the Ages*, Calcutta, 1950.

Sarkar, Jagdish Narayan, *Mughal Economy (Organisation and Working)*, Calcutta, Naya Prakashan, 1987.

———, *The Art of War in Medieval India*, New Delhi, Munshiram Manoharlal, 1984.

Satish Chandra, *Medieval India: Society — The Jagirdari Crisis and the Village*, Delhi, Macmillan & Co., 1982.

———, (ed.), *Essays in Medieval Indian Economic History*, New Delhi, Munshiram Manoharlal, 1987 (Indian History Congress Golden Jubilee Year Publication Series, Vol. II).

Sharma, S.R., *Mughal Empire in India*, Agra, Laxmi Narayan Agrawala, 1972.

Sharma, Sri Ram, *Religious Policy of the Mughal Emperors*, Calcutta, 1940.

Shelat, J.N., *Akbar*, Vols. I and II, Bombay, Bharatiya, 1959-64.

Siddiqui, Iqtidar Husain, *Some Aspects of Afghan Despotism in India*, Delhi, 1966, Three Men Publication, 1969.

———, *Mughal Relations with the Indian Ruling Elite*, Delhi, Munshiram Manoharlal, 1983.

Siddiqui, N.A., *Land Revenue Administration Under the Mughals*, Bombay, 1970.

Singh, M.P., *Town, Market, Mint and Post in the Mughal Empire, 1556-1707*, New Delhi, Adam Publishers and Distributors, 1985.

Sinha, P.P., *Raja Birbal, Life and Time*, Patna, Janaki Prakashan, 1980.

Smith, V.A., *Akbar, The Great Mogul, 1542-1605*, Oxford, 1917 (reprint), Delhi, S. Chand & Co., 1970.

Spear, P., *A History of India*, Vol. II, Penguin Books, 1981.

Srivastava, A.L., *Akbar the Great*, Vols. I, II and III, Agra, 1962-67, Shivlal Agrawal.

Srivastava, M.P., *Social and Cultural Trends in Islamic India*, Allahabad, Vohra Publishers and Distributors, 1989.

Storey, C.A., *Persian Literature — A Bio-Bibliographical Survey*, London, 1935-1953.

Tarachand, *Influence of Islam on Indian 1939*, Culture, Allahabad, 1946.

Tripathi, R.P., *Rise and Fall of the Mughal Empire*, Allahabad, 1956.

———, *Some Aspects of Muslim Administration*, Allahabad, 1965.

Varma, R.C., *Foreign Policy of the Great Mughals*, Agra, 1967.

Verma, H.C., *Medieval Routes to India: A Study of Trade and Military Routes*, Calcutta, 1978.

Walia, T.M., *Mughal Empire in India*, New Delhi, Enkay Publishers, 1988.

Wellesz, Emmy, *Akbar's Religious Thought Reflected in Mughal Painting*, London, 1952.

Wilson, H.H., *A Glossary of Judicial and Revenue Terms*, London, 1885.

Zareen, Fauzia Abbas, *Abdul Qadir Badauni — As a Man and Historiographer*, Delhi, Idarah-i-Adabiyat-i-Dilli, 1987.

Select Articles

Ahmad, Tasneem, Nadir-u-Asr, Mansur, *Indo-Iranica*, Calcutta, 1972, pp. 51-55.

Ahmad, Tasneem, Akbar's Love for Painting in the Light of His Doctrine of Sulah-kul, *PHC*, 1987, pp. 73-80.

Ahmed, Bashir, Akbar and His New Policy, *JSUR*, Art Series, Vol. I (1961), pp. 54-56.

Alvi, R.A., New Light on Mughal Cavalry, *Medieval India — A Miscellany*, Vol. II, Bombay, Asia Publishing House, 1972.

Ahmad, Aziz, Akbar, Heretique or Apostat, *JAS*, 1961, pp. 221-38.

Ahmad, Qazi Mukhtar, Was Bairam Khan A Rebel? *Islamic Culture*, Hyderabad, June, 1947.

Ansari, A.A., The North-West Frontier Policy of the Mughals Under Akbar, *JPHS* 4 (1956), pp. 36-63.

Arora, Parmanand, Akbar's Popularity, *JPHS* 10, 2 (1929), pp. 1-3.

Ali, M. Athar, *Akbar and Islam 1581-1605, Islamic Society and Culture: Essays in Honour of Professor Aziz Ahmad,* Ed. Milton Israel and N.K. Wagle, New Delhi, Manohar, 1983.

———, Foundations of Akbar's Organisation of the Nobility: An interpretation, *Medieval India Quarterly*, 1961, pp. 290-99.

Azimjanova, S., New Data Concerning Khatt-i-Baburi, *PICO*, 1964, Poona, IV, 1970, pp. 203-8.

Banerjee, S.K., Social Reform of Akbar, *IHR*, 29 (1953), pp. 51-55.

———, Mariam Ki Kothi or Sunhera Makan of Fatehpur Sikri, *JPHS*, 17 (i) 1944, pp. 103-10.

Beames, J., On the Geography of India in the Reign of Akbar, *JABS*, 52, I (1984), pp. 215-32.

Billimoria, N.B., Was Akbar Literate? *JSUR*, 5, 5 (February, 1942), pp. 229-32.

Buckler, F.W., A New Interpretation of Akbar's Infallibility Decree of 1579, *JRAS* (1924), pp. 591-608.

Das, S. Nirman, A Short Account of Akbar, *JSUR*, 2 (1942), pp. 162-63.

Desai, A.N., Population and Standard of Living in Akbar's Time, *IESHR*, 9, (1972).

———, Population and Standard of Living in Akbar's Time — A Second Look, *IESHR*, 15; 1. (1978).

Grover, B.R., Nature of Land Rights in Mughal India, *IESHR*, (1963).

———, Nature of the Dehat-i-Taaluqa (Zamindari-Villages) and the Evolution of the Ta'aluqdari System During the Mughal Age, *IESHR*, 2, (1965).

Hasan, S. Nurul, The Mahzar of the Akbar's Reign, *JUPHS*, 16; (1943), pp. 125-37.

———, Zamindars Under the Mughals, *Land Control and Social Structure in Indian History*, ed. by L.F. Frykenberg, London, 1969.

Heston, A.W., The Standard of Living in Akbar's Time — A Comment, *IESHR*, 14; 3, (1977), pp. 391-96.

Irfan, Habib, Cartography in Mughal India, Medieval India — A Miscellany, Vol. IV, Bombay, Asia Publishing House, 1977.

———, The Mansab System (1595-1637), *PIHC*, 1967.

———, Zamindars in the Ain-i-Akbari, *PIHC*, Trivandrum, (1958).

Jafar, S.M., Religious Views of Akbar and Aurangzeb as Disclosed by Contemporary Archives, *PPHC*, I. (1951), pp. 271-75.

Khan, Iqtidar Alam, The Middle Classes in the Mughal Empire, *Social Scientist*, Trivandram, 1976.

———, The Nobility Under Akbar and the Development of His Religious Policies, 1560-80, *JRAS*, 1968, pp. 29-36.

———, Wizarat Under Humayun, 1545-55, *Medieval India: A Miscellany*, Vol. I, Department of History, AMU, Aligarh, 1969.

———, The Mughal Court Politics During Bairam Khan's Regency, *Medieval India: A Miscellany*, Vol. I, AMU, Aligarh, 1971.

Khan, Iqtidar Alam, The Turko-Mongol Theory of Kingships, *Medieval India: A Miscellany*, Vol. 2, Aligarh, 1972.

Krishnamurthi, R., Akbar's Philosophy of Life, *IHR*, 20 (1944) pp. 53-58.

———, The Inaugural Meeting of the Divine Faith of Akbar, *PIHC*, 23 (1944), pp. 137-43.

Menon, K.P., The Personality of Akbar, *Islamic Culture*, Hyderabad, 3 (1927) pp. 412-24.

———, Socio-Religious Background at the Advent of Akbar: A New Approach, *JUPHS*, 19 (1946), pp. 109-47.

Moosvi, Shirin, Evolution of Mansab System Under Akbar, *JRAS* (London), 2 (1981).

———, Todarmal's Original Memorandum on the Revenue Administration, March, 1582, *PIHC*, Dharwar (1988) pp. 237-48.

Naqvi, Hamida Khatoon, Incidents of Rebellions During the Reign of Emperor Akbar, *Medieval India: A Miscellany*, Vol. II, Bombay, Asia Publishing House, (1972), pp. 152-86.

Qaisar, A.J., Note on the Date of Institution of Mansab Under Akbar, *PIHC*, 24th Session, (1961).

———, Distribution of Revenue Resources of the Mughal Empire Among the Nobles, *PIHC*, (1965), pp. 237-42.

Samaddar, J.N., Akbar's Illiteracy, *BORS*, 3 (1920) p. 443.

Saran, P., Socio-Religious Background at the Advent of Akbar: A New Approach, *JUPHS*, 19 (1946), pp. 109-47.

Satish Chandra, Some Aspects of the Growth of Money Economy During the 17th Century, *IESHR*, 3; 4 (1966).

Saxena, B.P., Ideals of Mughal Sovereigns, *JUPHS*, (1941) pp. 89-104.

Sharma, S.R., Akbar's Religious Policy, *IHQ*, 2 (1987) pp. 302-22.

———, Tarikh-i-Muhammad Arif Qandhari, *JRAS*, 1933, pp. 807-11.